THE IDEA OF A COLONY:
CROSS-CULTURALISM IN MODERN POETRY

Edward Marx

THE IDEA
OF A COLONY

Cross-Culturalism in Modern Poetry

UNIVERSITY OF TORONTO PRESS
Toronto Buffalo London

© University of Toronto Press Incorporated 2004
Toronto Buffalo London
Printed in Canada

ISBN 0-8020-8799-X

Printed on acid-free paper

National Library of Canada Cataloguing in Publication

Marx, Edward
    The idea of a colony : cross-culturalism in modern
poetry / Edward Marx.

    Includes bibliographical references and index.
    ISBN 0-8020-8799-X

    1. English poetry – History and criticism.   2. Commonwealth
poetry (English) – History and criticism.   3. Primitivism in literature.
4. Exoticism in literature.   5. Pluralism (Social sciences) in literature.
I. Title.

PN1271.M37 2004   821.009'3552   C2004-900286-4

University of Toronto Press acknowledges the financial assistance to its publishing
program of the Canada Council for the Arts and the Ontario Arts Council.

University of Toronto Press acknowledges the financial support for its publishing
activities of the Government of Canada through the Book Publishing Industry
Development Program (BPIDP).

Contents

Acknowledgments

This book, which began as a dissertation, has gradually taken shape according to an evolutionary process all its own. W.B. Yeats, another compulsive reviser, wrote of hammering one's thoughts into unity; Yone Noguchi, who might have revised more, preferred 'the book which reveals the process of how the thoughts and wisdoms worked and struggled.' Any success I may have had in reducing the noise of hammering and struggling in the pages that follow owes much to the help of the many individuals who have contributed to the shaping process. My first thanks go to my adviser, Louis Menand, a self-professed proponent of the brick-by-brick school of writing who nevertheless showed exemplary patience over more than a decade of revision, reorganization, and reconstruction. Meena Alexander and John Brenkman were also generous with their help during the supervision of the dissertation stage, and I am grateful to Karl Beckson, Vincent Crapanzano, James DeJongh, Barbara Fisher, Jarrod Hayes, Dorothy Helly, Christine Hutchins, Shoshana Milgram Knapp, Binita Mehta, Susan McCabe, Lisa Nakamura, Joan Richardson, Michael Rothberg, Gordon Thompson, Joe Wittreich, and Carina Yervasi for their helpful commentaries on various chapters. The CUNY Graduate School English Program and Professor Morton N. Cohen generously provided financial support in the form of a Morton N. Cohen Dissertation Assistance Award.

Earlier versions of chapters in this book have appeared in the *Wallace Stevens Journal*, the *Journal of Commonwealth Literature*, the *Langston Hughes Review*, *Women's Poetry, Late Romantic to Late Victorian: Gender and Genre*, and *Women and British Aestheticism*. I would like to thank the editors and anonymous readers of these journals and critical anthologies, particularly John Serio, John Thieme, Dolan Hubbard, Isobel Armstrong, Virginia Blain, Talia Schaffer, and Kathy Psomiades. Grateful acknowledgment is made to the Wallace Stevens Society, Oxford University Press, the University of Leeds, the Afro-American Studies Program of

Brown University, Macmillan Publishers, Ltd., and the University of Virginia Press for permission to reprint portions of those essays here. Material appearing in this book has also been presented at a number of conferences, and I would like to thank the organizers and participants of *Rethinking Women's Poetry, 1730–1930* at Birkbeck College, *The Kipling Conference: One Hundred Years of Kim* at Magdalen College, Cambridge, the ALA conference *Twentieth Century American Poetry: Developments and Definitions*, and the MLA panels, *Cross-Culturalism in Asian Literatures* and *Outside Modernism* – especially Angela Leighton, Meenakshi Mukherjee, Yoshinobu Hakutani, Jacqueline Brogan, Nancy Paxton, Marianna Torgovnick, and Bart Moore-Gilbert. Helpful responses to research queries were provided by Shoshana Milgram Knapp, John Jealous, Elaine Showalter, Terry Castle, William Radice, and the Sarojini Naidu Trust, Hyderabad. My colleagues and students at CCNY, York College, The University of Minnesota, Kyoto University, and Nara Women's University have contributed to the development of this book in ways too numerous to name. The final stages in the evolutionary process would not have been possible without the support and hard work of my editors at University of Toronto Press, and the incisive comments of the anonymous readers of the manuscript.

Grateful acknowledgment is made to New Directions Publishing Corporation for permission to reprint material from Ezra Pound's *Pavannes and Divagations* (copyright © 1958 by Ezra Pound), *The Cantos of Ezra Pound* (copyright © 1934, 1937, 1940, 1948, 1956, 1959, 1962, 1963, 1966, and 1968 by Ezra Pound), *Personae: The Shorter Poems of Ezra Pound*, ed. Lea Baechler and A. Walton Litz (copyright © 1926 by Ezra Pound), *Ezra Pound and Dorothy Shakespear: Their Letters, 1909–1914*, ed. Omar Pound and A. Walton Litz (copyright © 1976, 1984 by the Trustees of the Ezra Pound Literary Property Trust), and Ezra Pound and Ernest Fenollosa, *The Classic Noh Theatre of Japan* (copyright © 1959 by New Directions Publishing Corporation). Grateful acknowledgment is made to Alfred A. Knopf and Random House, Inc., for permission to reprint material from Wallace Stevens's *Collected Poems* (copyright © 1923, 1947, 1950, and 1954 by Wallace Stevens), *The Necessary Angel* (copyright © 1951 by Wallace Stevens), and *Letters*, ed. Holly Stevens (copyright © 1966 by Holly Stevens).

THE IDEA OF A COLONY:
CROSS-CULTURALISM IN MODERN POETRY

Introduction

On what strange froth does the gross Indian dote,
What Eden sapling gum, what honeyed gore,
What pulpy dram distilled of innocence,
That streaking gold should speak in him
Or bask within his images and words?

Wallace Stevens[1]

I think that the crusade of the Western poetry, if it is necessary, as I believe it is most momentous, should begin with the first act of leaving the 'words' behind, or making them return to their original proper places.

Yone Noguchi[2]

'We no longer know the history of the poetry of the first half of the century,' Cary Nelson observed in his 1989 study, *Repression and Recovery.* 'Most of us, moreover, do not know that the knowledge is gone.'[3] One could say that the history of early twentieth-century poetry has never really been known; it is the poetry itself that has been forgotten. Our knowledge clusters around a handful of major modernist poets, whose works provide a challenging field for the efforts of scholars and students, and readers of modern poetry tend to venture down poetic roads less travelled less often than we might. The conservative tendency of modern poetry studies has accompanied a larger waning of interest in modernist poetry in general: the productions of the early twentieth-century avant-garde have lost much of their power to shock us; they have become historical relics, like the first airplanes. The major modernist poets continue to be read, but in recent decades the most interesting developments in modern poetry scholarship have come not from specialists in the field but from outside. Poets such as H.D., Marianne Moore, and Mina Loy were scarcely studied before the advent of feminist literary studies; without the rise of Black studies, the Harlem Renaissance might never have been 'discovered'; without Marxist literary criticism, Cary Nelson's rediscovery of the radical poets of the twenties and thirties would have been unthinkable. These changes have taken hold within modernist studies slowly and against considerable resistance: the broader recovery envisioned by Nelson remains distant, and there is a great deal of work to be done before modern poetry studies can be said to have accommodated the more recent approaches of multiculturalism, postcolonial studies, and gender studies. The study of modern poetry has become curiously old-fashioned.

This book began in an attempt to rethink modern poetry from some of these more recent perspectives and particularly from the perspective of postcolonialism. Its primary objective is to explore the relationship between two propositions: (1) that the formative years of modern poetry coincided with the climax of what is usually called 'High Imperialism,' and (2) that the most visible link between modernist poetry and the world of empire may be found in modern poets' fascination with non-Western cultures. Neither of these propositions is, in itself, particularly controversial: the interesting problem is rather the one that forms between them, namely, the problem of the relationship between the modern poet's fascination with non-Western cultures and the cultural moment of modernism and imperialism.

Cross-Cultural Modernisms

It is not a problem that lent itself to simple answers, but interesting problems rarely do. The first conclusions I reached were (1) that the fascination with non-Western cultures in the modernist period could almost invariably be categorized as exoticism or primitivism, and (2) that the non-Western interest peaked between 1912 and 1914, a period coincident with the years of modernist poetry's emergence as a movement in England and America. The fascination with the exotic and primitive was clearly not restricted to the field of poetry; on the contrary, it was a development felt simultaneously and broadly throughout European and American culture, a development that has been examined from a number of different perspectives within a wide range of cultural fields. A brief review of some of the more notable events:

- In anthropology: Lucien Lévy-Bruhl's *Les fonctions mentales dans les sociétés inférieures* (1910) and Franz Boas's *The Mind of Primitive Man* (1911) inaugurate new perspectives on primitive psychology; James Frazer, knighted in 1914, publishes the third edition of *The Golden Bough* in twelve volumes (1911–15), ending the age of comparative anthropology (less flatteringly known as 'armchair anthropology'); the new arrival Bronislaw Malinowski begins teaching at the London School of Economics and publishes his first book, *The Family among the Australian Aborigines* (1913); his subsequent emphasis on fieldwork will revolutionize the discipline; Emile Durkheim's *Les formes élémentaires de la vie religeuse* (*Elementary Forms of the Religious Life*, 1915) becomes a founding work of the new discipline of sociology.

- In psychology: Sigmund Freud argues in *Totem and Taboo* (1912) that a prehistoric primal scene is the basis of father-son relationships. Carl Jung, breaking with Freud in 1913, develops an alternative theory derived in part from Lévy-Bruhl's theory of primitive mentality and insights gained from a variety of non-Western cultures.
- In the visual arts: The influence of *art nègre* on Matisse and Picasso, beginning around 1907, marks the beginning of an international primitivist modernism. The 1913 Armory Show in New York, which introduces modernism to the American public, features primitivist works by Matisse, Gauguin, Henri Rousseau, Marsden Hartley, and Max Weber. A show of 'African Savage Art' is mounted the following year at Alfred Stieglitz's influential 291 Gallery.
- In music: Stravinsky's *Sacré du printemps* (*The Rite of Spring*), a ballet based on a central motif of primitive sacrifice, provokes riots at its first performance (1913).
- In popular literature and film: Edgar Rice Burroughs's *Tarzan of the Apes* (serial 1912; book 1914) celebrates the superiority of a White boy raised by apes. D.W. Griffiths's *Birth of a Nation* (1914) depicts African Americans as a dangerous savage race insensible to civilization.
- In literary studies: The Cambridge Ritualists led by Jane Harrison and Gilbert Murray reinvent the study of classical literature using cultural anthropology to explain ancient Greek and Roman culture; Jessie Weston and others apply similar methods to medieval European literatures.

It is thus hardly surprising that modern poetry should have taken a similar interest in the primitive and the exotic during these years. Some of the more notable examples: Ezra Pound begins editing Ernest Fenollosa's translations of Chinese poetry and Japanese Noh drama (1913–15), developing a poetic theory based on Fenollosa's conception of Chinese ideograms. W.B. Yeats begins developing a new approach to poetic drama based on Japanese Noh drama (1914–16). Bengali poet Rabindranath Tagore wins the Nobel Prize. T.S. Eliot, a graduate student in philosophy at Harvard, reads Frazer, Durkheim, Jane Harrison, and Lévy-Bruhl in Josiah Royce's seminar, and studies Sanskrit and Indian philosophy with James Woods and Charles Lanman; he later uses elements drawn from these studies in his most famous poem, *The Waste Land* (1922).

The Primitive and the Exotic

To work toward an understanding of what this burst of interest in the primitive and the exotic might mean, we must first define what we mean by these terms. Simply put, something is *primitive* if it is in some way originary; something is *exotic* if it is in some way 'outside': foreign, strange, or unfamiliar. Both terms express valuations, but in a curiously ambivalent way – as terms of either approval or derision – and both imply an opposing term: the primitive is paired with the civilized or modern; the exotic with the familiar or local.

Primitivism and exoticism are, in other words, halves of binary oppositions. Postcolonial theory is premised on the analysis of binary oppositions representing cultural difference, most famously Edward Said's analysis of Orientalist discourse as 'a style of thought based upon an ontological and epistemological distinction made between "the Orient" and (most of the time) "the Occident."' This particular binary opposition becomes, for Said, the basis for uncovering 'Orientalism as a discourse' and, in turn, 'the enormously systematic discipline by which European culture was able to manage – and even produce – the Orient politically, sociologically, militarily, ideologically, scientifically, and imaginatively during the post-Enlightenment period.'[4]

Said's approach has proven very useful for scholars interested in discovering the relationship between literary works and colonial culture, but its widespread application has raised serious methodological questions. Although the approach known as 'colonial discourse analysis' remains a useful one, Said's view of a monolithic Orientalist discourse has proven especially problematic. Looking at the instances of primitivism and exoticism cited above, for example, it seems impossible to imagine that they might be contained within a single discourse.[5]

A more precise application of Foucault's theory of discourse (from which Said's is loosely derived) would view Orientalism, and primitivism and exoticism, not as individuated discourses in themselves, but rather as *discursive strategies*, repeatedly deployed in a variety of discursive contexts. It was this approach that I adopted when I began to explore and organize the forms of exoticism and primitivism in modern poetry, and to trace out their connections with colonial discourse and the culture of imperialism. Focusing on discursive strategies made it possible to identify different sets of forces and connections operating in the different instances of cross-cultural poetry under consideration. But there was a disadvantage to this approach: giving up the idea of a single discourse also meant giving up the idea of an underlying structural principle that might explain the coherence of this apparently interrelated cluster of cross-cultural interests.

It took some time to realize that these patterns did not yield themselves to rational analysis because they were intrinsically unconscious and irrational. 'When we speak of fluctuations of taste,' Wallace Stevens once said, 'we are speaking of evidences of the operation of the irrational.'[6] The unconscious and the irrational, along with their associated psychological phenomena, seemed to turn up frequently in conjunction with the primitive and exotic, but the usual explanation was that the modernists were interested in the irrational and unconscious. The modernist interest in the irrational and unconscious was thus subsumed into the conscious, rational project of modernism. Freudian psychoanalytic theory offered explanations of some cross-cultural phenomena, but not others. A way out of this dilemma finally turned up from the unexpected direction of Jungian analytic psychology.

How the Shadow Knows

What drew my attention to the Jungian model was the concept of 'the shadow,' the archetype associated with the personal (rather than collective) unconscious.[7] The usefulness of the shadow concept for an explanation of cross-cultural phenomena derives from three features: (1) its organization through binary oppositions; (2) its association with projection; and (3) its ability to link personal and collective (i.e., cultural) forms of repression.

Unlike the Freudian view of repression, organized around the libidinal drive theory, Jung's energic theory presented repression in the form of binary oppositions. Whereas Freud approached repression as a kind of resistance or blockage, Jung saw repression as including mental functions that remain in undeveloped and archaic form owing to the conscious development of opposing functions, as well as mental contents that are excluded because of their incompatibility with the conscious persona (the Jungian equivalent of the ego). The unconscious, Jung argued, remains part of the libidinal economy, and makes its presence known, often in unexpected or disruptive ways under conditions of psychological stress.

One of the most common ways in which repressed contents make their appearance is through projection. 'Although, with insight and good will, the shadow can to some extent be assimilated into the conscious personality,' Jung writes, 'experience shows that there are certain features which offer the most obstinate resistance to moral control and prove almost impossible to influence. These resistances are usually bound up with projections, which are not recognized as such, and their recognition is a moral achievement beyond the ordinary.'[8] 'Simply described,' writes Jungian analyst Naomi Quenk, 'projection involves attributing to others an unacknowledged, unconscious part of ourselves – something that lies outside of our conscious awareness. What we project onto others can be negative, repugnant, and undesirable – or positive, admirable, and wholesome. In either case, the "projector" unconsciously identifies someone who possesses at least some of the unconscious quality in question, but then exaggerates the degree to which that quality is actually present.'[9] Jung did not, strictly speaking, invent the idea of psychological projection – ideas that souls can be projected onto objects in various ways are found worldwide and were subjected to extensive scientific investigation by nineteenth-century psychical researchers – but it was Jung who grafted projection onto the Freudian unconscious and thereby formalized the psychological notion as we now commonly employ it when we refer, for example, to people 'projecting their unconscious fears and desires onto others.' The association of projections with *racial and cultural* others has been commonplace since at least the 1940s. 'Projecting his own desires onto the Negro, the white man behaves "as if" the Negro really had them,' Frantz Fanon observed.[10] Surprisingly, however, the concept of projection has rarely been applied in the study of primitivism and exoticism. The origins of this curious oversight can also be traced to Jung. Jung fails to recognize the *primitive as projection* because he believed that *projection was primitive* – more precisely, the remnant of a primitive mental state. This oversight is easily overcome, however, and this study should demonstrate the centrality of projections in modern cross-cultural poetics. The projection and shadow concepts go a long way toward explaining two of the central paradoxes of primitive and exotic objects that often prove confusing to analysts: first, how it is that these objects can be both *attractive and repellent* (often simultaneously), and second, how they can appear to be (again, often simultaneously) both *real and imaginary*.

The second point requires further comment, for it is imperative to dissociate the idea that the primitive and exotic are *psychological projections* from the idea that they are *purely subjective creations*: that the objects they purport to describe do not exist, or that their existence is merely incidental or irrelevant. Chinua Achebe points out one of the dangers of such views in his essay 'An Image of Africa: Racism in Conrad's "Heart of Darkness,"' criticizing Conrad's depiction of a dehumanized Africa which serves as 'merely a setting for the disintegration of the mind of Mr. Kurtz.' 'There is a preposterous and perverse kind of arrogance,' Achebe writes, 'in thus reducing Africa to the role of props for the breakup of one petty European mind.'[11] What Achebe calls 'props,' Jungian analysts refer to as the hook upon which the projection is placed. It is crucial for the analyst to dissociate the projection from the hook, and neither can be dismissed as irrelevant. For this reason, it is difficult to regard as entirely adequate the formulation of Elazar

Barkan and Ronald Bush that 'as for "primitives," they never existed. Only Western "primitivism" did, invented in heated arguments about human society.'[12] While such formulations perform the necessary dissociation of projection from hook, they fail to account for its association: one does, after all, need a suitable hook. We need to explain why, if the primitive and exotic *do not exist*, it is also the case that *they must exist*. The short answer is that the function of the primitive is precisely to serve as the point where the conscious, rational mind breaks down in its own unconscious irrationality. So-called modern civilized man urgently needs to locate this point of breakdown (for everything is based on it) and cannot do so without first projecting it onto a suitable hook. Africa not only provides props for the breakup of a European mind, but also the prop on which the European mind is constituted. This, I think, accounts for why Marianna Torgovnick gets along better by being of two minds about the primitive; though she distrusts the word, she cannot finally do without it because 'we would need a viable alternative to designate the kinds of societies it describes.'[13] But this leaves Torgovnick in the awkward position of the man in the Woody Allen joke who complains to his psychiatrist that his brother thinks he is a chicken, but says he can't turn him in because he needs the eggs. We cannot live with the primitive and the exotic, nor can we do without them. The perverse arrogance Achebe sees in Conrad is indistinguishable from a profound, self-destructive, and very genuine need. The civilized man's quest for the primitive usually ends in his becoming a god or being devoured by cannibals, and these amount to the same outcome: that of expulsion from conscious rationality.

Although the shadow is often viewed in terms of the individual personality (as Conrad allows us to see in the destruction of Kurtz), the application of the concept is much broader. Jung understood the personality to be a set of floating archetypes, themselves 'crystallized features of the collective unconscious' that have evolved within the collective psyche and 'correspond to certain general characteristics of the physical world.'[14] (When poststructuralists say that 'the subject is constituted by language,' or when Lacan says that 'the unconscious is structured like a language,' they are making similar points about the relation between the individual and the collective, although the poststructuralist prefers to leave the correspondence to a physical world in doubt.) Since the persona, for Jung, is 'a more or less arbitrary segment of the collective psyche,' the shadow of the persona is also part of the collective psyche. And in Jung's view, the basic organizing principle of the whole psychic system is energy, the Jungian libido, organized around paired opposites. 'Life is born only of the spark of opposites.'[15]

Paired oppositions are undoubtedly among the most basic intellectual functions, as innumerable philosophies, from Taoism and pre-Socratic philosophy to deconstruction, have recognized. Paired or binary oppositions also form the basis of our most advanced methods of cultural critique: they form the basis of Hegel's dialectics, of Saussure's signifier; of Derrida's deconstruction, of Bhabha's hybridity. What distinguishes the Jungian perspective on binary processes from Taoism or deconstruction is its psychological focus: the perception that human minds incorporate binary processes in characteristic ways. 'All consciousness, perhaps without being aware of it, seeks its unconscious opposite, lacking which it is doomed to stagnation, congestion, and ossification.'[16]

In the Jungian account of repression, when one pole of a binary opposition is privileged, the other pole is repressed. In the individual personality, repression typically involves the exclusion of the deprivileged element from the conscious identity formation, forcing it to operate as part of the unconscious, where it may become part of an autonomous complex, and may erupt into consciousness in various ways: through projection, for example, or in dreams. When repressed contents erupt into consciousness they often appear *numinous*, a word Jung borrowed from Rudolf Otto, who used it to describe the dual aspect of religious experience as '*mysterium tremendum et fascinans*' in *The Idea of the Holy* (*Das Heilige*, 1917). This numinous quality, so often possessed by primitive and exotic objects, is a useful indicator of their unconscious origin.

From the Personality to the Other

The concept of the shadow is also associated with Jung's theory of personality types. Jung began his *Psychological Types* (1921) by distinguishing two opposing attitude types, introversion and extraversion, and further distinguished personality types according to the individual's dominant psychological function, producing the typology of eight personality types that is now widely used in the form of the Myers-Briggs Type Indicator (MBTI). An individual's dominant function preference, drawn from two pairs of opposed functions (feeling vs. thinking, and intuition vs. sensation), implies an opposed, repressed 'inferior function' that plays a prominent role in the shadow of the personality.[17] Jung calls the type theory a 'useful compass' in psychological analysis, and I think it is possible to make a good case for its broader application in literary criticism, and particularly lyric poetry, which, among literary genres, bears the strongest imprint of the author's personality, notwithstanding Eliot's objection that poetry 'is not the expression of personality, but an escape from personality.'[18] (Stevens, at least, knew that 'there can be no poetry without the personality of the poet.')[19] Although I cannot develop the broader case for Jung's personality type theory here, I will make some use of it. My assumption is that we can expect to find distinctive forms of primitivism and exoticism among members of each personality type. Extraverted thinkers such as Sigmund Freud, or Conrad's Kurtz, tend to find their primitive in the form of 'the oceanic,' because the oceanic is the numinous form of their shadow function of introverted feeling. For an introverted feeling type such as W.B. Yeats, in contrast, the exotic takes the form of spiritual voices, which may be described as projections of repressed extraverted thinking. An extraverted intuitive such as Ezra Pound finds the exotic in repressed introverted sensation, and so on. Although I expect readers to regard these diagnoses sceptically, I hope to draw attention to their potential usefulness as an aid in structuring and developing interpretive hypotheses.[20]

It should be stressed that personality type is not the whole personality, nor is Jung's personality type theory the only theory of personality. The weaknesses of the Jungian account of personality are particularly apparent in the area of early childhood development, where the efforts of the Freudian school have been far more productive. The importance of the infantile stage, crucial to understanding the personality orientation of several of the poets considered in this study, has made it necessary to follow a Freudian or post-Freudian line in many cases. One indispensable Freudian concept in the context of this study is the distinction between 'primal repression' (the repression of the infantile connection to the mother prior to the formation of the ego) and the so-called 'ordinary repression' established as a function of the ego. Thus, where primal repression has seemed the decisive factor, I have tended to adopt the Freudian model of personality, or rather that of the post-Freudian school broadly referred to as 'object relations theory,' which considers the developing personality as a relational process through which subject and object are formed through the infant's interactions with the maternal environment. In several chapters, I also find it useful to employ the Lacanian model, structured around object relations, but with a particular focus on the mediating role of language. Lacan's theory is particularly relevant here because of its emphasis on the derivation of the symbolic field of language from the infantile object relation. Lacan's identification of the Other as the defining characteristic of the symbolic offers a Freudian alternative to the Jungian shadow. Both contribute to an understanding of the ways the cross-cultural is bound up with forms of repression. Combining these various approaches enables us to arrive at a broad theory capable of identifying and distinguishing common forms of cross-culturalism in terms of the various stages and sites of repression: primal repression, repression within the personality, and cultural repression.

The Cultural Unconscious

One of the most important contributions of the Jungian approach to this theory stems from its ability to link the individual and cultural levels of repression. Jung recognized that repressive phenomena are not restricted to the individual personality but may be found in other identity formations such as those associated with national identity, where attempts to exclude constituent elements produce effects that resemble neurotic symptoms at the systemic level.[21] In effect, all the binary oppositions we use to construct our worlds (and this includes most of what we call 'culture') are potentially subject to the effects of the shadow. The attraction of the shadow concept in explaining the dynamics of repression derives from its ability to easily reconfigure its frame to suit different levels of analysis and follow effects of repression from the inner psychic economy to the outer world of psychically formed objects. It provides the link between the biographical and cultural levels of analysis in this study – and we cannot understand the way the primitive and the exotic function in practice without understanding them from both personal and cultural perspectives.

At the cultural level, we may expect to find similar sorts of shadow effects wherever we can identify a dominant cultural tendency organized around a binary opposition. Here, Frantz Fanon has provided an important corrective to Jung's tendency to overemphasize the instinctual basis of the collective unconscious: 'the collective unconscious, without our having to fall back on the genes,' Fanon argues, 'is purely and simply the sum of prejudices, myths, collective attitudes of a given group.'[22] Jung may well be right about an instinctual collective unconscious, but for the present, the link between the psychological and the genetic remains conjectural, while the link between the psychological and the cultural is relatively easy to discern. Jungian analysts have begun discussing a cultural unconscious, but remain divided over the question of whether it should be considered part of the personal unconscious or part of the collective unconscious.[23] Of course, only the shadow knows, and since the persona is, for Jung, already a part of the collective, the question does not stand in the way of the development of a Jungian cultural studies. In fact, I would suggest, this Jungian cultural studies already exists, albeit under other names. Cultural theorists working across a broad range of disciplines have been for several decades exploring the ways societies dominated by rational, White, civilized, modern, law-abiding men project irrationality, unconsciousness, animality, criminality, and sexual perversion onto ethnic and gendered others. The point is not that these cultural analyses are necessarily true (indeed, we should never automatically assume they are) but simply that they are hypotheses organized around the mechanisms of the Jungian cultural unconscious.

To construct a general theory of modern cross-culturalism along these lines is not especially difficult once we have phrased the question in the right way. We simply need to look at the relationship between the main forms of cross-culturalism (primitivism and exoticism) and their opposites, and the question almost answers itself. Isn't exoticism – the powerful desire to explore, possess, or be subsumed by otherness – an opposing force to imperialism, viewed as a kind of aggressive explosion of local or national culture? Isn't modernism – the relentless, progressive drive to make it new – necessarily accompanied by a shadow of primitivism, reflecting deep anxieties about the loss of cultural foundations? The savage poet and the primitive artist are thus the inseparable doubles of their modern counterparts and together form a single cultural movement; it is only when they are separated that primitivism appears as a neurotic effect within the economy of modernism, and modernism as an unexpected characteristic of primitive objects.

Just as we can take the shadow concept inward to the level of personality and outward to explain these broader cultural movements, we can also apply it at the level of discourse, language, and text. Few writers have explored the shadow at the discursive level with such precision and artistry as Homi K. Bhabha, whose concept of 'hybridity' traces with extraordinary agility the effects of the shadow in colonial discourse. Hybridity, as Bhabha describes it, is the characteristic of colonial discourse which renders it incomplete: the seam through which the pull of the other threatens the wholeness of the colonial subject. It is 'the sign of the productivity of colonial power, its shifting forces and fixities,' and at the same time, 'it is the name for the strategic reversal of the process of domination through disavowal.'[24] Hybridity is not merely a name for a disorientation or 'imperial delirium' of the colonizer's discourse, for it infects all discourses produced by colonialistic interaction, but its effects in the discourse of Western colonialism are particularly marked by 'the disturbance of its authoritative representations by the uncanny forces of race, sexuality, violence, cultural and even climatic differences.'[25] As Bhabha argues, it is not sufficient to merely mark out the discriminatory processes of hybridity as a disruption in Western discourses of culture; rather, hybridity must be seen as that which produces both recognition and disavowal, which in turn constitute all cultural discourses: 'to see the cultural not as the *source* of conflict – *different* cultures – but as the *effect* of discriminatory practices – the production of cultural *differentiation* as signs of authority – changes its value and its rules of recognition.' Bhabha's practice of colonial discourse analysis 'reverses the effects of the colonialist disavowal, so that the other "denied" knowledges enter upon the dominant discourse and estrange the basis of its authority – its rules of recognition.'[26]

Derrida's deconstruction and Bhabha's hybridity find a parallel, as Jungian literary theorist Susan Rowland argues, in individuation, the term Jung uses to describe the development of the personality. 'Jungian oppositions are not logically exclusive contradictions but function as a deconstructive web where pairs of terms are antagonistic and complementary. Opposition in Jung's work is a tension between things alike and interchangeable: individuation deconstructs such logical hierarchies as the opposition of conscious and unconscious into a non-hierarchical relationship.'[27] Like deconstruction, which Derrida has argued is not a method, a system, or a practice, individuation, too, is simply what happens. Individuation is a process over which we may have some control, as Yeats believed –

> By the help of an image
> I call to my own opposite, summon all
> That I have handled least, least looked upon.[28]

Or maybe not: individuation may be merely the working out of a biological mechanism, as Wallace Stevens supposed. In either case, individuation, as the integration or reintegration of the repressed, is a process central to the work of the modern poet.

This brings us back again to Cary Nelson's question about the possibility of recovering the repressed alternative histories of modern poetry. The chapters that follow are arranged as a series of narratives focusing on individual poets and movements, each developing the approach I have laid out in this introduction in a somewhat different fashion. The organization of a book exploring irrational phenomena does not easily resolve itself into a linear sequence, and my arrangement of chapters is intended as a compromise between several possible arrangements. A chronological arrangement highlights the cumulative continuities of poetic cross-culturalism, but because of the fairly narrow and, in some cases, overlapping time frames, I have shifted the order somewhat to highlight certain geographical shifts in cross-cultural interests, which tend to follow the larger movements of Western colonialism from the Near East and India to the Pacific Islands, and then to East Asia and Africa.

European exoticism emerged largely out of Europe's relations with the Near East, and the first chapter, 'The Spell of Far Arabia: Flecker's Islamic Near East,' although focusing on a somewhat later work – Flecker's verse play *Hassan* (1915) – appropriately addresses this formative space of the English exotic tradition. I read *Hassan*, as I read a number of the texts treated in this book, as an expression of personality issues rooted in the author's childhood; in this case, restaging the author's personal drama of inadequacy and punishment, projected onto the exotic background of the Near East. This drama of failure is then contrasted, in 'The Ends of the Earth: Kipling's Afghanistan,' with the drama of heroism staged in Kipling's early Afghan-border poetry. I argue that Kipling evokes in these exotic scenes of heroic masculinity strategies of childhood personality adaptation that he reexperienced in an early, memorable journalistic assignment in the border city of Peshawar.

Indian exoticism is the focus of the next three chapters. Chapter 3, 'The Exotic

Transgressions of "Laurence Hope,"' looks at the reception of Violet Nicolson (sometimes called Kipling's female counterpart), whose pseudonymous 'Indian love lyrics' offered an irresistibly seductive projection of repressed violence, eroticism, and confessionality in a late Victorian culture of propriety and reserve which tended to exclude, organize, and repress these tendencies. The fourth chapter, 'Everybody's Anima: Sarojini Naidu as Nightingale and Nationalist,' uses Jung's concept of the anima to explain the formation of Naidu's poetic and political persona in relation to her series of powerful male mentors. Chapter 5, 'The Tagore Era,' considers Tagore's phenomenal Western fame and precipitous decline in connection with the repression and attempted rediscovery of spirituality within materialistic Western modernity.

In chapter 6, 'The Childhood That Never Was: Rupert Brooke's Primitive Paradise,' the Pacific Islands become the site for the exploration of Brooke's troubled issues of sexual identity. Chapter 7, 'The Infant Gargantua on the Wet, Black Bough: Pound's Chinese Object Relations,' uses object relations theory to argue that Pound's exotic preoccupations, along with certain of his racist tendencies, and even his famous Imagist doctrine, can be linked to problems of early childhood development associated with his repressed feelings for the Black and Chinese servants who served as his maternal substitutes.

American primitivism is the subject of the final three chapters. Chapter 8, 'The Red Man in the Drawing Room,' shifts the frame to the relationship between primitivism and American nativism, looking at the acrimonious debate over *The Path on the Rainbow*, the first 'modernist' anthology of Native American verse, and ends with an analysis of T.S. Eliot's contribution to the debate through the figure of the Red Man in the drawing room who, I argue, embodies repressed aspects of Eliot's personality. The ninth chapter, 'The Last Nostalgia: Wallace Stevens in the Shadow of the Other,' argues that the primitive and exotic play a key role in Stevens's psychological poetics. Stevens, in his elaborate psychoanalytic poetics anticipating, in many respects, the theories of Lacan, explores the roots of the psychological link between poetry and imperialism. Chapter 10, 'Forgotten Jungle Songs: Ambivalent Primitivisms of the Harlem Renaissance,' looks at the Black poets who turned their ambivalently embodied primitive projections against the repressive patriarchal law of White modernity that formed them, and thus inaugurated the transition into postmodernity.

Chapter One

The Spell of Far Arabia: James Elroy Flecker's Islamic Near East

'His dreams of the East and Greece were born with him ... but his hankering long antedated his travels,' wrote J.C. Squire of James Elroy Flecker in his introduction to Flecker's *Collected Poems*, published in 1916, a year after Flecker's death.[1] Flecker's exotic fantasies were undoubtedly formed in his childhood, and I will suggest that they grew out of his troubled relationship with his father, who was also his schoolmaster at Dean Close from the time he was eight years old. Flecker, his biographer John Sherwood writes, 'was far too individualist, far too egotistical to mix happily with the normal boy life of a public school, and he was very sensitive to the fact of being the Headmaster's son. Passionate and lacking in self-control, he was a trial to his masters since he could not take rebuke in any form and his hastiness, inaccuracy and carelessness often got him into trouble ... The school staff knew they had to be strict with him and James Elroy saw his father as the real source of any punishment which a master might inflict. His resentment grew accordingly, and his capacity for avoiding untidy and careless work diminished.'[2] Flecker seems to have become interested in literary exoticism during this period. Squire notes the influence of the poetry of Sir Richard Burton on the young Flecker, who, 'when still a boy, had copied out the whole of his long "Kasidah,"' and cites 'an unpublished poem written when he was twenty in which voices call him "to white Ægean isles among the foam" and the "dreamy painted lands" of the East.'[3] Nevertheless, exoticism is not a prominent characteristic of Flecker's early poetry; it becomes a focus of his work around the time of his decision to undertake a career in the diplomatic service in the Near East in 1907.

In 1907, having recently completed his course at Oxford, Flecker was, his biographer John Sherwood notes, 'having little success in living by his pen.' Flecker got the idea of entering a career in the Levant Consular Service from his Oxford friend W.D. Peckham, who had done so. 'What attracted him most, perhaps,' Sherwood writes, 'was that the entrants to the service spent their first two years studying oriental languages – and he enjoyed languages – at Cambridge, which seemed likely to prove congenial. Early in the spring he wrote to his father to say that he had decided to try for a Student Interpretership in the Foreign Office. He would "much rather be in this than the Home Civil." [4]

In June of 1907, Flecker published an essay on the exotic Anglo-Indian poet 'Laurence Hope' (Violet Nicolson) in the *Monthly Review*, an essay which suggests an important link between Flecker's Near Eastern career plans and his poetic aspirations. Flecker begins the essay by observing that Laurence Hope 'has succeeded where most modern poets have failed ... She has created for herself a world of admirers, a multitude of initiants – a Public.' 'Therefore,' he writes, 'she is bound to fascinate those who diligently inquire into the modern mind, and who love to grasp the elusive psychology of the present.'[5] Flecker's own interest must have extended beyond disinterested scientific inquiry: what 'Laurence Hope' had achieved was precisely what Flecker the aspiring poet needed and lacked: a public. Flecker does not conclude that Laurence Hope's exoticism was the only source of her appeal – though he cynically concedes that 'an outworn Byronism, a desperately sentimental affection for the sonorous names of the fantastic East, can partly explain this popularity,' and later warms to praising her poetry in exoticist terms as 'a matchless lotus of the East, a new and entrancing fragrance.'[6] But if Laurence Hope, with her flawed poetry of exotic passion flavoured with sadomasochism, could achieve popular success as a poet in spite of 'sadly failing in the most elementary knowledge of verse structure,'[7] certainly Flecker, with his extensive knowledge of classical prosody and his own passionate interest in the arts of flagellation, must have felt he could do so as well. And indeed, he was later to observe to his friend Frank Savery that he expected to 'go down to fame (if I go) as a sort of Near East Kipling.'[8]

Truc Mussulman Was I

Exoticism of the Near East has a special significance in the history of English literature. Exoticisms tend to hover around a particular geographical region or set of objects which has a special meaning within the culture. In the English literary tradition (and in numerous other European literatures) that special role is assigned to the Islamic Near East. As Edward Said put it, 'from the end of the seventh century until the battle of Lepanto in 1571, Islam in either its Arab, Ottoman, or North African and Spanish form dominated or effectively threatened European Christianity.'[9] The Crusades of the eleventh to thirteenth centuries, the rise of the Ottoman Empire from the beginning of the fourteenth century, and the expulsion of the Moors from Spain at the end of the fifteenth century provided the backdrops to the production of the Islamic other.

It was in the eighteenth century that Near Eastern exoticism acquired its characteristic modern forms through the vogue of the 'Oriental tale,' an enormously popular and prolific genre inspired by the *Arabian Nights* stories, first translated into French by Antoine Galland in 1704. By 1714, it was in its fourth English edition, accompanied by a host of successors and imitators including two English versions of de la Croix's *Persian and Turkish Tales*. The vogue of the Oriental tale was fading by the end of the eighteenth century, but the tales were to find new life in the poetry of the Romantics in the early nineteenth century.[10] Beckford's *Vathek, An Arabian Tale* (1786), a poem originally written in French and translated into English with the author's assistance, Landor's *Gebir* (1798), Southey's *Thalaba the Destroyer* (1801) and *Curse of Kehama* (1810), and Byron's *The Giaour* and *The Bride of Abydos* (1813) are among the notable poems of the period set in the Near East. Thomas Moore's enormously popular *Lalla Rookh* (1817) became the classic of the genre, at least through the Victorian era. Most of these poems had their origins in the European Oriental tales. Landor's *Gebir*, published anonymously in 1798, was based on a story in Clara Reeve's *The Progress of Romance* (1785) entitled 'The History of Chaoba Queen of Egypt,' which in turn derived from a seventeenth-century French translation of a twelfth-century Arabic tale.[11] Similarly, Southey's *Thalaba the Destroyer* was based on Henry Weber's translation from a 1792 French collection entitled *New Arabian Tales*.[12] Byron's Near Eastern works were unusual in being derived from the poet's own experiences in the region and relatively recent historical events.[13] Even the Victorians felt the pull of the Oriental tale. 'Many a sheeny summer-morn, / Adown the Tigris I was borne,' Tennyson wrote in 'Recollections of the Arabian Nights':

> True Mussulman was I and sworn,
> For it was in the golden prime
> Of good Haroun Alraschid.[14]

Thanks to his extensive exposure to this Near Eastern literary exoticism, Flecker knew a great deal more about the world of the *Arabian Nights* than he did about the contemporary Near East and the Levant Consular Service.

In an uncollected poem of late 1907, Flecker wrote,

> Far far away some brown mysterious priest
> Holds the arcana of the timeless East,
> And further yet are isles where I would be,
> Poised like red lilies on the Austral sea.[15]

The following year Flecker enrolled at Cambridge, studying Persian under Professor E.G. Brown, author of *A Literary History of Persia* (Flecker's student translations of Jalalu'ddin Rumi and from Sa'di's *Gulistan* appear in his *Collected Poems* and *Collected Prose*, respectively), and at the same time Turkish and Arabic. Though not notable for his social popularity, he developed a friendship with Rupert Brooke, who later proposed his inclusion among the so-called Georgian poets.

Two years later, Flecker sailed off to Constantinople to enter the Consular Service, meeting en route the woman who would later become his wife, Hellé Skiadaressi, daughter of a prominent Athens physician. A few months after his arrival, he was diagnosed with tuberculosis. There is no doubt that his declining health throughout his years in the Near East contributed to his indifferent professional performance, but there is ample evidence that his dissatisfaction stemmed from a more general sense of disappointment in his encounter with the exotic. Although he had done well on his language exams at Cambridge, tying for first place among the six student interpreters and taking a first class, he did poorly on his intermediate examination in Turkish in 1911 and the following year 'failed disastrously' in his final examination for promotion to Vice-Consul.[16] In 1912, he was able to secure sick leave to return to England, where he made unsuccessful attempts to find academic and literary work. A last attempt to secure a transfer to the consular General Service was rejected, and despite his evident desire to return to England by any means, parental pressure, backed by the threat of forfeiting the £500 bond he had been required to post on entering the service, sent him back to Beirut to take up again his Turkish studies.[17]

Around this time, Flecker drafted an 'Open Letter to the Poets of England,' which, according to Sherwood, he intended to send to the *English Review*.[18] In the 'Open Letter,' Flecker criticizes the 'hatred of civilisation' which 'is an old commonplace of Poets, especially of highly civilised ones.' He advises the poets of England to

> Come and live out of England and learn to rejoice in your country. Come and live for a year, not in the Lebanon, where civilisation has had its say, but in Turkey proper. Test the surface of a Turkish road and the smells of a Turkish town and learn for the first time to glory in the order and cleanliness of civilisation which you seem to take for granted. Stay long enough to overcome the first impression of the picturesque – which results from mere indifference – and let the sordid misery of those filthy stalls and flyblown wares sink into your soul. Learn to believe automatically every story of horror and oppression that you hear. They are all true. Seek for the magic of the Arabian Nights and you will learn that the East changes – all that belonged to a civilisation dead long years ago.[19]

He was later to confess to J.C. Squire that 'that he had not greatly liked the East – always excepting, of course, Greece – and that his intercourse with Mohammedans had led him to find more good in Christianity than he had previously suspected.'[20] His disillusion of this period is expressed in his poem 'Brumana,' where he blames the 'traitor pines' of England's southern shore for murmuring of 'older seas, / That beat on vaster sands,' and 'Lands / Where blaze the unimaginable flowers.'[21]

Discussions of exoticism have frequently called attention to a characteristic pattern in the literature of exoticism where the traveller arrives at the supposed exotic location only to find he has arrived too late: the exotic has disappeared, moved on, or perhaps it was never there at all. The theme of the belated traveller, in Ali Behdad's phrase, becomes a standard feature of orientalist literature in what Behdad calls 'the age of colonial dissolution.' 'Traveling in the Orient at a time when the European colonial power structure and the rise of tourism had transformed the exotic referent into the familiar sign of Western hegemony, these orientalists could not help but experience a sense of displacement in time and space, an experience that produced either a sense of disorientation and loss or an obsessive urge to discover an "authentic" Other.'[22] Flecker's 'Open Letter' cited above is a classic example of the sense of disorientation Behdad identifies.

Looked at from a Jungian point of view, however, the failure of the exotic object to meet expectations may be understood as a consequence of its status as a projection. The exotic object provides a suitable hook upon which to place the projection, but the hook can never fully support the projection, which originates in the subject's unconscious. The closer one gets to the hook, the more apparent this inadequacy becomes. The 'obsessive urge to discover an "authentic" Other' noted by Behdad is a likely reaction to this realization of inadequacy.

We can understand these reactions as the first three stages of what Robert Bly calls 'five stages in exiling, hunting, and retrieving the shadow.' The first stage, that of the establishment of the projection, is followed by a second stage in which the projection 'rattles,' as Bly (following Marie Louise von Franz) describes it; the third stage is 'that state of mind in which the distressed person calls on the moral intelligence to repair the rattle.'[23] In our context, this would involve a redoubled attempt to locate the exotic in the place where it is supposed to be, the 'obsessive urge' described by Behdad. The fourth stage 'in which we feel the sensation of diminishment'[24] is implied in what Behdad describes as the melancholic quality associated with the failure of the exotic quest.[25] The possibility of resolution is only achieved at the fifth stage, which Bly calls 'retrieving the shadow.' Jung describes this elusive 'realization of the shadow' as 'a suffering and a passion that implicate the whole man.'[26]

Flecker's Exotic Poems

By the time of his return to Beirut in 1913, Flecker had already written all the Near Eastern poems for which he would be remembered. It remained for him to assemble them, together with other poems, into *The Golden Journey to Samarkand* (1913) and to complete his play, *Hassan*, inspired by a comic Turkish tale about a Jewish magician. Two poems, 'Yasmin' and 'The Golden Journey to Samarkand,' appear in both volumes. In addition, *The Golden Journey to Samarkand* contains a number of other Near Eastern poems: notably, 'The Hammam Name,' 'Saadabad,' and 'The Gates of Damascus.'

By the time Flecker wrote these poems, translations of Near Eastern poetry into English had been around so long they scarcely qualified as exotic. From the 1770s the Oriental tales in their prose and verse forms had been accompanied by scholarship on Near Eastern languages and translations of Persian poetry. The poems of Hafiz, Sa'di's *Gulistan*, and Ferdowsi's *Shah Nameh*, or *Book of Kings*, were among the more frequently translated works. Some of these translations were intended as training texts for the language studies of young East India Company hopefuls, and the growth of the East India Company, which used Persian in its correspondence with the Mughal regime, certainly fuelled their production, but their interest extended well beyond the colonial context. Ralph Waldo Emerson himself translated poems by Hafiz and contributed a preface to Francis Gladwin's translation of *The Gulistan, or Rose Garden* (1865); later translators of Sa'di's collection of prose and verse aphorisms included Richard Burton, Edwin Arnold, and Launcelot Cranmer-Byng. Ferdowsi's great Persian historical epic was mined by Matthew Arnold for his 'Sohrab and Rustom,' while Edmund Gosse found in an apocryphal story of the poet the theme for his 'Ferdowsi in Exile,' a poem originally written as a preface for Helen Zimmern's *Epic of Kings, Stories Retold from Firdausi* (1882). Later, Edward Fitzgerald's *Rubáiyat of Omar Khayyám* (1859) found an immense if somewhat belated *fin de siècle* audience for its Decadent themes. Richard LeGalliénne published a collection of *Odes from the Divan of Hafiz* in 1903.

Flecker's translation efforts were not numerous, and are derived from relatively obscure sources, but they brought to bear a rare combination of linguistic and poetic abilities. 'The Hammam Name' is a straightforward translation of a homoerotic poem by the eighteenth-century Ottoman poet Mehemmed Emin Beligh of Larissa; however, its homoeroticism is masked by Flecker in his attribution of the poem as 'from a poem by a Turkish Lady.'[27] The poem is an excellent example of Flecker's skill in verse translation; Gillanders's comparison of the poem to Gibbs's ponderous precursor demonstrates Flecker's success in retaining not only a semblance of the original rhythm and rhyme-scheme, but also the playful tone of the original.[28]

The poem 'Saadabad,' which takes as its title the site of the summer palace of Turkish Sultan Ahmed III, is partly a translation of a *sharqi*, or ballad, by Ahmed's court poet, Nedim, and partly a personalized elaboration of the poem's theme by Flecker, written in 1910 when he and Hellé (the 'Daughter of the Golden Isles') were themselves approaching the site, in the 'Valley of the Sweet Waters of Europe.' In these early days of Flecker's career, the poet could still look upon the journey east with anticipatory pleasure, and Constantinople approached by sea was still the 'Rose of cities dropping with the heavy summer's burning dew.'[29]

'The Gates of Damascus,' which was not a translation, came out of Flecker's visit with Hellé to the Syrian city for Christmas in 1911. The poem, which Flecker called his 'greatest poem' in a letter to Frank Savery, celebrates the variegated possibilities of travel offered by the walled city's four gates. Each of the four gatekeepers sings a song disclosing the particular opportunities of success offered by his gate: the Eastern Gate, 'Portal of Bagdad' and 'Doorway of Diarbekir,' offers passage to caravans travelling through the desert on the long journey to the Persian capital, while the West Gate leads to Lebanon and 'the dragon-green, the luminous, the dark, the serpent-haunted sea,' beyond which strange lands may be found. The North Gate, leading to Aleppo, offers opportunities to merchants: there, 'thou shalt sell thy wares for thrice the Damascene retailers' price, / And buy a fat Armenian slave who smelleth odorous and nice,' while the South Gate leads to Sinai and thence to Meccah, where the Hajji has 'turned in prayer with aching heart and eyes that burn.' There, 'God shall make thy body pure, and give thee knowledge to endure / This ghost life's piercing phantom-pain, and bring thee out to life again.'[30] The poem situates the English reader in an exotic space looking outward to the possibilities of further exploration, mediated by the native informant who speaks to the reader not as other but as a fellow traveller.

In the Damascus bazaars, the Fleckers quite ruined themselves, as he wrote home – Hellé bought James Elroy a camel-hair burnouse while he reciprocated with Bedouin jewellery, and they 'also got embroidered saddlebags, a water skin, a pair of bellows, a silk scarf, coffee cups of the true Eastern kind' – 'so,' Flecker wrote, 'I am working hard with a poem or two to cover expenses.'[31] Thus, it is perhaps not surprising that the exotic wares of merchants play a prominent role in 'The Gates of Damascus.' The poem itself becomes a means of transforming financial loss into gain.

The exoticism of the merchant's caravan becomes even more compelling in 'The Golden Journey to Samarkand,' where the famed city of Silk Road trade,

further east than Flecker ever dreamed of going, becomes a quite mystical destination. The journey ends Flecker's play, *Hassan*.

That Was the World for Whippings!

Near Eastern exoticism in the English theatre has a long history that I can only
touch on very briefly here. With the establishment of the British East India Company in 1600, interest in the Persian roots of the Mughul dynasty was reflected in
such plays as Marlowe's *Tamburlaine* (1590) and Dryden's *Aureng-zebe* (1675).
Arabian Nights tales lent themselves to theatrical adaptation beginning in the late
eighteenth century and persisted into the era of film. Islamic characters were also
featured in the imperialist drama and melodrama of the nineteenth century. J.S.
Bratton, in her introduction to *Acts of Supremacy: The British Empire and the
Stage, 1790–1930*, describing the psychological function of this imperialist theatre in very similar terms to those I have suggested, also links them to questions
of class conflict. 'On to the transgressive and hostile imperial subject on stage the
audience could project all sorts of anti-social characteristics, and these could well
be the same evils which were condemned as characterising the working class, and
which also present problems of control in the individual psyche. The stage, therefore, offered a framed and bracketed space in which licence, violence, irresponsibility, physicality and other enjoyable but anti-social acts or sensations could be
savoured and then rejected and denied.'[32]

The story of *Hassan* revolves around the tragicomic adventures of Hassan, a
purveyor of sweetmeats in the Baghdad of Haroun ar Rashid, hopelessly in love
with Yasmin, a young widow. In the opening scene, Hassan confesses his love to
Selim, who offers to obtain for him a love philtre, but instead betrays him by
seducing Yasmin for himself. Discovering his friend's duplicity, and mocked by
Yasmin, Hassan is thrown into despair. He is discovered in this condition by the
Caliph's minstrel, and subsequently drawn into the Caliph's incognito evening
adventure, which ends up at the home of Rafi, King of the Beggars. As it happens, Rafi is planning an imminent rebellion against the Caliph because the girl
he loves has been taken into the Caliph's harem. The incognito Caliph and associates are imprisoned by Rafi, and it is Hassan who comes up with a means of
escape, after which he is rewarded by a position as advisor to the Caliph. Yasmin
now professes her love for Hassan, but he remains embittered, and his sympathy
toward the rebellious Rafi, whose true love for the harem girl he recognizes, leads
to his expulsion from the court. Rafi and the harem girl are subjected to a cruel
death by torture, Yasmin goes off with the Black executioner, and Ishak, the
Caliph's minstrel, persuades Hassan to accompany him to Samarkand.

Acquiescing in this exotic journey, for lack of a better alternative, the disillusioned Hassan provides a suitable figure for the poet. 'The Golden Journey to Samarkand,' the poem that ends the play, retains Flecker's earlier, exoticized conception of travel, while at the same time displaying the cynical awareness of exoticism as seduction characteristic of his later perspective. In the poem's prologue (left out of the play's final version), the 'Poets of the proud old lineage' 'beguile your pilgrimage' with 'Tales, marvellous tales / Of ships and stars and isles where good men rest,' offering a compelling vision of commerce as destiny. This is juxtaposed to the voice of Ishak ('a pilgrim' in the earlier version), who has broken his lute to 'write no more qasidahs in praise of the generosity of kings.' With his intention to 'try the barren road, and listen for the voice of the emptiness of earth,' he is after a more spiritual reward:

> We travel not for trafficking alone:
>   By hotter winds our fiery hearts are fanned:
> For lust of knowing what should not be known
>   We make the Golden Journey to Samarkand.[33]

The exotic appeal of the journey is both materialistic and spiritual, and Hassan is ultimately caught up in the momentum of the journey. Samarkand, the great commercial crossroads between West and East Asia, offers the stimulating mystery of an exotic quest for the disillusioned.

The proportion of verse in *Hassan* is small but central to the play. The most notable poem is the ghazal ('Yasmin' in Flecker's verse collections) sung by Hassan beneath Yasmin's window in the play's second scene – among the very few examples of the intricate ghazal form in English and almost certainly the best.

> How splendid in the morning glows the lily; with what grace he throws
> His supplication to the rose: do roses nod the head, Yasmin?
> But when the silver dove descends I find the little flower of friends,
> Whose very name that sweetly ends, I say when I have said, Yasmin,
> The morning light is clear and cold; I dare not in that light behold
> A whiter light, a deeper gold, a glory too far shed, Yasmin.
> But when the deep red eye of day is level with the lone highway,
> And some to Meccah turn to pray, and I toward thy bed, Yasmin.
> Or when the wind beneath the moon is drifting like a soul aswoon,
> And harping planets talk love's tune with milky wings outspread, Yasmin,
> Shower down thy love, O burning bright! for one night or the other night
> Will come the Gardener in white, and gathered flowers are dead, Yasmin![34]

Although Flecker neglects the authorial signature generally expected in the last line pair, the complex internal rhymes, plays on words, and patterns of imagery suggest a sophisticated appreciation of the workings and possibilities of the form.[35]

Critics have noted the prominent elements of sadomasochism in *Hassan* – indeed, prominent enough to inspire an article in the *Medical Press and Circular* in 1924, and a subsequent backlash against the play's popularity.[36] Flecker's personal interest in sadomasochism is a recurring subtext of John Sherwood's biography, though Sherwood does not actually identify the 'clear evidence' mentioned in his preface 'that caning and being tied up and caned formed an essential part of his married love-making.'[37] There are ample indications of Flecker's interest scattered throughout his writings, perhaps most notably in the digression on 'The Excellence of Whipping' in his novel, *The King of Alsander*, which displays what Gillanders calls 'undisguised enthusiasm.'[38] Whipping as 'an instrument for forming character by the Spartans, Romans and Russians is reviewed, and especially in its use in the East.'[39] 'But the East, the golden East in the golden days' – Flecker writes – 'that was the world for whippings!'[40]

But it is *Hassan*, I would argue, that most effectively stages Flecker's personal psychodrama, delineating its form as a circuit of desire, failure, escape, punishment, control, and ambivalence. The play stages the formation of personality as a series of enticing but hopeless alternatives explored through a series of double failures: Hassan loses the object of desire through his own foolishness, but also because it is unattainable; it is unattainable because the love object is either unworthy (Yasmin) or doomed by the law of the father (the Caliph's harem girl); Hassan is thus miserable when powerless because he cannot attain his object, and miserable when powerful because the object has become worthless. Hassan's idealism is gradually destroyed through scenes of whipping, torture, and death which he must either inflict or endure, in the process of which his dawning understanding accompanies a growing sense of alienation. His ambivalent departure at the end of the play may be a hopeful new beginning or merely one that will begin the circuit of desire and failure once again.

In Jungian terms, Hassan's personality is organized around the dominant sensing and feeling functions (he is a sweetmeat seller who wants to be loved), while his shadow side is represented by repressed intuition and thinking. Hassan's problem with intuition begins the play, while the play's narrative world, with its perverse and inescapable plots, may be taken as a projection of his repressed thinking: his drama is that he is punished by an unintuited logical complexity. Although Hassan's experience takes place in his external world, it is effectively an encounter with his unconscious shadow: he ventures out into the unknown, encounters that which he lacks, is exalted and crushed, and brought back to himself. In the end, he ventures out again.

Chapter Two

The Ends of the Earth: Rudyard Kipling's Afghanistan

The preceding chapter examined the common exoticist theme of the belated traveller as a characteristic shape of the encounter with the shadow, and suggested that the experience of failure in the encounter with the exotic object may be understood as a symptom of its non-identity with the unconscious projection. In Flecker's life and in his play, *Hassan*, this non-identity is reflected in the themes of disappointment, failure, and punishment. But the belated traveller is by no means the only fate of the exotic quest. It is, of course, an alternative to another fate, that of the successful heroic journey. Jung considered the heroic journey a mythical representation of the completed encounter with the unconscious, completed in the sense that the persona connects with the collective unconscious (finding the treasure) but is not subsumed by it (devoured by the monster) and is subsequently able to reconstitute the adapted, conscious persona (return with the treasure). The heroic quest is thus a representation of what Jung called the 'transcendent function' – the tendency of the mind to pursue balance by resorting to the unconscious in cases of irreconcilable conflict. If the heroic journey represents the successful encounter with the unconscious, the belated traveller theme would seem to represent the unsuccessful encounter. Yet while the hero and the failure seem to epitomize opposing outcomes in the encounter with the unconscious, failure and success prove on closer examination to be less distinct than they might appear. The unconscious is never delivered over in its entirety to the conscious persona, and thus the heroic deed is always tainted to a greater or lesser extent by a sense of inadequacy or dishonesty. Conversely, the failed encounter is a more truthful representation of the impossible task of apprehending the unconscious in its totality, and from this perspective, the fact that Hassan recognizes this truth and survives may be taken as a successful outcome.

Kipling, on the other hand, is the heroic writer of the exotic *par excellence*. In this chapter I hope to establish that Kipling's exotic poems are predominantly and even compulsively heroic in the Jungian sense, and that they celebrate Kipling's 'successful' personality adaptation through a series of frightening childhood crises, while at the same time compulsively covering over the traces of fear and failure involved in these adaptations. I will also examine the reasons Afghanistan served as Kipling's primary exotic region.

Teach Us to Rule Ourselves Alway

The ordeals of Kipling's childhood are well known; born in Bombay, he enjoyed a stimulating and emotionally satisfying upbringing in an artistically inclined family for his first six years, before being abandoned by his parents at a depressing English boarding house and then sent off to a military boarding school at the age of twelve. I would like to suggest that Kipling responded to these traumatic transitions by altering his personality orientation while maintaining the obligatory stiff upper lip. In this series of transitions, the 'little friend of all the world' was first severed from his emotional attachments, resulting in his self-reinvention as a bookish introvert, while deteriorating eyesight and a hostile environment forced him to shift his perceptual framework from the sensory to the intuitive, a shift marked by a nervous breakdown in early adolescence (in his autobiography he explicitly reports becoming worried about 'shadows and things that were not there' and the supernatural would remain a strong interest).[1] The reconfigured personality was then pushed in a more active direction in the military school environment at Westward Ho, where he achieved a level of social integration. Thus, in reaching his teens, Kipling had run the gamut of personality types in his effort to survive through adaptation, and the ordeal, though traumatic, would prove crucial to his life and to his literary career. We find traces of its lessons throughout his work:

> Teach us to rule ourselves alway,
> Controlled and cleanly night and day;
> That we may bring, if need arise,
> No maimed or worthless sacrifice.[2]

When Kipling left school to rejoin his family in Lahore at the age of sixteen and took a job as junior editor of the *Civil and Military Gazette*, he seemed to have two opposing personalities. The ostensibly dominant personality was a dependable and dutiful hard-working administrator type, while his shadow side, individualistic, spontaneous, exuberant, and creative, was typically expressed through what Jung calls 'active imagination.' Yet it is this highly developed, daring shadow side that appears as the stronger personality when we consider

Kipling's writing. Kipling's partial integration of his personal shadow, I have suggested, gives his work its characteristic heroic quality, and this heroic quality, in turn, may be seen as the source of his peculiar, powerful sense of irony – an irony based on an ability to see that personalities are always both fascinating and ridiculous from opposing points of view. But it was an all-consuming irony, and it meant that Kipling's efforts to embody his own shadow were obliged to hover perpetually between the heroic and the ridiculous.

Waiting for the Amir

On 29 March 1885, nineteen-year-old Rudyard Kipling, special correspondent to the *Civil and Military Gazette* of Lahore, was waiting to observe the arrival of the Afghan Amir Abdur Rahman Khan and his entourage, en route to Rawalpindi to hold a highly publicized durbar with the new viceroy, Lord Dufferin. 'Although a little nervous about his first big thing, I think he will do well,' his father, Lockwood Kipling, had noted in a letter when Ruddy had departed from Lahore two weeks earlier.[3] Peshawar, at the edge of the Northwest Frontier Province, was to be the Amir's first stop in British territory after arriving over the Khyber Pass. No one knew exactly when the Amir would arrive, and Kipling, during his first days in Peshawar, had ventured out to inspect the trains and the Amir's bungalow and began writing reports for the *Gazette* which appeared under the title 'To Meet the Ameer.'

A British lieutenant had gone through the Pass with the government carrier pigeons, 'but these useful birds have so far brought us no certain news about anything in particular,' Kipling noted in his dispatch of 27 March. 'When Abdul Rahman has actually set foot within the limits of Peshawur, we may be certain of his arrival. Till then, anything that may be written, rumoured or telegraphed, is of less than no value.' Earlier that day, however, two of the Amir's Sirdars (commanders) had arrived at the camp. 'Neither Kazi Kootb-ud-din nor Aga Hyder-Shah were pleasant to look upon, as they squatted on their charpoys and asked all manner of questions regarding the arrangements of the camp,' Kipling noted, yet look upon them he did: 'The Aga was clad in a camel's hair garment adorned with gold stripes, and his lower limbs were encased in what looked remarkably like European trousers,' while 'the kazi, who lounged about picturesquely in a corduroy waistcoat with brass buttons and a pair of snowy-white pyjamas, was meager, red-haired, and much lined and seamed with exposure.' Some efforts were made to interview the pair, though Kipling acknowledged that 'it is difficult to interview Kizilbashes satisfactorily.' 'A complimentary allusion to their silver mounted swords and belts – magnificent pieces of workmanship – was "cornered" promptly by the remark, that in *their* part of the world "arms were the ornament of a man."' 'This somewhat inapposite codicil was thrown in, possibly to soothe the feelings of the degenerate white man who walks about with a cane,' Kipling noted dryly. As for when the Amir might arrive, 'The Amer was a *Badshah* [king] and could come in when he liked,' the interviewers were told.[4]

If the Amir was not intentionally prolonging his arrival in order to flaunt his power, it certainly appeared that way to Kipling and his British compatriots, who were painfully aware of their political dependence on the Amir in holding the line against Russian advances. The durbar was to be a gaudy display of British military strength and support for the Amir, but painful memories of the British defeat in the recent Second Afghan War of 1878–80, which had crushed British hopes for expansion of the empire further into Afghanistan, simmered beneath the surface. Keeping the Viceroy waiting in Rawalpindi was seen as a humiliation, for, as Kipling noted, 'according to all Oriental notions of etiquette, the superior always arrives after the inferior.'

Kipling found Peshawar strange and depressing, naming it 'The City of Evil Countenances,' as he titled an article written on 28 March after venturing out into the marketplace near the Edwardes Gate where he found 'a scene worthy almost of a place in the Inferno ... everywhere repulsive to every sense.' There, in 'the vast human menagerie between the Gate and the Ghor Khutri,' 'faces of dogs, swine, weazles and goats, all the more hideous for being set on human bodies, and lighted with human intelligence, gather in front of the ring of lamp-light where they may be studied for half an hour at a stretch.' Not that the observer received a very warm welcome: 'As an Englishman passes, they will turn to scowl upon him, and in many cases to spit fluently on the ground after he has passed.' Kipling was particularly impressed by 'one burly big-paunched ruffian, with a shaven head and a neck creased and dimpled with rolls of fat,' who was 'specially zealous in this religious rite – contenting himself with no perfunctory performance, but with a whole-souled expectoration, that must be as refreshing to his comrades, as it is disgusting to the European.' Kipling describes him posing magnificently on a culvert, part of the expensive drainage system the British regarded as their great contribution to 'a proverbially thankless race.' Kipling was aware that 'it is easy to wax cheaply patriotic on this theme, as easy as it is to draw entirely erroneous conclusions from an evening stroll through one of the most wonderful cities on earth,' and that 'the rancorous expectoration of our red-bearded friend ... may mean anything you please,' but he limits his own reading of this expressive act to the observation that 'neither security to life and goods, law, order, discipline, or the best blood of England wasted on their care, reconcile the calibans of the city of evil countenances to the white stranger within their gates.' Peshawar was a revolting, incomprehensible place filled with repulsive people who seemed to hate him as much as he was disgusted by them: an ideal place, in other words, for Kipling to locate his border zone to the exotic – a place of overcoming fear, in which he must hold his ground even as repulsive natives spat upon his civilized ideals.[5]

The following morning Kipling ventured as close as he would ever come to Afghanistan, to the town of Jamrud, two or three miles from the entrance to the Khyber, where he took in the view from the 'elevated and decidedly airy point of vantage' at the fort: 'never did the Afghan hills look more rugged and forbidding than now.' There was still no reliable news of the Amir. 'A descent into the maelstrom of camp followers near the police barracks, keeps the blood from stagnation, and reveals incidentally some curiosities of character.' He was impressed with the camp followers' notion of camp pitching, and found an Afridi boy who proudly showed him his Colt revolver. Many decades later, in recalling his early journalistic assignments in his autobiography, Kipling transformed the border encounter with the gun-toting Afridi boy into a full-fledged 'walk into the Khyber, where I was shot at, but without malice, by a rapparee who disapproved of his ruler's foreign policy.'[6] At 10 o'clock, the Amir's train finally arrived, and Kipling pressed his way through the Afghan crowd to record his impressions of the affably smiling leader and his cavalry: 'wild picturesque men on wild horses – to whose appearance it is impossible to do justice, while writing on the spot.' Golam Hyder, the Amir's commander-in-chief, was particularly impressive, in a uniform of gold braid, his saddle-cloth 'a blaze of gold and velvet, with monograms and devices, *ad lib*, on its surface.' 'Their speech, of course, is utterly unintelligible, and they are all talking and staring about them. One or two have calmly pulled up their horses to look at the Englishman by the wayside. They point like children, and their remarks would, no doubt, be immensely amusing to listen to.'[7] The Amir's entourage represented something far more ambiguously fascinating than the border town of Peshawar, something resplendent, powerful, and at the same time, childish.

Kipling's Domesticated India

In considering the place of the exotic in modern English verse, Kipling's Indian poetry is, for many, the first topic that comes to mind. On closer examination, however, the exotic proves surprisingly absent in Kipling's two main bodies of Indian verse, which he categorized under the headings *Departmental Ditties* and *Barrack-Room Ballads*. The *Departmental Ditties* are satirical studies of Anglo-Indian life and culture, written primarily for the Anglo-Indian audience during Kipling's seven years as a journalist in Lahore and Allahabad, while the *Barrack-Room Ballads* are verses purporting to express the voices of the British soldiers of the Indian Army, mainly written during the two or three years after his return to

England in 1889. Both groups of poems take as their subject groups of people relatively familiar to a British or American audience. The *Departmental Ditties* focused on administrative Anglo-India and, as Ann Parry observes, 'barely acknowledged the existence of native India,' being 'solely concerned with such day-to-day preoccupations of Anglo-Indians as pay, promotion and the vagaries of government departments.'[8] In their original form (ten space-filling verses published in Lahore's *Civil and Military Gazette* in early 1886, expanded in subsequent editions to around fifty) the *Ditties* were intended as light amusement for Anglo-Indian readers, and for the most part satirized pretensions to power within the administrative group. India provided a backdrop of local colour, a mildly exotic flavour in some poems and an atmosphere of unreality in others. Indian characters were deployed mainly to highlight the effects of misguided British policies.

The later series of *Barrack-Room Ballads* takes up the voice of the common British soldier in India mainly for the benefit of the home audience. The topos of the barrack-room, like that of the department, was also a relatively familiar one to English audiences, and the stronger shock-value of the barrack-room verses is due more to their unaccustomed and provocative naturalism than to any unfamiliar exoticism, although a kind of no-nonsense exoticism does enter into a few of the poems where Indians appear as comrades-in-arms, military opponents, and sexual partners. The basic non-exoticism of the poems, however, is symbolized in the topos of the barrack-room itself, a moveable institution of military life, just as the department had offered a convenient symbol of the administrator's role in a compartmentalized administrative power structure. The poems are more interested in questions of class than of race, and perhaps their greatest accomplishment was in showing how ridiculous each class appears from another class's perspective: the common soldier is positioned against 'the Widow at Windsor' and both come off as simultaneously endearing and ridiculous.

What we therefore find, for the most part, in these two categories that together make up the bulk of Kipling's Indian poetry is an already-domesticated exotic: poems set within structures designed to instil a sense of familiarity. For Kipling, the familiarity and non-exoticism of India were personal: since he had spent his first six years there, it would have made a poor choice as a hook for his own exotic projections; on the contrary, India became for him a site of nostalgia. Although Kipling did attempt with some success to grapple with the otherness of India in a few of his stories and, perhaps most successfully, in his novel *Kim*, he made few attempts to do so in his poetry. There, the exotic is relegated to a small position and strongly marked by a particular orientation not toward India as such but rather, as I have suggested, toward the Indian frontier. For Kipling, based in the Panjab, this meant primarily Afghanistan, the volatile region to the northwest.

If we begin with Kipling's South Asian verse as a whole, a body of work essentially complete by 1896, and subtract the two categories of poems mentioned above, we are left only with the *Other Verses* of *Barrack-Room Ballads and Other Verses*, those 'once popular' poems that Peter Keating says have 'probably few enthusiastic readers' today,[9] and if we further subtract from this group the poems not set in the region, what remains is a series of seven poems, of which five are related to Afghanistan: 'The Ballad of East and West,' 'The Ballad of the King's Mercy,' 'The Ballad of the King's Jest,' 'With Scindia to Delhi,' and 'The Lament of the Border Cattle Thief.' These poems, all involved with the border regions of Britain's Indian Empire, are now relatively unknown – primarily, I think, because their contexts, comprehensible in a day when Kipling's readers knew their Marathas from their Mughuls, or at least thought they should, are now obscure to most readers. But they are interesting to rediscover today in order to recover those contexts, and because they represent the only substantial group of Kipling's poems reflecting a type of interest that can be labelled 'exotic.' And, as we shall see, the exotic border space that appears in the poems is heavily invested with qualities associated with Kipling's shadow personality, and the confrontations Kipling stages in these border regions explicitly invoke Kipling's fear-overcoming Peshawar experience of 1885.

Five Afghan Poems

'The Ballad of East and West' is the most famous of these poems, and not only for its well-known refrain: it offers a breathlessly told, compelling narrative based on vivid characterization and a rhythmical structure which complements the movement of the narrative. In the story, the son of a British colonel makes a heroic solitary attempt to rescue his father's horse, stolen from camp by an Afghan border rebel named Kamal. After a chase that severely tests his courage, the colonel's son meets up with Kamal, and, although he falls into Kamal's power, he displays bravery and, instead of being killed, is rewarded. The poem thus stages what I have described above as Kipling's heroic adaptation strategy.

Kamal, the mysterious rebel leader, has stolen the horse of the colonel of the Guides, a famous contingent based at Mardan, a few miles northeast of Peshawar. The Colonel's son initiates a quick discussion among the Guides concerning Kamal's whereabouts, and is informed by the son of the native commander:

> At dusk he harries the Abazai – at dawn he is into Bonair,
> But he must go by Fort Bukloh to his own place to fare,
> So if ye gallop to Fort Bukloh as fast as a bird can fly,
> By the favour of God ye may cut him off ere he win to the Tongue of Jagai.[10]

These places do exist: looking toward the hills surrounding Peshawar, Kipling would have been able to identify the approximate locations of Abazai and Buner, though he never got any closer than this. The apparently casual scattering of obscure place names is a common exoticist strategy, a convenient device to display the writer's often spurious familiarity with mysterious and inaccessible places. The Colonel's son then rides off alone – an improbable act, since he is surrounded by his own troops, any of whom could easily accompany him, but one necessary to the plot, the improbability of which also serves to suggest that the territory here is a psychological one. Moreover, it explicitly harks back to Kipling's own solitary adventure as a correspondent when he travelled heroically alone to a fort near the Afghan border in order to intercept the Amir. Less explicitly, I would suggest, the story harks back to Kipling's solitary adventures of self-fashioning in childhood.

In Jungian terms, the quest of the Colonel's son is an act of intuition, the psychological function most strongly associated with the more elusive aspects of Kipling's personality. The Colonel's son must use intuition, rather than relying on his senses, to head off Kamal, and in fact he relies on the intuition of a fellow guide who advises him of Kamal's probable route. He is successful in tracking Kamal, but is then led on a wild chase until his horse is exhausted, leaving him at Kamal's mercy. What saves the Colonel's son is the mastery of his own body, his ability to control his emotion of fear, his willingness to risk death (all associated in the poem's gendered logic with the renunciation of the feminine) and his acceptance of the transformation of his body into a token of exchange (gendered as masculine). Empowered by this masculine self-mastery to invoke the law of the (colonial) father, the symbolic order in which the death of the son will be valued and 'a thousand swords' will seek retribution, the Colonel's son succeeds in devaluing Kamal's physical mastery. Both men now face a life-threatening crisis, and Kamal defuses the situation by invoking the lost phallic mother with his question, 'What dam of lances brought thee forth to jest at the dawn with Death?' and then beginning a scene of gift exchange which will symbolically repair the castration and restore the lost mother. Although the 'dam of lances' is the only woman to be mentioned, the poem is, after all, structured around the theft and recovery of a mare that properly belongs to the father, no doubt filling in for the absent *mère*, a point reinforced by its explicit eroticization:

'Take up the mare for my father's gift – by God, she has carried a man!'
The red mare ran to the Colonel's son, and nuzzled against his breast;
'We be two strong men,' said Kamal then, 'but she loveth the younger best.
So she shall go with a lifter's dower, my turquoise-studded rein,
My 'broidered saddle and saddle-cloth, and silver stirrups twain.'[11]

Kamal's rather improbable decision to allow the mare's supposed sign of love to determine the outcome of this very volatile situation makes more sense if we view it in the context of the Oedipal resolution. Faced by the castration threat, the son has relinquished the mother to the Other (the father), hoping to regain access to the mother within the imaginary space of the symbolic. And indeed, his hope is fulfilled as he symbolically reclaims the love of the lost mother through the love sign of the *mère* (although a mere mare). In this masculine symbolic order, it seems quite natural for the exchange to end by producing a son: Kamal's, directed to accompany the Colonel's son as protector and to become a faithful member of the guides 'Till Death or I cut loose the tie.' Thus a conflict of birth (i.e., race) is resolved by symbolic exchange governed by the name of the father and death, as we see in the paradox of the famous refrain:

> Oh, East is East, and West is West, and never the twain shall meet,
> Till Earth and Sky stand presently at God's great Judgment Seat;
> But there is neither East nor West, Border, nor Breed, nor Birth,
> When two strong men stand face to face, tho' they come from the ends of the earth![12]

East and West cannot meet in the sense of becoming identical or equal (in Kipling's racially organized world) but they can meet in the sense of standing face to face (i.e., coexisting within the order of the symbolic), for the symbolic is nothing but a system of difference. What enables this recognition, reserved for the 'two strong men' who have mastered the game of the symbolic law of the father (entered into by mastering feminine bodily weakness), is the transformation of the maternal Thing beyond the symbolic that is constituted by difference (the labial Border, Breed, and Birth that constitute difference) into a token of exchange. This is clearly impossible, but the poem shows that it can be done.

The next poem we consider, 'With Scindia to Delhi,' is not concerned with Afghanistan *per se*, but rather with a historical battle that took place in Panipat (a town along the Jumna river north of Delhi) against an Afghan invasion in 1761. The battle, referred to as the third battle of Panipat, has been regarded as a turning point in Indian history, as it weakened the Maratha alliance, the strongest Hindu military power in the subcontinent, and one that would otherwise have presented strong resistance to British incursions into central India. The battle (which has an interesting if somewhat tangential connection to *Kim*, in that the battle was one of those in which the gun Zam-Zamah was used) pitted the Maratha alliance against an Afghan force led by Ahmed Shah Abdali, who brought a force of about forty thousand armoured men supported by such innovations in military technology as camel-mounted swivel-guns. The Maratha resistance ostensibly brought together the forces of the three Maratha rulers under the nominal leadership of Peshwa Balaji Bajirao; these were Mahadji Scindia of Gwalior, Damaji, eldest son of the Gaekwar of Baroda, and Malhar Rao Holkar of Indore. The poem is unusual among Kipling's poems in that its protagonists are entirely Indian – a circumstance that makes more sense if we read it as an allegory of a frequent and painful British experience that would have been difficult to address directly in a poem: the experience of defeat by an Afghan army.

The Maratha empire had been established by Shivaji in the 1640s, but with the death of Shivaji's grandson, power had passed to the Peshwa, or prime minister, and regional Maratha powers had subsequently become more or less independent, as is certainly evident in the poem: Holkar, 'the harlot's traitor son the goatherd Mulhar Rao,' as Kipling calls him, fled the battlefield, and Damaji followed soon afterward. Holkar receives Kipling's full scorn for his cowardly behaviour, while Mahadji Scindia is presented as a heroic figure for continuing the fight. Though severely injured, he managed to escape: Kipling's poem follows an unidentified 'Maratta trooper' who accompanies him in his post-battle ride to Delhi.

Kipling's source for the poem was an obscure historical novel entitled *Lalun the Beragun* by Mirza Moorad Alee Beg, pseudonym of an eccentric Madras-born English Theosophist named Godolphus Mitford, published in Bombay in 1884, the year of the author's death.[13] The poem follows Mitford's story in portraying Scindia attempting to carry with him a favoured *beragun* (a woman of the *bairági*, a caste of wandering Hindu ascetics), Lalun, whom he intends to make his queen. But they are chased by an Afghan warrior, Lutuf-Ullah, who gains as Scindia's mare nears exhaustion. The girl begs Scindia to sacrifice her to aid his escape, and when he refuses, she throws herself from the horse;

Then Scindia checked the gasping mare that rocked and groaned for breath,
And wheeled to charge and plunged the knife a hand's-breadth in her side[.][14]

The confusion over whether 'her' refers to Lalun or the mare is no doubt intentional – the reader is left to ponder the meaning of Scindia's act as he falls unconscious under the dying horse.

Kipling's sympathy with Scindia is no doubt connected with Scindia's courage under fire, but it is also connected with his rather extravagantly emotional behaviour. That Scindia may be regarded as a projection of Kipling's partially repressed feeling function is evident from his tinkering with the ending of the poem, which diverges considerably from Mitford. There, Scindia, 'paralyzed by his extremity, could only lean forward in his saddle and feebly call out to Lalun to come back for God's sake' before Lalun is carried off by Lutuf Ullah, and while Mitford has no information about 'her weal or her woe – the tears she shed or the treatment she experienced in the Afghan tower of the chief of the Populzaees' – he reports that in the British Afghan war of 1879 'the last descendant of our heroine and Lootf-Oolah was shot by an Irishman in the endeavor to reach and carry a British gun.'[15] This bit of information is likely to be as fictive as Kipling's conclusion, but the interesting point is that Kipling's change in the narrative seems designed to rescue Scindia from the pathetic and hopeless emotional paralysis, the sinking into feminine weakness, of Mitford's ending. In Kipling's version, Scindia's act is desperate and irrational, but he remains in control as long as he remains conscious.

Whereas 'The Ballad of East and West' and 'With Scindia to Delhi' present model cases of the heroic and tragic consequences of mastering feminine emotions, 'The Ballad of the King's Mercy' offers a cynical but informative view of the way weakness of personality may be manipulated by a person who possesses mastery of self. The poem's narrative, set in Kabul, tells how the Amir, intuiting the disloyalty of a secretly rebellious Afghan, Yar Khan, manipulates him into revealing his disloyalty by requiring him to perform a humiliating task: executing a Hindu who has assaulted a Pathan. The Amir patiently waits until Yar Khan seeks retribution; he is then arrested and slowly tortured by stoning until he publicly begs for a merciful death. Granting this death is the 'King's mercy,' a phrase intended somewhat ironically.

The ignominious Yar Khan would seem an unlikely figure for Kipling to identify with. But we may recall parallel elements in the story of Kipling's encounter with the Amir at the durbar: like Yar Khan, he suffered from feelings of humiliation and impatience. Yar Khan is, in effect, the Kipling who acts on these feelings and dies a horrible death as a result.

The need for restraint is explicitly the theme of 'The Ballad of the King's Jest,' a poem well known because its story is the seed of a major plot strand in the novel *Kim*. Here again Kipling makes extensive use of his brief frontier visit, as is clear from the opening lines:

> When spring-time flushes the desert grass,
> Our kafilas wind through the Khyber Pass.
> Lean are the camels but fat the frails,
> Light are the purses but heavy the bales,
> As the snowbound trade of the North comes down
> To the market-square of Peshawur town.[16]

The poem, set at Peshawar and Jamrud, tells the story of a King who, though not identified by name, is clearly the Amir (as the reference to 'Gholam Hyder, the

Red Chief' – the Amir's commander-in-chief – indicates), and revolves around the rumoured presence of 'a gray-coat guard on the Helmund ford.' It is based on an actual event, the Russian occupation of Pandjeh, near Herat, which had been under discussion at the Amir's durbar. In reality, it was Lord Dufferin's private secretary who kept him 'dancing on the mat for half a day' refusing him news, while in the poem it is the more exotic Mahbub Ali the muleteer who defers the narrator's desire for gossip, telling him the story of a certain Wali Dad who once warned the Amir of an impending Russian attack and was duly appointed to stand vigil awaiting their arrival, until after seven days he finally goes mad and dies.

> Friend of my heart, is it meet or wise
> To warn a King of his enemies?[17]

One can imagine this sort of helpful lesson about staying out of the political line of fire coming from a viceroy's private secretary, and it is interesting to see the way it evolves into the voice of Mahbub Ali, first, in the poem, where it is accepted without comment by the unidentified speaker, and later, in the novel, where it is disregarded by Kim. Kim is the positive figure of Kipling's incompletely achieved shadow – the Kipling who would have disregarded the secretary's advice not to meddle, the Kipling who would have gone into the Khyber Pass to find the Amir rather than hanging around dejectedly at the border, the Kipling who manages to become Indian without sacrificing his White racial identity. But in Kipling's world, for every Kim or Colonel's son who overreaches and succeeds spectacularly, there is a Yar Khan or Wali Dad who fails miserably. These poems, like so much of Kipling, profess to offer lessons in how to get into the one group rather than the other.

The last Afghan poem of this group, 'The Lament of the Border Cattle Thief,' returns to the Afghan frontier, this time taking up the case of an imprisoned cattle thief of the Zukka Khel, considered to be 'the strongest and most turbulent clan' of the Afridi, themselves distinguished for their violent ways among the various Pathan subgroups. Kipling's cattle thief is no exception, and is spending his disagreeable confinement planning revenge on both the 'Young *Sahib* with the yellow hair' and the 'Fat herds below Bonair' (this being the third poem of the group to evokes the two obscure towns of Abazai and Buner). 'For every cow I spared before – / In charity set free –' the cattle-thief promises, 'If I may reach my hold once more / I'll reive an honest three.'[18] Incarceration is clearly not an ideal solution for this character, and in part, this is a bit of journalistic railing at misguided public expenditures. But again, I would suggest, Kipling manages to identify with the border cattle thief – there is something irresistibly independent about him, and he is certainly no one to trifle with. If Afghanistan is the region associated with Kipling's shadow personality, the border cattle-thief serves as an apt figure for the irrepressible unconscious and the impossibility of policing borders within the personality. Borders will be crossed, and attempts at repression simply compound the damage.

Looking at Kipling's conception of the exotic through this series of Afghan scenes and characters reveals a series of efforts to confirm and reaffirm the unique configuration of personality that enabled Kipling's special contribution to colonial literature and identity, which might be described as an ideology that transforms childhood trauma into heroism, based on the idea of overcoming the self and fear of the other in the right sorts of ways. This ideology, however, is finally indistinguishable from the personal mythology through which Kipling claims ownership of a success accomplished not in the space of the real, but rather in a place arranged by his parents, the real agents of Kipling's rescue and abandonment. The events that take place in the imaginary Afghan space, with its conspicuously displayed factual referents, all work toward the construction of this personal mythology of overcoming and its associated ideology. As do the characters: the Colonel's son as idealized man of action, overcoming fear and reaping rewards; the cowardly Holkar, who helps create an opening for foreign conquest; the heroic Scindia, who nobly survives the fight but barely escapes falling victim to his own emotional weakness; the unfortunate Wali Dad and Yar Khan, who are punished for overreaching; and the border cattle thief, whose existence is a constant reminder that the other cannot be fully repressed. All of the successes contain traces of failure: the Colonel's son and Scindia both ought to have been killed and only survive miraculously, while the failures are all to some extent sympathetic. The disturbing trend of Kipling's later work can be located in the progressive erasure of the traces of failure from his heroic ideology, and the general conflation of his personal mythology with the ideology of British imperialism. His autobiography, written in the 1930s, has him shot at during his Afghan border experience, and his former schoolmate G.C. Beresford complained of Kipling's presentation of himself as 'a hearty, hefty, athletic person to match his propaganda of imperialism and jingoism, instead of what he was – a podgy, spectacled highbrow.'[19]

Chapter Three

The Exotic Transgressions of 'Laurence Hope'

When we think of the poetry of British imperialism, we tend to think of the male poets who sang its praises or criticized its methods – poets such as Kipling, Henley, Newbolt, Lyall, and Blunt, perhaps Yeats – or the male poets enthralled by the exotic, Edwin Arnold or James Elroy Flecker. But the colonies also produced many women poets, although their names have been largely forgotten – women such as Emma Roberts, whose *Oriental Scenes, Sketches, and Tales* appeared in 1832, Mary Carshore of Rajapore, whose *Songs of the East* was published in 1855, and Mary Leslie, whose *Sorrows, Aspirations, and Legends, from India* appeared in 1858. These women poets were not often taken seriously, nor, it would seem, were they often encouraged to take their own work seriously: 'the Authoress,' Mary Carshore acknowledged in the preface to *Songs of the East*, 'must naturally feel a diffidence and hesitation in thus venturing to appear before the world, and cannot be without many doubts and fears as to her success.' It is difficult to gauge the success of these 'unpretending little volume[s]' in India, with their picturesque accounts of quaint native customs and patriotic sentiments, but there can be little doubt that they found no substantial audience outside of the Anglo-Indian community and only a small one within it. But one woman poet, Violet Nicolson, did break the success barrier with her three volumes of 'Indian Love Lyrics,' published between 1901 and 1905; she did so, however, by posing as a man, by breaking the conventions of Victorian propriety, and by catering to the home audience's interest in the exotic. Through the poems, the reader at home could vicariously experience the fantasy of the Oriental despot's power, particularly his sexual omnipotence, with all of its inherent possibilities of violence, cruelty, exoticism, and erotic passion:

You are my God, and I would fain adore You
  With sweet and secret rites of other days.

> Burn scented oil in silver lamps before You,
>   Pour perfume on Your feet with prayer and praise.[1]

Or experience the transgressive thrill of visiting an exotic Indian temple, where

> Strange, weird things that no man may say,
>   Things Humanity hides away; –
> Secretly done, –
> Catch the light of the living day,
>   Smile in the sun.
> Cruel things that man may not name,
> Naked here, without fear or shame,
>   Laughed in the carven stone.[2]

The urges of the repressed West clearly had the run of things in Laurence Hope's India.

The early success of *The Garden of Kama* was aided by the popularity of Amy Woodforde-Finden's musical arrangements of 'Four Indian Love Lyrics' the following year, the most popular of which was 'Kashmiri Song':

> Pale hands I loved beside the Shalimar,
> Where are you now? Who lies beneath your spell?
> Whom do you lead on Rapture's roadway, far,
> Before you agonise them in farewell?
>
> Oh, pale dispensers of my Joys and Pains,
> Holding the doors of Heaven and of Hell,
> How the hot blood rushed wildly through the veins
> Beneath your touch, until you waved farewell.
>
> Pale hands, pink tipped, like Lotus buds that float
> On those cool waters where we used to dwell,
> I would have rather felt you round my throat,
> Crushing out life, than waving me farewell![3]

With its hint of forbidden, tragic interracial passion and lush Oriental atmosphere, 'Kashmiri Song' remained popular for decades.

The poems, with their eroticism and violence, were not only different from earlier Anglo-Indian poetry, they went far beyond anything previously seen in England, or in America, where they were also widely acclaimed and often reviled.

They portrayed a world of primal sexual and aggressive urges acted upon, where passion outweighed reason, where politeness and reserve did not exist:

> When I have slowly drawn my knife across you,
>   Taking my pleasure as I see you swoon,
> I shall sleep sound, worn out by love's last fervour,
>   And then, God grant your kinsmen kill me soon![4]

It was a world in which all of the transgressive desires of the West found free expression, a veritable playground of the unconscious, and it was all happening, apparently, in India. 'Let the reader who desires to enjoy the real beauties of this collection, never forget as he reads, that these are the love songs of young Eastern blood, whose laws of conduct were framed to fit their temperament, not ours,' John Lane stressed in an advertising circular for the second book, *Stars of the Desert*.[5]

The Real Thing, or a Clever Simulation?

But were the translations authentic? The confusion was aptly expressed by an early reviewer in the 15 March 1902 *Athenaeum*, who wrote, 'It is not clear to us precisely what Mr. Laurence Hope means by "arrangement," or whether Valgovind, Mahomed Akram, Zahir-u-Din, Taj Mahomed, and others, to whom many of these verses are ascribed, are more than projections of his own poetic personality.' In spite of this doubt, the reviewer goes with it: while several passages 'betray an Anglo-Indian rather than a native inspiration,' the reviewer concludes, 'Mr. Hope has caught admirably the dominant notes of this Indian love poetry, its delirious absorption in the instant, its out-of-door air, its melancholy' and 'brings us into a region of native feeling and imagination never yet fully explored.'[6] Francis Thompson, in his unsigned review published on the same day, concurred: 'They are essential translations, in the best sense; and the measure of their literal fidelity concerns us as little as in the case of FitzGerald.'[7] Edith Thomas also cited Fitzgerald in her 1902 review in the *Critic*: 'The genius of the translator, or the adapter, is so flexibly great, in both the cases cited, that we are made, *first*, to feel the equivalence and kinship of human emotion and desire wherever on this earth they have their action and being; and, *afterwards*, to discern the special marks of race differentiation and the outlines of the strange landscape in which they have their setting.' Thomas thought Mr Hope's poems transmitted remarkably well this 'racial' temperament – 'the wondrous lethal fascination and the "Inherent Cruelty of Things" in the ancient land of Vishnu.' The *Indian Love Lyrics*, she suggested, could be thought of as a worthy addition to 'the aggregation of such temperamental songs of a race as "The Roumanian Folk-Lore Songs," or the recent Celtic revival by Mr. Yeats and others.'[8] The critic William Morton Payne, writing in the January 1903 *Dial*, was not so easily persuaded: 'It is a pretense easy of penetration that would have us think of Mr. Laurence Hope's collection of "India's Love Lyrics" as translations, or even paraphrases, of Eastern originals. The title-page admits that Mr. Hope has "collected and arranged" these poems; it might as well have said outright that he is their author.' And yet Payne allows that 'they are Indian in theme, no doubt, and Indian in their warmth and color, as well as in their sentiment and imagery.'[9]

The authenticity question was, in other words, necessary but irrelevant. From a Jungian perspective, authenticity may be regarded as a necessary stage in the establishment of a site or 'hook' for the projection of unconscious contents. Projection may be understood as a game played between the ego and the unconscious that requires the acquiescence of the ego; the game is up once the ego discovers the numinous object to be merely a projection. But even if the inauthenticity of the projected object is later discovered, the mechanism of repression and the unconscious origins of the repressed contents will not be exposed and will remain intact as long as the ego can justify the original belief in the projected object: to put it in simpler terms, the projection survives the mistake. Thus, exoticism tends to treat authenticity as a formality, a stamp of approval that validates the site of the exotic projection that, once granted, has served its purpose. Afterward, any further considerations of authenticity are likely to be actively discouraged; if they succeed, and approval is revoked, the projection can find an alternative hook or continue without one. In short, just as a racist's belief in Black cannibals is not altered by proof that his Black neighbour is not one, the erotic, violent India of Laurence Hope cannot be affected by a failure to find the India described in the poems.

The main objection to exoticism's cavalier attitude toward authenticity, of course, came from the supposed exotic objects themselves, who naturally resented being made the bearers of Westerners' repressed unconscious projections. The only review that seriously grappled with the authenticity question appeared in the *Calcutta Review* in April 1904. Though the anonymous review had the general title 'Western Interpreters of Eastern Verse,' it was actually a sustained attack on the authenticity of Laurence Hope's *The Garden of Kama*. India had been the land of opportunity for many – soldiers, civilians, and writers, the reviewer suggests. 'But, there is one class of writer, who has made "opportunity" of India, in a way we cannot but resent. I refer to those who indulge a taste for the forbidden, and – indecent, by sheltering behind a misrepresentation of a country their knowledge of which may be summed up in the bare fact that it is the home of elemental passion.'[10] Laurence Hope is not at this point named, though it is clear that she is the sole representative of the type, of which, indeed, no other example is offered. 'We read into the things we see, that which we bring to them,' the writer concedes. It was therefore the obligation of the 'interpreted' to question the accuracy of the interpretation, and the reviewer attempts to demonstrate that the 'essence' of the East depicted in the poems is not the true essence of the East:

> All the world throbs to one pulse in the East. Men and women take the mystery of God's great Life-gift, as simply as does the flower or animal life around them. The West, with its taint of the 'civilized,' its cleavage between human and animal and vegetable, its suggestions of the improper – born, of necessity, of its highly developed civilization – looks on, and reads into the wondrous work of creation, thoughts of ugliness and ill. Not all the West, of a truth; but this 'West' to which I now refer.[11]

The reviewer proceeds to cite representative passages from the early Vedic hymns, from the erotic Radha-Krishna poetry of the twelfth century, from seventeenth-century Maratha poetry, and from Persian poetry. Nowhere does the reviewer find poetry like that of Laurence Hope, with its 'monotonous passion, and unbeautiful suggestion.' There were other problems to be found in the details. 'In truth are these things difficult to be known by strangers: but why then write love-lyrics which you call *Indian?* Label them otherwise.'[12] The point was well taken. The 'Indian Love Lyrics' are certainly a misrepresentation of Indian life, if they are indeed taken as being representative – and they were: even, paradoxically, when their authenticity was questioned. The potential damage of such misrepresentations was utterly lost on most critics, whose obliviousness reaffirmed the unspoken belief that it was the West's prerogative to represent the East in whatever fashion it pleased. This sort of critique, therefore, was entirely and even wilfully absent from criticism of the poems in British and American periodicals. When Laurence Hope's third book was reviewed together with C.F. Usborne's more authentic but less popular *Panjabi Lyrics and Proverbs* in the *Spectator*, the reviewer was forced to contend with Usborne's statement that he had consulted 'a native' about Laurence Hope, and had been informed that, although it was beautiful poetry, the sentiment seemed entirely Western. 'This is enough to make the rashest critic pause,' wrote the reviewer 'for the conventional comment on "Laurence Hope's" books is that they breathe the authentic spirit of the East. Yet we think we can understand the point of view. It is the sentiment of the East; but the form of its expression, the self-consciousness, the clear analysis, the wider horizon, are entirely Western.' For it was, the reviewer observed, 'impossible to imagine any Oriental attaining so articulate and passionate an expression.'[13]

There were a number of other ways of getting around the authenticity problem. Brian Hooker, a minor poet and librettist, wrote in the *Bookman* in 1909: 'it is not, of course, of the smallest importance whether her Oriental atmosphere and detail are in fact accurate and correct, any more than it matters whether the Celtic Revival school reproduce correctly the spirit of old Celtic literature.' The claim of Irish writers to reimagine the Irish past might seem self-evidently different from a British woman's right to represent India's present, but this distinction was lost on Hooker and other critics of the day. The autonomy of the Western fantasy of the East was not something Hooker was willing to undermine:

> She holds the gorgeous East in fee; and through her we hear our own dreams of it – of fierce joys and pains, a swarming vividness of life, a fate cruelly smiling, death-cries trodden under the feet of interminable generations and sultry fevers of desire. It is a new dream, intensely modern and a little unhealthy; but it has a tone and colour of its own, and it will find a place in our literature and live there.[14]

Hooker's language captures perfectly the paradox of the exotic: the poems are at the same time both dream and reality, a projected fantasy that becomes, through the poet's creative intensity, a reality destined to live a life of its own. Such language, of course, practically unmasks the exotic as a Western fantasy, but it avoids this unmasking by relocating the basis of the authenticity claim within the framework of aesthetics and psychology: the poems are authentic because they are psychologically and aesthetically compelling. In an age of aestheticism this was not seen as a substitute for authenticity: it was authenticity. Arthur Symons doubted whether the poems 'have, for sheer fidelity, any parallel in European literature.'[15]

Biographical Fragments

It is easier to account for the poems' reception than to explain how they came to be written in the first place. What we know about the life of Violet Nicolson is rather sketchy.[16] The daughter of Colonel Arthur Cory of the Bengal Army, she was born Adela Florence Cory in England in 1865 (her father was then on leave). With the exception of her English birth and early separation from her parents, her childhood was remarkably similar to Kipling's: she and her sisters were raised in England by relatives, and she spent part of her teens at a boarding school in Italy before, at the age of sixteen, rejoining her family in Lahore, where her father, now retired, was coeditor of the *Civil and Military Gazette*. Poems written in her early teens show her already sublimating the loneliness and depression that would plague her throughout her life into an identification with romanticized sacrifice and suffering. Whereas Kipling dealt with his childhood crises through a heroic self-overcoming, Nicolson adapted through self-denial and the idealization of suffering.

When Colonel Cory fell ill, the family was forced to return to England (Cory was replaced by the young Kipling), but after the Colonel's recovery the family returned to India, and the Colonel took up the editorship of the *Sind Gazette* in Karachi. Adela and her sisters, Vivian (who later became the popular and exotic novelist 'Victoria Cross') and Isabel, assisted their father with the newspaper. In 1889, at twenty-three, she married Colonel Malcolm Hassels Nicolson, forty-six, of the Bombay Army, commander of a native regiment, veteran of the Second Afghan War, and an expert linguist. After several years of regimental duty in various regions of northwest India, Colonel Nicolson became Commanding Officer of a small cantonment in Central India, and two years later was promoted to General and transferred to Mhow, the headquarters of the Western Command (located in the Native State of Indore), where he served as Commanding Officer from 1895 to 1900. As the General's wife, Violet Nicolson occupied a prestigious position, but she was regarded as eccentric. The Scottish writer Violet Jacob, who lived in Mhow for several years, described her in 1897 as 'a tiny, fair, very strange woman, vilely and impossibly clothed.' 'I always find her rather interesting,' she added, 'though of course everyone mocks at her and I can't help doing it myself sometimes at the really absurd figure she makes.'[17] Rumours have naturally developed about Violet Nicolson's transgressive behaviour during these years – Somerset Maugham wrote a well-known story based on her supposed affair with an Indian prince, while others claimed she and Amy Woodforde-Finden had been lovers.[18]

Nicolson's second book, *Stars of the Desert*, appeared in 1903 while the Nicolsons were in London following a sojourn in North Africa. During that year she had some interaction with literary society (notably meeting Thomas Hardy at the home of Blanche Crackanthorpe). In 1904 the Nicolsons returned to India, but in August Malcolm died during a routine prostate operation. Two months later, Violet committed suicide, swallowing a corrosive poison. A friend wrote to Hardy, who wrote an anonymous obituary for the *Athenaeum*. This was later expanded at the request of her publisher, William Heinemann, into a preface for her third book.[19] Heinemann, however, declined to use the preface in the volume, which appeared in 1905 as *Indian Love* in England, and as *Last Poems: Translations from the Book of Indian Love* in the United States.

The Scandal of Confession

Despite the poet's elaborate devices of concealment – the pseudonym, the pretence of translation, the fictionalized characters – it is apparent, and was apparent even to some of her contemporaries, that the poems were deeply personal, even confessional. The 'Dedication to Malcolm Nicolson' that prefaces her last collection invited such speculations, while providing at the same time an ambiguous disclaimer:

> I, who of lighter love wrote many a verse,
>   Made public never words inspired by thee,
> Lest strangers' lips should carelessly rehearse
>   Things that were sacred and too dear to me.
>
> Thy soul was noble; through these fifteen years
>   Mine eyes familiar, found no fleck nor flaw,
> Stern to thyself, thy comrades' faults and fears
>   Proved generosity thine only law.
>
> Small joy was I to thee; before we met
>   Sorrow had left thee all too sad to save.
> Useless my love —— as vain as this regret
>   That pours my hopeless life across thy grave.[20]

Even today, when we are accustomed to confessional poetry unflinchingly exploring private and emotionally fraught aspects of poets' personal lives, Nicolson's 'Dedication' remains disturbing; how much more so it must have seemed in an age of propriety and restraint. The reviewer in the *Academy* was among those who disapproved of 'the painful revelation in the latest poems.' 'The dedication and some of the other verses,' the reviewer observed, 'force an active imagination to read between the lines matters which the mind instinctively feels it is intrusive in formulating. Some women of emotional temperament have this lack of final reticence under the pressure of sorrow, and seem to take a fierce pleasure in inviting the whole world to gaze upon their holy of holies.' The 'Dedication' was only the tip of the iceberg: 'There are pieces in it which, despite her warning, it is impossible not to connect with her life,' wrote Henry Bruce. Another critic found 'the sense of tragedy and personal pain' to be 'so strong that wandering, or rather, being compelled, into a Hospital "theatre" during an operation would scarcely be a more unwelcome experience.'[21]

But the horror of confession was the flip side of the qualities that fascinated the critics: her sincerity and passion. 'She is so hotly in earnest that it seems beside the mark to criticise her for technical carelessness, or an occasional lapse into the obvious,' wrote the *Academy*'s reviewer. Flecker, too, thought that sincerity and passion were the key qualities of this 'sincere but imperfect artist,' observing that 'very often the glow of passion transfuses lead into gold.' 'The passion and fire of Laurence Hope's lyric inspiration is astonishing,' Harold Williams remarks. The very significance of *The Garden of Kama*, the 1902 *Athenaeum* reviewer observed, was 'the tremulous, irrecoverable deliciousness of young passion.'[22]

Indeed, a number of reviewers complained that the later books failed to maintain the same level of passionate intensity. Francis Thompson, who admired the 'elemental and barbaric passion' of the first book, expressed disappointment that in the first part of *Stars of the Desert*, 'the passion lacks conviction, there is a note of Western weariness and unvitality masquing in hotness of phrase,' and relief that toward the end of the book, 'the authenticity of passion returns.'[23] The *Athenaeum*'s reviewer of the third book, *Indian Love*, thought that the passion was 'beginning to seem forced, the colour is fading. It would seem that the vein which the author worked successfully was nearing exhaustion.'[24] But the poet's suicide helped to persuade many of the authenticity of her passion: her explicit figuration of her suicide as *sati* in the suicide-note dedication to her last volume was clearly intended to link her own fate to the fates of her tragic heroines. For Hardy, 'the tragic circumstances of her death seem but the impassioned closing notes of her impassioned effusions,' and the *Academy*'s reviewer hoped 'that in these three volumes of tropical verse, which are like the white-hot lava from a crater, a vexed and passionate spirit has dissipated its inquietude.' Some reviewers, of course, found the level of passionate eroticism excessive and even intolerable. The 1905 *TLS* reviewer, who found that the poems 'touch on one side the love of women – the women of the Western's East; on the other the jungle-lusts of the tiger,' returned gratefully to 'that other Laurence, Mr. Binyon, thankful that there are more ways than one of making and singing love.' Even Arthur Symons conceded that the poems 'crave an antidote.'[25] One might conclude from these opposing reactions to Laurence Hope's confessional excess on the one hand, and to her sincerity and passion on the other, that passion and sincerity were qualities felt to be relatively repressed within British and American culture at the turn of the nineteenth century.

It was not only that the poems were full of intense feeling, although this was part of the attraction; it was also that the poems were about experiencing another culture through its structures of feeling. It is useful to recall Jung's view of feeling as a rational, judging function 'differing from intellectual judgment in that its aim is not to establish conceptual relations but to set up a subjective criterion of acceptance or rejection.'[26] The poems of Laurence Hope show feeling to be not only capable of extraordinary intensity, but also great power as a means of understanding and interacting with the world. What the poet knows of India she knows primarily through feeling rather than intellect.

Moreover, the poet is generally accepting of India and its customs, and conversely, rather critical of the West. Feeling is a function with strong connections to social custom; extraverted feeling, Jung explains, 'is always in harmony with objective values': usually 'traditional or generally accepted values of some kind.'[27] Thus, it was extraordinary and shocking that Violet Nicolson was so strongly drawn to *non-Western* structures of feeling. This feeling for the East over the West was implicit in the first book, but quite explicit by the third book, as in the following lines from a poem that celebrates the poet's return to India:

> These are my people, and this my land,
> I hear the pulse of her secret soul.
> This is the life that I understand,
> Savage and simple and sane and whole.[28]

'It is a new note in English poetry, but it is not an English note,' Arthur Symons observed. 'These, after all, are not the accents of the races that rule the world.'[29]

Chapter Four

Everybody's Anima:
Sarojini Naidu as Nightingale and Nationalist

In April 1917 *Poetry* magazine 'discovered' Sarojini Naidu's first book of poetry, *The Golden Threshold*, first published a dozen years earlier. In part it was Arthur Symons's glowing introduction that caught the attention of the reviewer, Eunice Tietjens, yet Tietjens, at the time deeply entranced by the Orient, was also captivated by the 'elusive personality of this young Hindu woman,' whose poems she found 'strangely alluring.' 'These are subtle, delicately-wrought lyrics, self-conscious with the same quiet poise that pervades the Hindu classics, a poise that disregards with mystic certainty the confusing sense of the plurality of the universe which colors so much western thinking.' Tietjens had got into the mystic certainty thing when Edgar Lee Masters gave her a copy of the *Bhagavad Gita* and 'changed the whole course of her spiritual existence,' and at the time of the review, she was just back from a trip to China and Japan, during which she had met Japanese poet Yone Noguchi and Bengali poet Rabindranath Tagore, 'whom so many of us hold in admiration little short of veneration.'[1] A passing reference to Naidu's 'more strongly nationalistic' poems seems to cloud this picture of the poet's commitment to the mystical oneness of the universe, but Tietjens has little interest in this, choosing rather to focus on one lyric in particular which 'might almost, in its color and imagery, be an incidental lyric in Kalidasa's *Shakuntala*,' the classical poetic drama which had been, since William Jones's eighteenth-century translation, the standard of comparison for Indian poetry.[2]

Several months earlier the *New Republic* had been sufficiently less enthusiastic (in these waning days of the 'Tagore craze') to title its review simply 'Another Hindoo Poet'; it was argued that, although written by 'a Hindoo woman of pure blood,' there was 'nothing specially Hindoo in the book now published; it is European in structure, and even in tradition it is European.' 'Girton and King's College have done their work thoroughly,' lamented the reviewer, who went on to argue that the British poet Laurence Hope was more authentically Indian than

Naidu: Laurence Hope, the reviewer suggests, 'needed just India for a setting – needed the cruel heat of the Indian day and the hallucination of the Indian night,' while 'Sarojini Naidu's poems might have suggested themselves in Connaught or Cornwall or even in New Jersey.' Naidu 'seems Indian by obligation: take away the Indian decoration, which is extraneous and not, in sum, very much, and what have you but some very musical western poetry – English poetry?'[3] Two reviews, only months apart, one proclaiming a poet who captured the supposed essence of classical Hinduism, the other refusing to acknowledge anything more than a decorative Indianness, both, however, fixated on the question of the authenticity of the poet's representation of India to a Western audience. Of these two opposing, but equally limited, views, the latter has had somewhat more weight in determining Naidu's place in the English canon, or rather, her lack of one. As the *Concise Cambridge History of English Literature* pronounced in 1941, 'Some of her songs are little more than exotically sentimental utterances that might have come from an English writer who knew the East by hearsay: but others give vivid vignettes of native life and some embody the spirit of Oriental devotion. In general her work is more remarkable for its command of English than for any revelation of India.'[4]

Naidu's failure to reveal something new about India has not been as much at issue in Indian appraisals of her work, where her alleged over-dependence on English Romantic poets as models has been considered her major failing. 'It was Sarojini's ill-luck that she wrote at a time when English poetry had touched the rock bottom of sentimentality and technical poverty,' the poet Nissim Ezekiel has written.[5] 'It is true,' writes M.K. Naik, 'that her verse, at its worst, suffers from sentimentality, vagueness, sloppiness, a lack of intellectual fibre and a cloying sweetness. It is also unfortunate that though she possessed a sharp wit and a fine comic sense, she did not allow these to function in her poetry. She failed to grow as a poet too, devoting in mid-career to politics what could have gone into poetry.'[6] Yet, Naik continues, her finest lyrics 'are not just a weak echo of the feeble voice of decadent romanticism; they are an authentic Indian English lyric utterance exquisitely tuned to the composite Indian ethos ... Of all her contemporaries she had perhaps the finest ear and her mastery of word-music is indisputable.'[7] Naik's description of her poetry as 'an authentic *Indian English* lyric utterance' – an authentic hybrid – displaces the (Western) question of whether she presents an authentic monocultural Indian voice. And yet it is the limitations of this hybrid voice that are consistently stressed in Naik's reading of her work, and indeed, in much of the recent Indian criticism of it.

Coming to Naidu's poems through this critical history, we may easily lose sight of what a remarkable and unique figure Naidu really was. What was involved in Naidu's efforts to acquire an English poetic voice at a time when English poetry offered limited openings for the Indian, and when both English and Indian poetry offered little hope of recognition for the female poet? Naidu's carving-out of a position for a female poetic voice, between the doubly silencing constraints of colonialist racialism and Indian patriarchalism, necessarily demanded concessions to both of these fields of power, concessions which have, predictably, subjected her work to intense criticism by readers approaching her work from feminist and postcolonial perspectives. In my reading of her work, I would like to focus on the difficulties Naidu faced in acquiring this poetic voice, and examine the way it enabled and empowered her participation in a field of Indian nationalist politics which restricted access to Indian women.

Sarojini Chattopâdhyây was born in 1879 in the native state of Hyderabad, where the ruling Nizam enjoyed a relatively independent status under an agreement which allowed the British Army to maintain a garrison there. Her Bengali Brahmin father, Dr Aghorenath Chattopâdhyây, had studied science at Edinburgh and returned to settle in Hyderabad, where he served as a physician under the Nizam and later founded Nizam College. In an unpublished autobiographical fiction entitled 'Sunalini: A Passage from Her Life,' Sarojini later recalled the intellectual ferment surrounding her father, epitomized in the moonlight gatherings of which

> he was the chief, the host of a coterie of men of all nationalities and creeds, of all sorts and conditions: wild young poets, with garlands round their hair intoning their delicious verses, and sage philosophers solving the deepest problems of humanity; saints, who had given up their lives to prayer and meditation on things occult, and astrologers who had studied the secret of the stars; atheists and theologians, princes and paupers, dreamers and alchemists, Hindu pundit, Moslem Mollah, and Christian priest: and while they closed in the heat of an endless discussion, a bewildering rapid and delightful interchange of thoughts and ideas utterly at war with one another, unheeded by any, and noticed by none, Sunalini would steal in behind her father's seat and breathlessly drink in the confused babel of wit.[8]

The often-discussed account of Sarojini's first reluctant, and then emphatic, embrace of English appears in Arthur Symons's introduction to *The Golden Threshold*: 'Sarojini was the eldest of a large family, all of whom were taught English at an early age. "I," she writes, "was stubborn and refused to speak it. So one day when I was nine years old my father punished me – the only time I was ever punished – by shutting me in a room alone for a whole day. I came out of it a full-blown linguist. I have never spoken any other language to him, or to my mother, who always speaks to me in Hindustani."'[9] This scene may be understood in Jungian terms as one of several personality-defining moments in which

Sarojini discovered her vocation as a poet. 'The poetic instinct, which I inherited from him and also from my mother (who wrote some lovely Bengali lyrics in her youth) proved stronger. One day, when I was eleven, I was sighing over a sum in algebra: it *wouldn't come right*; but instead a whole poem came to me suddenly. I wrote it down.'[10] What we see in these scenes is Sarojini, in order to remain in a relationship of positive feeling with her father (who hoped that she would be 'a great mathematician or a scientist'), rejecting the fascinating but confusing world of introverted sensation by becoming, in the first instance, a person who can speak English, and in the second, a person who can write poetry. Thus, as Sarojini recounted it to Symons, began her career as an English poet. She wrote 'a long poem *à la* "Lady of the lake,"' a poetic drama, a novel, and 'fat volumes of journals.'[11]

Sarojini's intuitive solution to the crisis of feeling brought on by her father's dissatisfaction was the first of a series of personality reinventions in which she reinvented herself in relation to a series of extraordinary men: the British poets Edmund Gosse and Arthur Symons, and the Indian leaders Gopal Krishna Gokhale and Mohandas K. Gandhi. These adaptations may be understood through the Jungian concept of the *anima*. The anima is an image, produced by the masculine-gendered unconscious, representing the inner attitude of the personality, and taking the female gender in opposition to the gender of the outward persona. It is more elusive than the shadow, for 'whereas the shadow can be seen through and recognized fairly easily, the anima and animus are much further away from consciousness and in normal circumstances are seldom if ever realized.'[12] The anima 'is represented in the unconscious by definite persons with the corresponding qualities' and is frequently projected onto a suitable object (mothers and wives being prime candidates) resulting in 'an absolute affective tie to the object.' The anima is not merely a factor in individual psychology: she also has an important cultural presence as a result of what Jung calls her 'supra-individual quality.' We find her as a frequent subject in cultural forms such as art, film, and music, where she may be recognized by her numinous quality, the 'mysterious factor' that points to her identity with elements repressed in the masculine personality. 'Most men, probably, who have any psychological insight at all will know what Rider Haggard means by "She-who-must-be-obeyed,"' Jung notes.[13] In contrast, woman's counterpart to the anima, the animus, 'does not appear as one person, but as a plurality of persons'; it 'is rather like an assembly of fathers or dignitaries of some kind who lay down incontestable, "rational," ex cathedra judgments,'[14] something quite like the 'coterie of men' Sarojini encountered in the paternal world of her childhood. Her self-reinvention as her father's anima-poet thus brought her into relationship with the larger field of the animus.

Sarojini graduated from the University of Madras at the age of twelve and in

1895, at the age of sixteen, was sent to England on a scholarship from the Nizam. Accompanied to England by theosophist Annie Besant,[15] she began her studies at King's College, Cambridge, but found the lectures tiresome, and after a brief stint at Girton, ceased to attend them.[16]

'What we wished to receive': Gosse and Symons

When Sarojini met Edmund Gosse in January of 1896, it was, she wrote him, the fulfilment of a premonition that 'the magical name [of Gosse] was to be one of the strongest and most inevitable influences on my life.'[17] Gosse was then a well-known critic and occasional poet, and Sarojini was undoubtedly aware of his earlier patronage of Toru Dutt, the Indian poet whose brief fame in the 1870s had been cut short by her tragic death. When Gosse read some of Sarojini's early work, he was impressed with her skill as a poet but felt disappointment and embarrassment at the content of the poems. 'Many were Western in feeling and imagery; they were founded on reminiscences of Tennyson and Shelley; I am not sure they did not even breathe an atmosphere of Christian resignation.'[18]

Gosse's response may be attributed to what Homi Bhabha has called the profound and disturbing effect of mimicry on the authority of colonial discourse.[19] Gosse's observation that Sarojini's poems 'had the disadvantage of being totally without individuality' confirms his uneasiness with a mimicry that, in Bhabha's words, 'conceals no presence or identity behind its mask.'[20] By offering a mimicry of English poetry, 'skilful in form, correct in grammar and blameless in sentiment,' as Gosse concedes, Sarojini threatens the autonomy of the English poem as a medium for the expression of an authentic English subjectivity. 'I laid them down in despair,' Gosse recalls. 'This was but the note of the mocking-bird with a vengeance. It was not pleasant to daunt the charming and precocious singer by so discouraging a judgment; but I reflected on her youth and her enthusiasm, and I ventured to speak to her sincerely. I advised the consignment of all that she had written, in this falsely English vein, to the waste-paper basket.'[21]

Her father had earlier withheld his approval until she embraced English; now Gosse, her surrogate English father, was withholding approval for her too-successful 'false' appropriation of English. Gosse then proceeded to outline to Sarojini a program for salvaging her poetic persona, a program which largely determined the course of her poetic career: 'what we wished to receive was, not a réchauffé of Anglo-Saxon sentiment in an Anglo-Saxon setting, but some revelation of the heart of India, some sincere penetrating analysis of native passion, of the principles of antique religion and of such mysterious intimations as stirred the soul of the East long before the West had begun to dream that it had soul.'[22] If Gosse's suggestion illustrates the Western desire for an authentic voice of the

Orient (a role that Tagore would come to fill), it did offer Sarojini a means of adapting her poetic talents to the English literary marketplace. She was 'to write no more about robins and skylarks, in a landscape of our Midland counties, with the village bells somewhere in the distance calling the parishioners to church, but to set her poems firmly among the mountains, the gardens, the temples, to introduce to us the vivid populations of her own voluptuous and unfamiliar province.' By these means, she would become, as Gosse saw it, 'a genuine Indian poet of the Deccan, not a clever machine-made imitator of the English classics.' The advice was 'instantly accepted and with as little delay as possible acted upon,' as Gosse recalls, 'with the docility and the rapid appreciation of genius.'[23] When Gosse expressed his approval of her new work, she wrote to him, effusively, 'You cannot know what these words meant to me, how people always colour my life, how when I am in the very depth of self-disgust and despair – as I often am – they will give me new hope and new courage – no, you cannot know! Poetry is the one thing I love so passionately, so intensely, so absolutely that it is my very life of life, and now you have told me that *I am a poet* – I am a poet! I keep repeating it to myself to try to realise it.'[24] The passage underscores Sarojini's need to have her poetic voice recognized and validated as a poet by a suitable authority figure. While it would be easy to dismiss this as a mere craving for something like parental approval, to do so would, I think, misrepresent what was really at stake: the claim of the Indian woman to the power of the poetic voice. This was, indeed, the crossing of the 'Golden Threshold,' which became the figure for her first volume of poetry, and for her entry into the nexus of colonial power relations.

Permission to cross the Golden Threshold was not granted without substantial costs, such as were characteristic of what Ashcroft, Griffiths, and Tiffin have called the second phase of postcolonial literature, a phase in which 'natives' are permitted access to publication under imperial licence. 'The institution of "Literature" in the colony is under direct control of the imperial ruling class who alone licence the acceptable form and permit the publication and distribution of the resulting work.'[25] Having renounced subversive mimicry, Naidu's verse, reconstructed by Gosse to conform to the interests of the colonial gaze, is licensed for publication. In the process, the poet is reconstructed as a figure of the primitive and exotic East, and a source of knowledge for the West. In his introduction to her second book, *The Bird of Time*, Gosse wrote:

> she is in all things and to the fullest extent autochthonous. She springs from the very soil of India; her spirit, although it employs the English language as its vehicle, has no other tie with the West. It addresses itself to the exposition of emotions which are tropical and primitive, and in this respect, as I believe, if the poems of Sarojini Naidu be carefully and delicately studied they will be found as luminous in lighting up the

dark places of the East as any contribution of savant or historian. They have the astonishing advantage of approaching the task of interpretation from inside the magic circle, although armed with a technical skill that has been cultivated with devotion outside of it.[26]

Naidu thus becomes, in Gosse's account, an informer to the West, like Kipling's Kim, a privileged revealer and interpreter of Eastern secrets 'inside the magic circle,' an illuminator – like Conrad's Marlow – of 'the dark places of the East.' Permission to cross the 'Golden Threshold' is exchanged for access into 'the magic circle,' figuring a double exchange of access into spaces respectively prohibited to the Indian poet and the Western reader.

Sarojini continued to be invited to the Gosses' – 'one of the most welcome and intimate of our guests' – and it was there in 1896 that she was introduced to another important poet, Arthur Symons, then at the peak of his fame as editor of the *Savoy*.[27] Sarojini and Symons became quite close that spring and summer, as their extant correspondence shows, although it is not entirely clear whether Symons – who met her just after his mother's death and an emotionally wrenching romantic breakup – conceived of her as daughter, lover, mother, or, as it appears, all three: a seventeen-year-old girl who 'had in her all the wild magic of the East,' someone 'to whom one could tell all one's personal troubles and agitations, as to a wise old woman,' and 'one of a few girls whom I made love to in different years who would have married me.'[28] One could hardly find a clearer example of anima relationship.

Appropriate to her role as Symons's anima, Sarojini's first important publication in England was a lush, exotic poem entitled 'Eastern Dancers' that Symons published in the *Savoy* in 1896. Sarojini had been initially disappointed with the *Savoy*, explaining to her fiancé back home, 'It is very brilliant, dazzling, but – these boys, are wildly extravagant, wildly audacious.'[29] But this was perhaps in the way of an apology to her fiancé; her poem 'Eastern Dancers' turned out to be as extravagant and audacious as anything in the magazine. It begins:

> Eyes ravished with rapture, celestially panting, what passionate spirits aflaming with
> fire
> Drink deep of the hush of the hyacinth heavens that glimmer around them in fountains of light?[30]

Symons seems to have toned down the poem, substituting 'passionate spirits' for the more logical 'passionate bosoms aflaming with fire' which appeared in Naidu's collection, *The Golden Threshold*.[31] 'Eastern Dancers' is not the sort of poem seventeen-year-old girls were expected to write in Victorian Britain, even in the age of Salomé. Indeed, the scene of the poem only makes sense if we regard the 'Eastern Dancer' as an exotic anima projection produced by the poet for the benefit of the male reader, more specifically, a Decadent Western male reader such as Arthur Symons. The performing dancers offer an appropriate hook for this projection since they perform in response to the observer's desire. They recall (and were perhaps inspired by) the dancers of Symons's poem 'Javanese Dancers' (inspired by the dancers at the 1889 Exposition Universelle in Paris): 'Like painted idols seen to stir / By the idolators in a magic grove.'[32] The conspicuous difference is that Sarojini has not only appropriated the role of the unconscious as originator of the exotic projection; she has also in some sense merged with the projection itself. In order to escape the problem of mimicking the (colonial male) subject, she has learned to become the (colonized female) other by mimicking the subject's projection of the other. Such a position may appear retrogressive from the standpoints of gender equality or decolonization, but it is nevertheless a position of extraordinary psychological power. Persuading the colonial male subject to relinquish control of the exotic projection to the colonized subject masquerading as exotic object may well be regarded as the crucial stage in the disruption of colonial identity and authority.

The Golden Threshold

During Sarojini's long sojourn in Italy and Switzerland she and Symons continued an intimate correspondence, and when she returned in the spring of 1898 they again became close. In August of that year, however, she decided that her intention to marry Dr Naidu had not changed, and determined to return to India despite her father's objections. Her views prevailed, and the wedding took place that December in Madras. She settled down to married life and having children – one each year from 1901 to 1904. For a while she neglected her poetry: 'I have written nothing yet,' she told Gosse in August 1899, and in December 1903 she had only 'five little poems' to send him, 'the only poems of the year.'[33] But one of these poems was an ode to the Nizam of Hyderabad presented at the Ramadan durbar: 'it is something quite novel in the annals of Indian tradition for a woman to present a poem to a sovereign in full durbar,' she explained to Gosse. The Nizam, a poet himself, fascinated her: 'you cannot find a figure more picturesque, more brilliant and alas more pathetic than the Nizam of Hyderabad,' she told Gosse; and she was now reconfiguring herself as the Nizam's anima-poet: 'I mean to recreate with all the golden bricks and mortar of verse the dead dramas and legends and passionate historic beauties of the Nizam's dominions.'[34] 'Do you know I have some very beautiful poems floating in the air,' she wrote Symons in 1904, 'and if the gods are kind I shall cast my soul like a net and capture them, this year.'[35] By spring she had a batch of eighteen poems, which she sent to Symons and Gosse for advice; and with their assistance a small edition was published the following year by William Heinemann.

Becoming Sarojini Naidu, the Indian poet, turned out to be a stepping-stone to other possibilities for Sarojini. Her entry into the political sphere in 1902, at the urging of the prominent nationalist leader Gopal Krishna Gokhale, followed in the wake of the triumphant appearance of Sarala Devi, a member of the Tagore family, at the Indian National Congress of 1901. Sarala Devi had composed a song 'in which she linked together the different provinces and combined the watchwords of the various races and creed[s],' and sang it on the opening day of the Congress. 'After the second stanza was sung, every person in the huge pavilion joined in the refrain.'[36] At the 1904 Congress, Naidu read her ode 'To India,' in which, borrowing from traditions of the patriotic songs invoking powerful maternal forces (notably the influential 'Bande Mataram' of Bankim Chandra Chatterjee), she projects the figure of Mother India rising and leading the fettered nations out of darkness:

O young through all thy immemorial years!
Rise, Mother, rise, regenerate from thy gloom,
And, like a bride high-mated with the spheres,
Beget new glories from thine ageless womb!

The nations that in fettered darkness weep
Crave thee to lead them where great mornings break ...
Mother, O Mother, wherefore dost thou sleep?
Arise and answer for thy children's sake!

Thy Future calls thee with a manifold sound
To crescent honours, splendours, victories vast;
Waken, O slumbering Mother and be crowned,
Who once wert empress of the sovereign Past.[37]

Naidu's poem filters out the explicit Hinduism of Bankim's song (which explicitly evokes two Hindu goddesses – Durga, the avenging demon-destroyer, and Lakshmi, goddess of prosperity). While the awakening Mother of the poem may be read in many registers – personal, political, and religious, among others – the aim of the awakening is explicitly toward the question of sovereignty. In becoming the poet who calls this politically awakening anima, Naidu transfers her authority as an English poet into a different sphere, where English is transformed from the language of mimicry or colonialist exoticism into a means of linking together the disparate linguistic populations of India. Reading the poem was a 'great awakening' for Naidu, as she explained to Gosse: 'so far from being the insignificant little provincial I had thought myself I was treated almost as a national possession ... my public was waiting for me – no, not for me, so much as for a poet, a national poet, and it was ready to accept me if I would only let it – if I would be a little truer to my own powers and realize the potency of all Art for good or evil.'[38]

On Behalf of Her Sisters: The Poet as Activist

In the decade following the publication of *The Golden Threshold*, Naidu continued to write poetry, publishing her second collection, *The Bird of Time*, in 1912. The following year, suffering from ill health, she was back in England. In London, Naidu renewed old literary friendships and made new ones, including the Japanese poet Yone Noguchi.[39] On 16 June 1913, she presided over the garlanding of Tagore by the Indian students of Great Britain; the London *Times* reported on her speech. Others present were Gokhale and 'the Hon. Mr. Jinnah,' future leader of Pakistan.[40] It was at her home that Ezra Pound was introduced, later that year, to Mary Fenollosa, a meeting which was to have an enormous impact on the development of modernist poetry.

The event which would have the most lasting impact for Naidu, however, was her first meeting with Gandhi in August of 1914.[41] Gandhi was also a disciple of Gokhale, and had just arrived in England after the first great triumph of his passive resistance program in South Africa. Naidu sought him out and found him in an unfashionable house in an obscure part of Kensington, 'a little man with shaven head, seated on the floor on a black prison blanket and eating a messy meal of squashed tomatoes and olive oil out of a wooden prison bowl' surrounded by 'battered tins of parched groundnuts and tasteless biscuits of dried plantain flour.' Naidu 'burst instinctively into happy laughter at this amusing and unexpected vision of a famous leader,' and Gandhi laughed back, and invited her to share his meal. Naidu recalled refusing, saying, 'what an abominable mess it is!'[42] Gandhi, however, had the opposite recollection: 'In she sailed, nevertheless, and without the least thought, squatted down by my side and even began to eat out of my dish!' Naidu's anima-like relation to Gandhi was most vividly manifested in their complementary attitudes toward abstinence and consumption. As Gandhi commented in 1918: 'Though not a millionaire's daughter herself, she has long enjoyed the luxuries of a princely home and cannot give them up. She may deliver an impressive speech on simplicity and voluntary suffering, and immediately afterwards do full justice to a sumptuous feast. But, I am quite sure, she will cast off the slough, if she falls in with a man of my type. Nature herself has made her of that deceptive fibre. I myself, when I first saw her, wondered,

"How can I take any work from this apparition!"[43] Naidu remained attached to conspicuous consumption (and seemingly incurable internal illnesses) throughout her life, growing ever fatter as Gandhi demonstrated ever more impressive control over a body diminished by fasting. Nevertheless, she proved hard-working indeed, and after the death of Gokhale in 1915, Naidu grew increasingly attached to Gandhi, 'a loving, loyal discipleship, which never wavered for a single hour through more than thirty years of common service in the cause of India's freedom,' and Gandhi increasingly dependended on her in later years.[44]

Naidu was indeed becoming everybody's anima. Performing in the role of anima for the masses was not a simple matter, particularly in a country as culturally varied as India, but a political figure is a very anima-like form of projection, and thus the transition was a natural development of her previous roles. A 1915 Indian National Congress speech supporting home rule illustrates her accommodation of the role:

> since it is the desire of so many people here present that some woman from amidst you, some daughter of this Bharat Mother, should raise her voice, on behalf of her sisters, to second and support this resolution on Self-Government, I venture – though it seems presumption so to venture – to stand before you and to give my individual support as well as to speak in the name of many millions of my sisters of India, not only Hindu, but Mussalman, Parsi and other sisters, for the sake of Self-Government which is the desire and the destiny of every human soul.[45]

Self-government, she argued, was inseparable from Indian unity, which demanded freedom not only from British rule but from 'that infinitely subtler and more dreadful and damning domination of your own prejudices and your own self-seeking community or race.'[46] She ended with a poem written for the occasion entitled 'Awake,' which added the call for unity to the message of the earlier poem 'To India,' and expanded on the awakening Mother India imagery of the earlier poem.

The call for unity among India's disparate ethnic and religious groups, and particularly between the powerfully divided Hindu and Muslim groups, was a central problem addressed by Naidu in her presentations at the December 1915 Congress. 'But fate has a curious and incalculable way of doing without political creeds in effecting her own solutions of the grave and crucial problems from and through personal experience and emotions,' she wrote a few weeks later, and this was no idle philosophy, for she wrote it in a letter to Dr Syed Mahmud, a young Muslim politician who had fallen desperately in love with her during the conference. Afterwards, Naidu sent him a copy of her latest book and advice to 'take your little bride as my gift to you, dear,'[47] and Mahmud had replied in a now-lost

letter that seemed to Naidu 'like the cry of a wounded creature in agony.' Nevertheless she could only reply with 'the mocking irony of the old taunt that rings
down the centuries "Physician heal thyself."' 'Would it not be easy for me –
fatally easy – to say "I will break these bonds that man has made in his ignorance
and cowardice. I will fling aside all duty, all responsibility and seek in yours what
has been mine since the beginning of Time."' But this was quite impossible, and
she implored Mahmud to pull himself together and not give in to weakness.[48]

'Awake' was the most overtly political poem included in the final volume of
poetry published in Naidu's lifetime,[49] *The Broken Wing* (1917). 'The Gift of
India' honours Indian soldiers killed in the Great War, and 'The Lotus,' dedicated
to Gandhi, might be read as a political allegory of India under colonialism. There
is a series of three memorial poems to the Nizam, Gokhale, and her father. And
Naidu continued to offer picturesque images of Indian life past and present in
poems like 'Wandering Beggars' and 'Imperial Delhi,' and expressions of Indian
religious views in such poems as 'The Prayer of Islam' and 'Kali the Mother.' But
the surprise is the last third of the book, a group of twenty-four love poems entitled 'The Temple: A Pilgrimage of Love,' noticeably reminiscent of the passionate poems of Laurence Hope.

> Why did you turn your face away?
>   Was it for love or hate?
> Or the spell of that wild miraculous hour
> That hurled our souls with relentless power
>   In the eddying fires of Fate?[50]

In light of the conspicuous absence of such poems in Naidu's earlier volumes, it
was difficult to explain why she found her poetic self, as Meena Alexander has put
it, 'in the grip of a sexuality so atavistic that desire equals destruction,'[51] until
Makarand Paranjape's discovery and publication of Sarojini's letters to Syed Mahmud. Reading 'The Temple' against these letters is to confront the very real
dimensions of sexuality as an irresistibly compelling source of creativity and at the
same time a destructive but liberating chaotic force wreaking havoc on the social
order. This dualism is inscribed in the tripartite structure of 'The Temple,' which
counterposes 'The Gate of Delight' to 'The Path of Tears,' and tries to resolve the
pair in the third part, 'The Sanctuary,' which explores the possibility of transcendence through love. This structure is reflected in the letters as well, and the title
poem, taken from a question evidently addressed to the poet by Gokhale – 'Why
should a song-bird like you have a broken wing?' – reads as an apology for pursuing erotic pleasure required for the production of poetry. Nationalism itself is
seen as 'renascence,' an erotic energy of renewal:

Shall spring that wakes mine ancient land again
Call to my wild and suffering heart in vain?[52]

In contrast to this celebration of the release of libidinal energies, the volume ends with a horrific declaration of utter self-sacrifice to love: 'Take my flesh to feed your dogs if you choose ... Am I not yours, O Love, to cherish or kill?'[53] Yet we need to read this, I would argue, not as an advertisement for traditional patriarchal gender roles, as has sometimes been suggested, or even as a declaration of utter self-abnegation, but, rather, as an act of self-reconstitution through active imagination. The limit of love, at least for the extravert, is found at the point where the self is extinguished – and we may have the sense that Naidu has pursued this impossible relationship out of a powerful need to confront this limit. While the poems explore the expression of love as self-negation from a variety of viewpoints, in the letters to Mahmud the dominant note is the need for self-control. 'It is true that much of social life is built on hypocrisy and an ignorance of the deep fundamental laws of the Soul but if we abide by the conventions of civilization – so called – it is *not* through weakness or cowardice but because some of us have the strength and courage to make the supreme self-sacrifice lest those [who] depend on us for their daily bread of body and spirit may die – if we fail them.' There is a conspicuous absence of anything that could be called 'feminine weakness' here, while, on the contrary, it is Mahmud who claims to feel 'lost and paralyzed.'[54] The desire to sacrifice the self for love is trumped by the need to salvage the self for a greater love. Having taken her spring passion to its imaginative limits, Naidu draws back to a recovered self and the lesser and greater sacrifices of devotion to country.

The renunciation of erotic passion was not without its price: both Naidu and Mahmud entered into a period of prolonged and dramatic physical sufferings which became the dominant theme of their correspondence over the next two years. In 1918, however, amid the gradual cooling of passion and Naidu's apparent desire to reconcile with her husband, their correspondence seems to have ended. Traces of her personal struggles during this period can be seen in her political speeches, as in one of March 1918 given to students at Jullundur, where she pressed women in her audience to seek strength in Indian tradition: 'Have you forgotten the heroic stories and scriptures of your own motherland? It was the privilege of India – to possess women – who were bolder and braver than men. Yes, even to-day the need is that we the women of India should be bold and go to Yama Savitri-like and beg of him a new life for Mother India.'[55] Such stories extolled traditional feminine virtues, but a conservative position regarding gender roles, historian Partha Chatterjee argues, was the price demanded by nationalist ideology in exchange for qualified acceptance of reforms in the material conditions of women, such as access to education, that were widely seen as representing a threat to the spirituality of the home. 'The new patriarchy advocated by nationalism conferred upon women the honour of a new social responsibility.'[56]

Exoticism is among the first characteristics of Naidu's poetry to catch the eye. I have suggested that from the Jungian viewpoint, the exoticism of Naidu's poetry is best explained in conjunction with the anima relationship. Naidu became a poet in relation to her father, then an exotic poet in relation to Gosse and Symons, later a political poet in relation to Gokhale and Gandhi, and finally, everybody's anima. The strategy has come under criticism by recent generations of Indian feminists. Susie Tharu calls attention to the 'peculiar formation of the Indian intellectual' which demands servility to a (colonial) order, and makes a poet like Naidu into both exhibit and exhibitor: 'our country is the spectacle, our lives a masquerade, and the poet must strain to keep it so.'[57] Naidu herself foresaw the necessity of this interrogation, wondering, in her poem 'At Dawn':

Children, my children, who wake to inherit
The ultimate hope of our travailing spirit,
Say, when your young hearts shall take to their keeping
The manifold dreams we have sown for your reaping,
Is it praise, is it pain you will grant us for guerdon?
Anoint with your love or arraign with your pardon?[58]

Chapter Five

The Tagore Era

In the summer of 1912, a new poet appeared on the English literary scene. Though fifty years old and a literary legend in his native Bengal, Rabindranath Tagore was almost entirely unknown in the West, and his sudden emergence as a leading literary figure was the most talked-about development in English letters in 1913. English literary society, colonial discourse, spiritualism, and international relations all came together to produce the new discursive object, 'Tagore,' and its associated event, the 'Tagore craze.' 'There is little doubt that what some people are largely calling the "Indian Renaissance," but which may be better described as the rise of Mr. Tagore upon the West, is, as yet, the most striking event in the poetry of the century,' declared the *Manchester Guardian* several weeks after Tagore was awarded the Nobel Prize in November.

Rabindranath Tagore had arrived in England with a small entourage, including his twenty-four-year-old son, Rathindranath, and Rathindranath's wife, Pratima, on 16 June 1912. He had been in England twice before (once during his studies in the late 1870s, again in 1890) and was hoping on this trip to recover his health after a long period of stress. He had by then amassed a considerable body of work in Bengali: poetry, songs, plays, novels, short stories, and essays. In other parts of India he was less well known, and only a few scattered fragments of his work had been translated into English. On the way to England Tagore occupied himself by translating some of his poetry into English, which he presented, shortly after his arrival, to Will Rothenstein, who had expressed an interest in seeing more of his work in translation when they had met during Rothenstein's trip to India a few years earlier. What Rothenstein found, when he read through the poems, was 'poetry of a new order' which seemed to him 'on a level with that of the great mystics.'[1] He communicated his discovery to his friend William Butler Yeats, who read the poems over, suggested a few emendations, and agreed with Rothenstein's assessment. 'The writing of European saints ... has ceased to hold our attention,' Yeats later wrote in his introduction to the poems. But the spiritualism of Tagore was different. 'This is no longer the sanctity of the cell and of the scourge; being but a lifting up, as it were, into a greater intensity of the mood of the painter, painting the dust and the sunlight, and we go for a like voice to St. Francis and to William Blake who have seemed so alien in our violent history.'[2]

Indian Religions in the West

Tagore was not, of course, the first to introduce Western readers to Indian religious perspectives. English, German, and French philologists had been working on classical Hindu religious texts since the late eighteenth century. Although initially their work was intended to support colonial projects, it quickly took on a life of its own, spurred on by the unexpected discovery of the common origin of Indo-European languages. 'It is quite amusing, though instructive also,' wrote the great nineteenth-century philologist F. Max Müller, 'to read what was written by scholars and philosophers when this new light first dawned on the world. They would not have it, they would not believe that there could be any community of origin between the people of Athens and Rome, and the so-called Niggers of India ... No one ever was for a time so completely laughed down as Professor Bopp, when he first published his Comparative Grammar of Sanskrit, Zend, Greek, Latin, and Gothic.'[3] Müller remembered the shock, both horrible and thrilling, of being present at the moment when this conceptual bombshell was dropped on him and his unsuspecting fellow students:

> I remember, I say, one of our masters (Dr. Klee) telling us one afternoon, when it was too hot to do any serious work, that there was a language spoken in India, which was much the same as Greek and Latin, nay, as German and Russian. At first we thought it was a joke, but when one saw the parallel columns of numerals, pronouns, and verbs in Sanskrit, Greek, and Latin written on the blackboard, one felt in the presence of facts, before which one had to bow. All one's ideas of Adam and Eve, and the Paradise, and the tower of Babel, and Shem, Ham, and Japhet, with Homer and Æneas and Virgil too, seemed to be whirling round and round, till at last one picked up the fragments and tried to build up a new world and to live with a new historical consciousness.[4]

These comments were part of Müller's lectures at Cambridge to students interested in Civil Service careers in the early 1880s, and Müller had no compunction in promoting ancient India at modern India's expense. 'Those who have spent many years of active life in Calcutta, or Bombay, or Madras, will be horror-struck at the idea that the humanity they meet with there, whether in the bazaars or in the courts of justice, or in so-called native society, should be able to teach *us* any lessons,' he concedes.[5] The Hindus, he argued, are regarded 'as an inferior race, totally different from ourselves in their moral character, and more particularly in what forms the very foundation of the English character, respect for truth.' 'So often has that charge of untruthfulness been repeated, and so generally is it now accepted, that it seems almost Quixotic to fight against it.'[6] But it was not necessary to do so, for, Müller argued, the modern Indian was utterly irrelevant: 'we are speaking of two very different Indias. I am thinking chiefly of India such as it was a thousand, two thousand, it may be three thousand years ago.'[7] This ancient India, Müller explained, had been inhabited by White Aryans, and it was therefore the literature of this ancient India that was valuable. 'We may call the literature of the former period *ancient* and *natural*, that of the latter *modern* and *artificial*.'[8] In the ancient literature, we find 'the Aryan man, whom we know in his various characters, as Greek, Roman, German, Celt, and Slav, in an entirely new character,' one that is 'passive and meditative' rather than 'active and political.'[9] This meditative view of life, Müller argues, 'though we cannot adopt it in this Northern climate, may yet act as a lesson and a warning to us, not, for the sake of life, to sacrifice the highest objects of life.'[10]

By the time Müller published these lectures in the early 1880s, interest in Indian religions had already spread far beyond the audience of colonial administrators. The American Transcendentalists were among those influenced by Hinduism: Emerson became interested in Hinduism as early as the 1820s. 'In the morning,' Thoreau recorded in his Walden journal, 'I bathe my intellect in the stupendous and cosmogonal philosophy of the Bhagvat-Geeta ... in comparison with which our modern world and its literature seems puny and trivial.'[11] Whitman wrote of Hindu scripture's 'far-darting beams of the spirit' in 'A Passage to India.' By the 1870s Müller was helping to satisfy the need for a broader range of reliable texts with his series of *Sacred Books of the East*, a vast compendium of scholarly translations of Hindu, Buddhist, Zoroastrian, Islamic, and Taoist texts eventually stretching to fifty volumes.

But the popularization of Indian religion and philosophy in the West was beginning to depend less on reliable texts than on charismatic religious leaders. The Theosophical Society, established in New York in 1875, prominently featured Hindu beliefs within its syncretic pantheon, and a number of influential poets, including Yeats, first encountered Indian thought through Theosophy and Indian Theosophists like Mohini Chatterjee, whom Yeats met in Dublin in 1886. The most impressive and influential of these was Swami Vivekananda, who made his dramatic first Western appearance at the World's Parliament of Religions in Chicago in 1893; Harriet Monroe, who was present, described his speech as 'a rare and perfect moment of supreme emotion ... human eloquence at its highest pitch.'[12] Vivekananda was the dominant force behind the establishment of Yoga in the United States, a practice that later became more firmly established in the 1920s with the establishment of the Self-Realization Fellowship and Vedanta Society in California by Paramahansa Yogananda and Swami Prabhavananda.

Indian religious thinkers played a dominant role in this Indian-Western religious cross-culturalism. Most if not all of the popular Western forms of Hinduism grew out of Hindu encounters with Western religion in the contact zone of colonial Bengal. One of the influential new forms of Hinduism to emerge out of this context was the Brahmo Samaj, established by Bengali reformer Raja Rammohan Roy in 1828 'for the worship and adoration of the Eternal, Unsearchable and Immutable Being, who is the Author and Preserver of the Universe.' The monotheism of the Brahmo Samaj was partly an effort to create a universal religion and partly an effort to return to a pure Hinduism based on the *Vedas* and, particularly, the *Upanishads*. In the West, Roy published several influential English books on the *Vedas* (they were read by Emerson and Thoreau), but was best known as a reformer, having successfully lobbied for the abolition of *sati* in 1828 and travelled to England to advocate further reforms in 1830.

Tagore's grandfather, a flamboyant merchant who had prospered in business with the British East India Company, was a close friend of Rammohan Roy, and after Rammohan's death in England in 1833, it was Tagore's father, Debendranath, who revived the Brahmo Samaj in 1841. Debendranath rejected the worldly lifestyle of his father, took up meditation, and was referred to in later life as the Maharishi. Swami Vivekananda came from a similar background – born Narendranath Dutta, son of a prominent Calcutta barrister, he joined the Brahmo Samaj while studying law in Calcutta. But Vivekananda received his most powerful inspiration from Sri Ramakrishna, a nearly illiterate priest at the Kalighat temple. Vivekananda was thus able to combine the more intellectual Brahmo tradition with the simple mysticism of Ramakrishna and present it with the rhetorical skill of an English barrister, and the package was irresistible. But Vivekananda's early death in 1902 left no successor of equal ability.

Gitanjali

Tagore was not primarily a religious thinker or a mystic, but his spiritual orientation was a prominent feature in his poetry, and the one he chose to foreground in *Gitanjali* (*Song Offerings*), his first collection of English translations, which drew upon several decades of his Bengali verse.

In Jungian terms, Tagore's personality type was that of the introverted intuitive: his inner intuition was the source of an inexhaustible stream of images, metaphors, allegories, and parables out of which he created succinct portraits of the human condition, and the introverted orientation to the self provided a central problematic of his lyrical work:

29

He whom I enclose with my name is weeping in this dungeon. I am ever busy building this wall all around; and as this wall goes up into the sky day by day I lose sight of my true being in its dark shadow.

I take pride in this great wall, and I plaster it with dust and sand lest a least hole should be left in this name; and for all the care I take I lose sight of my true being.

'As a rule, the intuitive stops at perception; perception is his main problem,' Jung notes, but by bringing an auxiliary, extraverted judging function into play, the introverted intuitive is able to relate himself to his vision and thus progress from merely aesthetic perception to moral understanding of the meaning of his vision.[13] Nevertheless, extraverted sensation falls in the shadow of the introverted intuitive personality, and it is appropriate that Tagore describes spiritual failure in the preceding poem as a loss of sight of the external world. And again, Tagore describes the attainment of unity of being as the experience of identity with the world of external sensation, a carrying outward of inner life into the external world:

69

The same stream of life that runs through my veins night and day runs through the world and dances in rhythmic measures.

It is the same life that shoots in joy through the dust of the earth in numberless blades of grass and breaks into tumultuous waves of leaves and flowers.

It is the same life that is rocked in the ocean-cradle of birth and of death, in ebb and in flow.

I feel my limbs are made glorious by the touch of this world of life. And my pride is from the life-throb of ages dancing in my blood this moment.

Here, the poet follows the circuit of life outward into the perceptible world, and is energized by the sense of its connection to other beings and to the cycle of birth and death. This energizing sensation of unity in the touch of the real is then carried back inward.

In describing his poems as 'song offerings,' Tagore was acknowledging their role as part of a spiritual practice. They offered an introduction to, and a reworking of, a tradition of Indian spiritual poetry – *bhakti*, or devotional poetry –

almost entirely unknown in the West. While *saguna bhakti* poetry addresses a god such as Vishnu or Shiva, a god 'with qualities' (hence the name), *nirguna bhakti* poetry addresses a god or godhead 'without qualities.' Many of the religious poems in *Gitanjali* may be considered in this latter category, although, as Mary Lago points out, they owe much to the poetic traditions associated with Vaishnavism, poems to the god Vishnu and his avatars, which would generally fall into the former.[14] The poems are addressed to 'Thou,' 'Lord,' 'my God,' or sometimes, a being allegorically personified as 'friend' or 'king.' The religious tone is set by the first poem in the volume, which begins, 'Thou hast made me endless, such is thy pleasure. This frail vessel thou emptiest again and again, and fillest it ever with fresh life.' This first poem, like a number of others early in the volume, is concerned with the relationship between poetry and the divine, the nature of inspiration.

In many poems Tagore speaks as the mystic, the spiritual poet devoted to communion with God:

38

That I want thee, only thee – let my heart repeat without end. All desires that distract me, day and night, are false and empty to the core.

As the night keeps hidden in its gloom the petition for light, even thus in the depth of my unconsciousness rings the cry – 'I want thee, only thee'.

As the storm still seeks its end in peace when it strikes against peace with all its might, even thus my rebellion strikes against thy love and still its cry is – 'I want thee, only thee.'

Jung notes the prevalence among introverted intuitive personality types of 'an extraordinary aloofness of the individual from tangible reality,' a potentially isolating characteristic.[15] But Tagore was acutely aware of the problem of achieving wholeness in personality: 'the one cry of the personal man,' he writes, 'has been to know the Supreme Person.'[16] For Tagore this need was frequently expressed as a movement outward, out of the reclusive, world-rejecting pose of the devotee:

11

Leave this chanting and singing and telling of beads! Whom dost thou worship in this lonely dark corner of a temple with doors all shut? Open thine eyes and see thy God is not before thee!

He is there where the tiller is tilling the hard ground and where the pathmaker is breaking stones. He is with them in sun and in shower, and his garment is covered with dust. Put off thy holy mantle and even like him come down on the dusty soil!

Deliverance? Where is this deliverance to be found? Our master himself has joyfully taken upon him the bonds of creation; he is bound with us all for ever.

Come out of thy meditations and leave aside thy flowers and incense! What harm is there if thy clothes become tattered and stained? Meet him and stand by him in toil and in sweat of thy brow.

Through such poems Tagore sought the shadow of his inner world of contemplation and devotion in an external world of work and sensation. The divine or transcendent appears in a variety of guises in the poems, most often as a resplendent king whose arrival is always anticipated, representing transcendence, unity, death. The poems are records of moments of self-realization, sometimes simple, sometimes difficult, small offerings of gratitude for the incommensurable gift of being.

The Tagore Craze

The precise date on which Tagore became an object of public interest may be fixed as Wednesday, 10 July 1912, when a dinner was held in his honour at London's Trocadero restaurant. The large gathering, over which Yeats presided, was written up twice in the *Times*: on Saturday in a brief descriptive notice, again on Tuesday in a longer article entitled 'The Triumph of Art over Circumstances.'[17] This second article celebrated the event as a moment of cross-cultural unity; Tagore is recorded as assuring the gathering of influential poets and writers that he was deeply moved, and had learned 'that, though our tongues are different and our habits dissimilar, at the bottom our hearts are one.' Rothenstein set to work arranging an edition of the poems, to be put out initially in a limited edition by the India Society, then by a commercial press. 'I personally feel certain that the book is going to take its place among the books of the world,' Rothenstein assured his friend William Butler Yeats, who was delegated to write 'a short & emphatic introduction.'[18] 'It is good news that you have chosen him to edit the English versions of your poems,' Sarojini Naidu wrote. 'To the European world they will be a revelation of the beauty and rapture of the Indian genius at its best.' She was sure that 'hundreds of yearning souls' would 'drink deep and find peace' through his work.[19]

Yeats completed his glowing introduction in September. 'These prose translations from Rabindra Nath Tagore have stirred my blood as nothing has for years,' he wrote.[20] Yeats had spoken to some Indian acquaintances about Tagore and was fascinated by the awe surrounding the Bengali poet and his remarkable family. He was deeply moved by the poems themselves – 'the work of a supreme culture, they yet appear as much the growth of the common soil as the grass and the rushes'[21] – and impressed by what he learned of their cultural vitality – 'these verses will not lie in little well-printed books upon ladies' tables, who turn the pages with indolent hands that they may sigh over a life without meaning, which is yet all they can know of life, or be carried by students at the university to be laid aside when the work of life begins, but, as the generations pass, travellers will hum them on the highway and men rowing upon the rivers.'[22] And he was impressed by their mysticism. The poems of Tagore were both alien and strangely familiar: 'A whole people, a whole civilization, immeasurably strange to us, seems to have been taken up into this imagination; and yet we are not moved because of its strangeness, but because we have met our own image, as though we had walked in Rossetti's willow wood, or heard, perhaps for the first time in literature, our voice as in a dream.'[23]

Tagore left England for the United States in October, shortly before the November publication of the India Society edition of *Gitanjali (Song Offerings)*, and there began working on further translations. 'There is a rich mine,' Rothenstein informed Yeats. Tagore hoped Rothenstein and Yeats would handle literary and financial matters, but 'he would very much care to have them bring in as much as possible, as he dedicates all the profits of his writings to his school.'[24] As expected, enthusiastic reviews called for a commercial edition; indeed, enthusiastic is a severe understatement: the *Times Literary Supplement* thought the book might reverse the decadence of modern poetry, blamed on poetry's failure to 'express the emotions stirred by ideas,' for 'that is the problem which troubles our poetry at present and seems to endanger its very existence; and it is no wonder that Mr. Yeats should hail with delight the work of an Indian poet who seems to solve it as easily as it was solved in Chinese painting of a thousand years ago.' The *Nation* thought it 'mystical poetry of the highest class': 'for those interested in the spiritual history of man ... the appearance of these poems is an event of great importance.' Poet Lascelles Abercrombie, writing in the *Manchester Guardian*, concurred, though he thought the poems too great to be the work of one man alone: 'the poems of Rabindra Nath could not credibly come except on the crest of some large and vital impulse moving thorough a nation.'[25] For the commercial edition, instead of using John Murray, publisher of the 'Wisdom of the East' series, as planned, Yeats persuaded his own publisher, Macmillan, to bring out the book, which appeared early in 1913. Yeats only encountered problems when he tried to persuade the Academic Committee to elect Tagore as a member; the proposal failed, in spite of his pragmatic suggestion to fellow Committee member Edmund Gosse that it would be 'a piece of wise Imperialism, for he is worshipped [in India] as no poet of Europe is.'[26]

Tagore Hook and All

Tagore had mixed feelings about modernist literary tendencies he viewed as being caught up in the problems of a spirituality-denying modernity. In a later essay he criticized modernism's impersonal 'aggressiveness and iconoclastic bluster,' while praising a pure modernism that sees the world 'with dispassionate absorption, free of personal attachment.'[27] Tagore's own contribution to modern poetry, when acknowledged at all, is not often cast in a modernist light. But there were certainly modernist elements in his poetry, though sometimes obscured by archaic diction, as in the following:

7

My song has put off her adornments. She has no pride of dress and decoration. Ornaments would mar our union; they would come between thee and me; their jingling would drown thy whispers.

    My poet's vanity dies in shame before thy sight. O master poet, I have sat down at thy feet. Only let me make my life simple and straight, like a flute of reed for thee to fill with music.

Yeats's poem 'A Coat,' written in 1912, must have been inspired by this poem:

I made my song a coat
Covered with embroideries
Out of old mythologies,
But the fools caught it,
Wore it in the world's eyes
As though they'd wrought it.

Yeats's song relinquishes its adornments less willingly than Tagore's, but similarly embraces the necessity of nakedness:

Song, let them take it
For there's more enterprise
In walking naked.[28]

Yeats's poem disrobes for practical, worldly reasons – there is 'more enterprise' in a naked song, shorn of mythological ornamentation – while Tagore removes his poetical adornments as a gesture of spiritual austerity toward a more direct relationship with the divine soul.

    Tagore also used the same extended metaphor in the aesthetic sense in a February 1913 note thanking Pound for a copy of *Personae*: 'your modern poetical literature has always seemed to me to have eaten the forbidden fruit, lost her simplicity and shamefully become conscious of her nakedness trying to hide herself in all manner of elaborate garbs woven of dead and decaying leaves. Your muse (pardon me for using this phrase) has come out, clothed in her own youthful body, full of life vigour, and suggestive of incalculable possibilities of growth.'[29] Interestingly, it is Pound's muse rather than Pound's poetry whose vigorous nakedness Tagore praises. But Pound probably did not appreciate this compliment. 'I'm fed up with Tagore,' Pound wrote Dorothy Shakespear on 8 May. 'I wish he'd get thru' lecturing before I get back. I don't want to be any more evangelized than I am already – which is too dam' much. And I much prefer the eagle's [Yeats's] gods to any oriental beetle with 46 arms.'[30] And he expressed his antipathy to Tagore's naked poetry metaphor, and Tagorean idealism generally, in a poem, 'Further Instructions,' published later that year in *Poetry*:

Come, my songs, let us express our baser passions.
Let us express our envy for the man with a steady job and no worry about the future.
You are very idle, my songs,
I fear you will come to a bad end.
You stand about the streets, You loiter at the corners and bus-stops,
You do next to nothing at all.
You do not even express our inner nobilitys,
You will come to a very bad end.

And I? I have gone half-cracked.
I have talked to you so much that I almost see you about me,
Insolent little beasts! Shameless! Devoid of clothing!

But you, newest song of the lot,
You are not old enough to have done much mischief.
I will get you a green coat out of China
With dragons worked upon it.
I will get you the scarlet silk trousers
From the statue of the infant Christ at Santa Maria Novella;
Lest they say we are lacking in taste,
Or that there is no caste in this family.[31]

Pound suggests here that his poem is already too naked; his naked poem, his 'half-cracked' and bestial poetic self too exposed, in need of a more elaborate and exotic dress reflecting taste and caste. The issues addressed in the poem – self-criticism, concern with money, employment, and caste – may be explained by Pound's situation at the time and particularly his relationship with Dorothy Shakespear, whose mother had informed him in no uncertain terms that he was destroying her daughter's life: as he did not have £500 a year, obviously Dorothy could not marry him; as things stood, Ezra was 'a great trouble' and she wished Dorothy 'had never been born.'[32] While Pound could recognize the validity of the Shakespears' practical concerns, he was, at the same time, disgusted by the reduction of love to a pecuniary matter. The sardonic attitude of the poem compasses both the self-loathing of his inability to provide for Dorothy and disgust with a world governed by rules of caste and propriety over poetry. In a world governed by caste and propriety, no one can afford to be naked, even the infant Christ, and Pound's naked song is merely shameless and 'devoid of clothing.' In such a world one overcomes the critical gaze of the world by one's style of dress. Pound's 'green coat out of China' points to the secret love of China he shared with Dorothy (a topic to be explored in the next chapter) and the early (pre-Fenollosa) stages of his alternative Chinese exoticism.

Pound had missed the first wave of excitement over Tagore; in spite of his growing intimacy with Yeats, he did not meet the Bengali poet until nearly three months after Tagore was introduced to literary London at the Trocadero, and when he did finally meet Tagore on 2 October 1912, he tried energetically to make up for lost time. 'I dined with Tagore on Wed. – discussed meetres etc. Spent most of yesterday P.M. (2–6) with him. Discussing prosody, watching Rothenstein paint his portrait, listening to him read & sing. Have arranged to print 6 poems in "Poetry" unless somebody raises a fuss.' Here, writing to Dorothy Shakespear, Pound admitted being impressed: 'He is very fine & makes me feel like a painted pict with a stone war club.' But he made it clear he was not going overboard in adulation: 'You have seen the eagle [Yeats] in a state of exhultation over this matter and you may readily judge the condition of my lighter and more volatile spirits. I send this off before I go into another fit of meditation.'[33] Writing to Harriet Monroe, however, he adopted a more deferential tone: 'I'll try to get some of the poems of the very great Bengali poet, Rabindranath Tagore. They are going to be *the* sensation of the winter.'[34]

As it turned out, the sensation of the winter was soon visiting Harriet Monroe himself, for in November, shortly after the publication of *Gitanjali*, Tagore accompanied his son Rathindranath to his university in Urbana, Illinois. On subsequent visits to Chicago and other American cities, his planned vacation turned into an impromptu lecture tour. Fortunately, Tagore had been writing a series of English essays on self-realization (published the following November as *Sadhana: The Realisation of Life*), which provided him with material for lectures he gave at Urbana's Unitarian church, and later at Harvard, where T.S. Eliot, as a student in James Woods's Indian philosophy course, was among the auditors.[35]

But Pound had meanwhile arranged to act as Tagore's intermediary to *Poetry*, and was attempting to immerse himself in Indic studies to solidify his position among the Tagoreans. In January Pound bought 'a huge history of Hindoostan' and lectured on Tagore in 'Mrs Fowler's new chinese drawing room,' where he was able to read some of the twenty-five newly translated poems Tagore had sent him, including 'a nice one about ducks.' He also began working with Kalimohan Ghose translating Kabir, a fifteenth-century Hindi poet whose mystical verse was favoured by Tagore, their collaboration appearing in the *Modern Review* of Calcutta.[36] But Pound's determination to dominate the Tagore industry was not truly in the Tagorean spirit of universal brotherhood. In a March 1913 letter to Harriet Monroe, Pound was appallingly clear about what he perceived to be his stake in the control of the Tagore industry:

> The *Current Gossip* (God what a sheet!!!!) seems to have taken Tagore hook and all. *Current Opinion* (March number). However, it serves as illustration of what I said a while back. These fools don't KNOW anything and at the bottom of their wormy souls they know they don't and their name is legion and if once they learn that we do know and that we are 'in' first, they'll come to us to get all their thinking done for them and in the end the greasy vulgus will be directed by us. And we will be able to do a deal more for poetry indirectly than we could with just our $5,000 per annum.[37]

The relationship between Pound and Tagore began to cool soon after Tagore's return to London in mid-April. Pound did not have much use for Tagore's spiritualism, and, in May, when Tagore began a series of weekly lectures at the Caxton Hall based on the *Sadhana* material, Pound began issuing ostensibly reluctant and well-meaning criticisms of Tagore in an effort to undermine his growing influence. 'As a religious teacher he is superfluous,' he explained to Harriet Monroe. 'We've got Lao Tse.' Nor did Pound think Tagore's philosophy had 'much in it for a man who has "felt the pangs" or been pestered with Western civilization': 'So long as he sticks to poetry he can be defended on stylistic grounds against those who disagree with his content. And there's no use his repeating the Vedas and other stuff that has been translated. In his original Bengali he has the novelty of rime and rhythm and of expression, but in a prose translation it is just "more theosophy." Of course if he wants to set a lower level than that which I am trying to set in my translations from Kabir, I can't help it. It's his own affair.'[38] In reality, however, it was Tagore who rejected Pound by choosing Evelyn Underhill, a well-known English mystic, to edit the collection of Kabir translations he had been preparing, a job Pound clearly wanted for himself. Pound claimed to pity Tagore, but his anger revealed itself through a passive-aggressive comment in a letter to Alice Corbin Henderson: 'I'm glad Tagore hasn't gone to pot personally. His work has and Yeats says he will no longer stand criticism, and that he has taken to composing in English, which will destroy all the advantage he had in using familiar idiom, and also le[a]d him to express only thoughts that will fit into such English as he knows. The descent from Yeats to Evelyn Underhill, was *facilis* like the more famous *descensus*. Poor Rabby.'[39] Pound's repressed anger is cleverly masked by his use of Yeats to wage his attack, but the point is easily discerned: in Pound's mind, Tagore had consigned himself to Hell by rejecting his help for that of Underhill.

In fact, Tagore was not trying to set himself up as a spiritual leader; he was simply bringing out other facets of his extensive literary work. He did deliver the *Sadhana* lectures again at London's Caxton Hall in June of 1913, but he was also promoting his work as a dramatist. On 9 May he gave a reading of his newly translated play, *Chitra*, to 'a large and deeply interested gathering that included ... many well-known men of letters,' as the *Westminster Gazette* noted in its glowing review,[40] and a week later, his play *The Post Office* appeared at the Abbey Theatre in Dublin. Both plays were being prepared for publication, as were two collections of short stories, *Glimpses of Bengal Life* and *The Hungry Stones*.

Tagore returned to India in September after spending the summer recovering from a minor operation. On 13 November the announcement that he had been awarded the Nobel Prize launched the second phase of his Western fame. Newspapers in Britain were generally pleased, if surprised, by the decision: 'The choice of the receipt of the Nobel Prize for Literature has furnished more than one surprise, but so far no selection has been quite as startling and significant as just announced,' wrote the *Manchester Guardian*. Popular British sentiments toward India appear to have been fairly benign at this time, and the press was inclined to set Tagore favourably against Kipling, the 1906 laureate: 'One might almost think that Tagore had been raised up for the express purpose of refuting Kipling's best-known line, "East is East and West is West, and never the twain shall meet."' In this anxious, pre-war climate, unity seemed much more desirable: 'beneath the distinctions, which although they seemed fundamental prove to be superficial, that separate the races, Mr. Tagore has struck down to the principles that unify the race.'[41] Only a few papers found it necessary to sound the note of Western cultural superiority, the pro-imperialist *Daily Telegraph*, for example, reminding its readers that 'no comparison can be made between his verse and that of West[ern] poets, and it is doubtful if, even in his wonderfully apt translation, Mr. Tagore's poems would have found a ready appreciation in England were it not for the fact that they resemble, although they can not be said to equal, the familiar models of Oriental literature contained in the Bible.'[42] The *New York Times* initially commented that it was 'the first time that this prize has been given to anybody but a white person,' but corrected this the next day by noting that 'Babindranath [*sic*] Tagore, if not exactly one of us, is, as an Aryan, a distant relation of all white folk.'[43]

The Nobel committee members, in taking up the recommendation of Tagore by Yeats's friend T. Sturge Moore, were particularly taken with the religious poems in *Gitanjali*, but were also familiar with Tagore's four English volumes published in 1913: *The Gardener, Glimpses of Bengal Life, The Crescent Moon,* and *Sadhana.* The committee was impressed by 'the perfection with which the poet's own ideas and those he has borrowed have been harmonized into a complete whole; his rhythmically balanced style ... his austere, by some termed classic, taste in the choice of words and his use of the other elements of expression in a borrowed tongue.' His poetry was seen by the committee as 'by no means exotic but truly universally human in character.'[44] The *Daily News and Leader* observed that 'The Nobel Committee is a conservative body, and the scepticism of Anatole France and the pessimism of Hardy are too unorthodox to find favour,'[45] an assessment borne out by the pronounced emphasis on the religious, and particularly the Christian, elements in Tagore's Brahmo perspective. In the Committee's presentation speech, oblique references to the not-always-visible fruits of the missionary movement led into a discussion of Tagore's father, 'one of the leading and most zealous members of a religious community to which his son still belongs,' the Brahmo Samaj, 'founded in the early part of the nineteenth century by an enlightened and influential man who had been much impressed by the doctrines of Christianity, which he had studied also in England.' Tagore was depicted in the speech as a prophet, 'a bearer of good tidings which are delivered, in language intelligible to all, from that treasure house of the East whose existence had long been conjectured,' but nevertheless, 'as far removed as anyone in our midst from all that we are accustomed to hear dispensed and purveyed in the marketplaces as Oriental philosophy.' Tagore's rejection of Hindu pantheism and of 'painful dreams about the transmigration of souls and the impersonal *karma*' was approvingly noted, as was his avoidance of 'a mysticism that, relinquishing personality, seeks to become absorbed in an all that approaches a nothingness.'[46]

Couldst Thou But Be a Bright Black Boy Again

Until the announcement of the Nobel Prize award, Tagore's English and American reception had been almost uniformly positive. To understand the intense appeal of Tagore we must set him and the ideals he represented against the characteristics of Western modernity in an age of industrial and imperial expansion, international political tensions on an unprecedentedly global scale, declining religious belief, dissociation of man from nature, and uncertainty about the future direction of poetry – an age in which the speed of changes in social organization and technology outpaced the capacities of cultural adaptation, an age of nervous disorders. Tagore seemed to offer compelling alternatives to all of these problems;

he exuded personal and spiritual groundedness and charisma; he stood as a glowing counter-example to the pretensions and purposelessness of the surviving poets of the 1890s, split between the aggressive imperialist poets and the effete Decadents. As long as Tagore was taken to represent these idealized qualities, seemingly lost under the pressures of modernity, and as long as these qualities were taken as repressed and thereby shrouded in nostalgia – a nostalgia Tagore personified by his status as a marginalized visitor from a colonized, suppressed, archaic nation – his attraction was nearly unassailable: he appeared as a kind of saint.

Tagore's appeal was in this sense more primitive than exotic, something akin to what Enlightenment thinkers saw in the figure of the Noble Savage. Rousseau, in his *Discourse on the Origins of Inequality*, had argued eloquently that by retracing the forgotten paths that led man from the state of nature to the civil state, it might be possible to find the solution to countless moral and political problems which the *philosophes* could not resolve, 'to explain how the human spirit and passions, altering imperceptibly, change their nature, so to speak; why our needs and pleasures change, at length, their objects; why, the original man having gradually vanished, society offers nothing more to the eyes of the wise than an assemblage of artificial men and manufactured passions which are the product of all these new relations and without any foundation in nature.'[47] Jung offers a psychological version of this argument: 'We can satisfy the demands of adaptation only by means of a suitably directed attitude,' he explains, but 'it may easily happen that an attitude can no longer satisfy the demands of adaptation because changes have occurred in the environmental conditions which require a different attitude.' The result is 'a damming up of libido,' in which 'the value of the opposed positions increases; they become enriched with more and more associations and attach to themselves an ever-widening range of psychic material.' The result is what he calls the regressive tendency.[48]

Indian religion tended to evoke this primitive-regressive response in Westerners, not because Indian religion was either primitive or infantile – indeed, its metaphysical and mythological aspects are extraordinarily elaborate and sophisticated – but because it retained a profound interest in forms of intense religious experience that had been all but eliminated in most modern Western religions, and to which, for the most part, Westerners could only relate through the remnants of their primally repressed memories of the infantile state. The regressive tendency, however, tends to bring out previously repressed contents – which are 'not only of an infantile-sexual character, but are altogether incompatible contents and tendencies, partly immoral, partly unaesthetic, partly again of an irrational, imaginary nature' – and can be a nasty business: 'what the regression brings to the surface certainly seems at first sight to be slime from the depths.'[49]

Westerners encountering Indian spiritual philosophies and philosophers often experienced a regressive tendency in one form or another, and this was certainly the case with responses to Tagore. 'An innocence, a simplicity that one does not find elsewhere in literature makes the birds and the leaves seem as near to him as they are near to children,' wrote Yeats, and indeed, Tagore often takes the child mind as an exemplary state of being. A collection of child verses, *The Crescent Moon*, followed on the heels of *Gitanjali*, and included one of *Gitanjali*'s finest poems (one of several chosen by Yeats to represent the Bengali poet in his *Oxford Anthology of Modern Verse* [1935]):

60

On the seashore of endless worlds children meet. The infinite sky is motionless over-head and the restless water is boisterous. On the seashore of endless worlds the children meet with shouts and dances.

They build their houses with sand and they play with empty shells. With withered leaves they weave their boats and smilingly float them on the vast deep. Children have their play on the seashore of worlds.

They know not how to swim, they know not how to cast nets. Pearl fishers dive for pearls, merchants sail in their ships, while children gather pebbles and scatter them again. They seek not for hidden treasures, they know not how to cast nets.

The sea surges up with laughter and pale gleams the smile of the sea beach. Death-dealing waves sing meaningless ballads to the children, even like a mother while rocking her baby's cradle. The sea plays with children, and pale gleams the smile of the sea beach.

On the seashore of endless worlds children meet. Tempest roams in the pathless sky, ships get wrecked in the trackless water, death is abroad and children play. On the seashore of endless worlds is the great meeting of children.[50]

Child psychologist D.W. Winnicott has written of his lifelong fascination with this poem, which aided him in his discovery of an infantile state in which play is a transitional state that is neither subjective nor objective, but rather situated in an in-between place 'on the seashore of endless worlds.'[51]

The concept of regression is useful in helping us understand the powerful responses to Tagore, and also the ways which identification with Tagore failed. If the encounter with Tagore was also an encounter with the unconscious, we might expect it to fail in one of three ways, which might be called negative identification, over-identification, and rejection of identification.[52] After the Nobel award placed Tagore in the limelight and conferred upon him a certain authoritative status, these failed identifications became more common, as resistance to Tagore and the associated threat of regression began to emerge from various directions and in various forms.

Of the poets who negatively identified with Tagore and his message, Joyce Kilmer, the spiritually inclined, recently turned Catholic poet from New Jersey, was perhaps the most vocal, mounting an attack on the 'Tagore Craze' in the journal *America*: 'If Tagore had been born in Brooklyn, he would never be a fashionable poet. There is a quaint exotic aroma about his poems, like sandalwood or stale cigarets or the back room of a Chinese laundry. He writes about temple-bells and water-jars and the desert: it is all so nice and Oriental! And then he teaches such a comfortable philosophy: just have a good time and love everybody and your soul will migrate and migrate and migrate until finally it pops off into the Infinite!'[5] Admittedly, it was not an easy leap from the Catholic belief in the fallen state of man to the Hindu conception of the soul's identity with God, and Kilmer had no intention of making it. 'Poems are made by fools like me,' he had stated the previous year in what was to be his most famous poem, 'But only God can make a tree.'[54] Kilmer's attack was happily played up by the *Literary Digest*, which thought it had at least 'an air of novelty': It was 'puzzling and offensive,' the *Literary Digest* agreed, to find Americans and Englishmen 'humbly kneeling before the clever Oriental journalist ... who would substitute fatalism for hope, Nirvana for heaven, and ... Krishna for Jesus Christ.'[55] The theological differences were genuine enough, but such attacks tended to collect unconscious racial and professional resentments in their expression. Whatever exotic experiences Kilmer might have had with 'sandalwood or stale cigarets or the back room of a Chinese laundry,' it is clear that they had no direct bearing on Tagore's work.

D.H. Lawrence was another writer who identified negatively with Tagore. For Lawrence, the primitive and exotic qualities of non-Western cultures were equated with instinctual sexuality and lust for power, both decidedly lacking in the ascetic, spiritual Rabindranath. In a letter to Lady Ottoline Morrell, he wrote: 'one is glad to *realise* how these Hindus are horribly decadent and reverting to all forms of barbarism in all sorts of ugly ways. We feel surer on our feet, then. But this fraud of looking up to them – this wretched worship-of-Tagore attitude – is disgusting.' Yet Tagore was not the decadent, barbaric Other that Lawrence needed to confirm his sense of superiority; he would have better luck in Mexico.[56]

Harold Monro, owner of the Poetry Bookshop and editor of *Poetry and Drama*, was calmer in his objection to 'stretching out our hands into the obscure East to a poet quite alien to us.' Monro thought Tagore 'a temporary foil, a clever excuse under cover of which we may procrastinate facing ourselves just a while longer,' for, 'even supposing he has something to give us, how can we expect to realize it?' Monro was prepared to concede that Tagore had 'left us some fine literature,' but deplored the throngs and adulation, the flattering with dinners and speeches, and the 'inappropriate' Nobel Prize. 'Among the foremost to throng him,' Monro suggested, had been 'the pseudo-mystics and the large and increasing seekers after exotic delights,' followed by 'the whilom disciples of Laurence Hope, and last a straggling rout of feasters with "What does it all mean? Can *you* understand it?"' Monro's simple answer was no. 'His revelation ... is not our own revelation. The boom was based on curiosity and has ended in delusion.'[57]

The disturbing 'wretched worship-of-Tagore attitude' was not merely the invention of the anti-Tagoreans. It derived from a tendency to regressively over-identify with Tagore. Tagore overwhelmed. This came out most clearly in responses to his American lecture tour of 1917, where he spoke on nationalism and directed a sharp critique at the institutions of Western culture: 'You pile system upon system, and when one system fails, you turn and devise another and yet another,' he told a Wisconsin interviewer; 'You are content to grovel in the sand and make therein little, narrow, intricate patterns, and content to dwell within the boundaries of these little patterns.'[58] Audiences were surprisingly receptive to this harsh criticism. The April issue of the *Modern Review*, which covered the tour, printed an extract from an unnamed Midwestern newspaper's review of his 'Cult of Nationalism' lecture: 'One felt that here was a dissector carving out our foolish boasts and our smug comfortabilities into their essentials, and finding, for the most part, little or nothing ... How paltry are the things we tolerate. How dirty. It is refreshing to meet this manly man of an outside world very near to us and more valuable, by far, than it is near.'[59] Such responses of ego-loss might be helpful on the road to self-awareness, but the immediate effect could indeed be a detrimental cult-worship form of ego-projection.

Initially, such tendencies toward over-identification were accepted by Tagore's Western supporters. 'It was pleasant to see homage paid so readily to an Indian; nothing of the kind had happened before,' Will Rothenstein recalled in his memoirs. But they did have a disturbing effect, and eventually led to unease and the rejection of identification among Tagore's early admirers. These early supporters had begun by supporting a marginalized figure, and his success exceeded expectations and provoked resentments. Rothenstein became convinced that Tagore was falling victim to the temptations of fame: 'I was concerned only lest Tagore's saintly looks, and the mystical element in his poetry, should attract the *Schwärmerei* of the sentimentalists who abound in England and America, and who pursue idealists even more hungrily than ideals.' It had seemed easy enough to protect Tagore at first. 'But great fame is a perilous thing ... Tagore, who had hitherto lived quietly in Bengal, devoting himself to poetry and to his school, would now grow restless. As a man longs for wine or tobacco, so Tagore could not resist the sympathy shown to a great idealist.'[60] The evil forces Rothenstein saw as plaguing Tagore might be understood as the projection of the shadow side of Rothenstein's own helpful, protective, selfless persona.

Jokes proved to be one of the most popular ways of dealing with the anxiety

Tagore provoked. *Punch* offered its obligatory Tagore parody in the form of 'Mr. Punch's Own Indian Poet,' while the *Evening Standard and St. James's Gazette* provided a set of comical rhymes illustrating the difficulty of pronouncing Tagore's name.[61] The serious poets were by no means above such amusements. In early 1914, Richard Aldington included Tagore in his series of verse parodies in the *Egoist*:

> Come, my songs, let us go to America.
> Let us move the thumbs on our left hands
> And the middle fingers of our right hands
> With the delicate impressive gestures
> Of Rabindranath Tagore.

Tagore's success was for Aldington merely a theatrical trick. Ezra Pound's entry into the mudslinging took the form of a comical short story, entitled 'Jodindranath Mawhwor's Occupation,' parodying the effete lifestyle of an aristocratic Bengali in the most unflattering manner.[62] Will Rothenstein participated in an interesting comic effort by way of a collaborative sonnet in which alternate lines were contributed by his wife, Alice, and his close friend, humorist Max Beerbohm, over the course of a lengthy exchange of letters:

(AR) Tagore, the nature once so clean we knew
(MB) Before you sailed from India's coral strand
(WR) That nature once we thought to understand
(AR) Is now become a thing for fashion's view,
(MB) Equivocal in form, subfusc in hue,
(WR) Obnoxious to the scent, a thing to brand.
(AR) What might it yet have been had not this land
(MB) Unfortunately made a pet of you?
(WR) Now turn a turbid ear to what I fain
(AR) Would tell you while there is yet time and hope.
(MB) Could'st thou but be a bright black boy again
(WR) Along the Ganges ghats where many a corpse
(AR) Would caution thee and tell thee to use soap
(MB) As do the Orpens (sometimes called the Orps)[63]

Here, the satirical Beerbohm injects the strongest elements of racialism, referring to Tagore as subfusc (dusky) in hue in the fifth line and sentimentalizing over the impossibility of the return of Tagore to his status as a 'bright black boy.' (Interestingly, it was always Tagore's 'Aryan features' that were commented on by the press.) But the Rothensteins are quite complicit in this ritualized denigration: Will with his introduction of the description, 'Obnoxious to the scent, a thing to brand,' Alice with her references to cleanliness and uncleanliness, reminiscent of the popular soap advertisements of the day which played on associations of race and purity by depicting people of colour.

The *Daily Citizen* inquired, in its review of the past year's books, 'Do Prizes and Petting Spoil Poets?': 'And what of our mystical poet-philosopher, Rabindranath Tagore? I hope Nobel Prizes and much petting will not spoil him, and that he will drop a certain tendency to affectation and return to the simplicity of his Gitanjali. So with Yoshio Markino, whose idiosyncracies and way of writing English get rather on one's nerves. Let him become again our laughing philosopher, and his work will be more valuable and more amusing.'[64] But Tagore did not remain the laughing philosopher: in 1916 and 1917, he embarked on an extensive tour of Japan and the United States, lecturing on nationalism and other controversial subjects. With this entry into the sphere of Western political discourse, it is not surprising that Tagore came to be seen as politically dangerous; this danger, however, emerged in a curious way: through allegations connecting Tagore to a radical plot involving a group of German-funded Indian revolutionaries in New York arrested and tried in San Francisco between November 1917 and April 1918. A letter produced in the trial claimed that Tagore had come to the United States at the suggestion of the revolutionaries and had tried to enlist support for their cause in Japan, and though the allegations were eventually revealed to be groundless, they 'did tremendous damage to Tagore in the USA' and 'virtually killed the sales of his books for several years,' according to Krishna Dutta and Andrew Robinson.[65]

In England, Tagore's transformation into a dangerous revolutionary was completed in 1919, when, in the wake of the notorious Amritsar massacre, he renounced the knighthood awarded to him four years earlier. (Even then, he had been regarded with some suspicion: Pound had written jokingly to Alice Corbin Henderson, 'Raby Tagore is knighted as I suppose you know. Some change in the official attitude toward Suspect No. 12 Class b.')[66] Tagore was reported in the British press as making a number of anti-British and anti-European statements: in January 1921, he was reported in the *Times* as having 'expressed his view that the League of Nations is a league of robbers' while on tour in Europe; three months later, back in England, he was recorded in the *Morning Post* as saying, in an address to Indian students, that 'Western civilization was of no benefit to native races.'[67] After his visit to Germany in 1921, suspicions that Tagore was a German sympathizer were fuelled by the mass adulation accorded him by the Germans. When he lectured for the first time in Berlin University in June 1921, the London *Daily News* reported 'scenes of frenzied hero-worship ... In the rush for seats many girl students fainted and were trampled on by the crowd.' His German publishers had to order two million pounds of paper on which to print his books, more than eight hundred thousand of which had been sold by October.[68]

The decline of Tagore's popularity in England and America should not be taken as a sign of the failure of his cross-cultural effort; on the contrary, the strong reactions he provoked should be taken as an indication that he succeeded, more than any other non-Western poet of the age, in touching a deep nerve. Had he wished to prolong his popularity, he might have managed it easily enough, but instead he chose to spend whatever cultural capital he accumulated through his success on projects of real consequence. Perhaps, as an exotic object, Tagore's popularity was in any case bound to decline. The opening to the repressed unconscious is a wound which the ego must eventually close, one way or another. A 1921 *Manchester Guardian* review of *The Fugitive* expresses the form of that closure well enough: 'We treasure the volume as we treasure a Persian carpet or a Japanese print; the colour is good, but we do not understand the thoughts of those quaint figures boating or fishing in the sunlight or in the rain.'[69]

Chapter Six

The Childhood That Never Was: Rupert Brooke's Primitive Paradise

In October 1913 the English poet Rupert Brooke, having spent the previous months travelling across the United States, departed by ship bound for the South Seas. Brooke was the flower of the emerging Georgian poets, and the leader of a group of youthful, rebellious, and idealistic intellectuals who enjoyed such primitivistic pastimes as nudism and camping out: 'the Neo-Pagans,' as Virginia Stephen, his childhood friend, dubbed them. Members of the group, including Brooke and James Strachey (later Freud's patient and translator), experimented with homosexuality and questioned received sexual mores of the time. As a member of this group of self-styled sexual radicals who had called into question patriarchal civilization, Brooke had already sought an oppositional position in relation to the sexual law of that civilization, and his voyage of escape and self-rediscovery can be read as a navigation between patriarchy and its Neo-Pagan critique, and between hetero- and homosexuality. For, in spite of his legendary good looks, Brooke's sexual frustrations, his biographers unanimously agree, had reached alarming proportions. Utopian nudity and frankness between the sexes according to a Platonic ideal had rendered most of his relationships with women in his circle sexually sterile. Brooke seemed unable to resolve in his own mind the sexual and Platonic. ('This uncertainty contributed heavily to his nervous breakdown in early 1912,' concludes biographer William Laskowski; Adrian Caesar adds that Brooke 'was deeply uncertain as to his sexual identity, but seems to have wished to choose either homosexuality or heterosexuality.')[1] Brooke's brief sexual relationship with Katharine 'Ka' Cox had ended disastrously and only exacerbated his confusion.

Problems of sexual orientation were endemic to Brooke's elite artistically inclined set. But certainly Brooke's mother contributed to her son's difficulties. 'Mrs Brooke,' Brooke's biographer, Nigel Jones, writes, 'was a distinctly unlovable person. Severe, hard and self-righteous, she combined an unbendable will with narrow moral rectitude and an energetic determination to rule the lives of others to a very unattractive degree.' She, like Brooke's 'henpecked and frustrated' father, was the child of a clergyman. Brooke regarded his father, William Parker Brooke, as a 'very pessimistic man, given to brooding, and without much inside to fall back on.' Rupert found alternative moral suggestions outside the home, but 'much of [his] driving energy was devoted for too many of his mature years to evading and avoiding his mother's unceasing vigilance.'[2] Many of Brooke's characteristic problems seem to have grown out of his troubled parental relations, notably his alternately idealizing and aggressive attitude toward women and the fascination with death that characterizes nearly all of his poetry. Adolescence in the homoerotic atmosphere of Rugby, where Brooke's father was a tutor, provided the finishing touches to his childhood sexual neuroses.

Brooke's decision to journey to North America and the Pacific Islands in 1913 has been read by his biographers as 'an attempt to purge himself completely of his unhappy affair with Ka' and 'a search for oblivion, to release Rupert from conflicts that arose in his motherland but could not be resolved there,'[3] and as 'an attempt to purge himself of what he perceived as the weaknesses in his character.'[4] On the ship, 'Three passionate Pacific women cast lustrous eyes towards me: but with a dim remembrance of the fates of Conrad characters who succumbed to such advances, I evade them.'[5] As he sailed out into the Pacific, he had Conrad, Kipling, and, most of all, Gauguin on his mind. 'You may figure me,' he had written to Edward Marsh shortly before leaving San Francisco, 'in the centre of a Gauguin picture, nakedly riding a squat horse into white surf.'[6]

Island Paradise

Of all the regions associated with the primitive, it was the Pacific Islands that were most powerfully associated with images of Edenic paradise: they were places without boundaries, places of unfettered desire where men and women went naked, freed from the constricting garments of civilization. The 'noble savage' appeared in English literature as early as 1670, when John Dryden used the phrase in one of his exotic dramas, *The Conquest of Granada*. His character declaims in the play's opening scene,

> I am as free as nature first made man,
> Ere the base laws of servitude began
> When wild in woods the noble savage ran.[7]

But the phrase is usually identified with Jean-Jacques Rousseau, who made the *bon sauvage* a key figure in his ethical and political philosophy. In the 1770s, a decade after Rousseau's *Discourse on the Origins of Inequality*, the voyages of Louis-Antoine de Bougainville and James Cook both visited the Pacific Islands, providing extensive material for the debate on the noble savage.

Conversely, the islands were also said to be places of excessive licence, of unspeakable rites and cannibalism. Missionaries, a presence in the islands since the late eighteenth century, encouraged the latter view, and 'made it their business to produce, to people the South Seas with the very beings that had, for expediency's sake, to be found there: depraved, brutish savages,' as Christopher Herbert has argued,[8] but they did have ample material to work with, including the probable cannibalistic consumption of the popular Captain Cook on the last of his three voyages.

By the late nineteenth century, the islands had been drastically transformed by the Euro-American presence. Melville, who rose to fame as the 'man who lived among the cannibals' on the strength of his semi-autobiographical *Typee: A Peep at Polynesian Life* (1846), blamed the missionaries and their self-serving ethnographic accounts, finding the alleged blessings of civilization highly questionable: 'the devoutest Christian who visits [the Hawaiian Islands] with an unbiased mind, must go away mournfully asking – "Are these, alas! the fruits of twenty five years of enlightening."'[9] Steeped in the Enlightenment tradition of the noble savage, Melville finds in the society of the Marquesas 'none of those thousand sources of irritation that the ingenuity of civilized man has created to mar his own felicity,' of which he offers a substantial if idiosyncratic list: 'no foreclosures of mortgages, no protested notes, no bills payable, no debts of honour ... no unreasonable tailors and shoemakers, perversely bent on being paid,' and so on. The 'artless vivacity and unconcealed natural graces' of the 'savage maidens' are contrasted favourably with the 'stiffness, formality, and affectation' of their Western counterparts.[10]

While Western writers quarrelled over the good and bad qualities of primitive life, islanders fought a losing territorial battle with Western missionaries and commercial interests. France's takeover of Tahiti and the Marquesas took place over several decades; we find in *Typee* an account of Melville's arrival in 1842 at the precise moment of French annexation. By an odd coincidence, half a century later, we find Gauguin, in his autobiographical account, *Noa Noa*, narrating his arrival in the same islands at the precise moment at which France formally assumed political control on the death of the last puppet king, Pomare V. Britain briefly annexed the Sandwich Islands (Hawaii) in 1843; afterward, Britain, America, and Germany remained content with shared exploitation of the islands until the 1890s, when the United States annexed Hawaii and divided Samoa with the Germans. As colonialism in the islands progressed, the images of fierce, man-eating natives were increasingly relegated to the background. And with the rise of tourism in the late nineteenth century, the attractions and seductions of 'the amorous islands' were increasingly foregrounded.

Babies and Coconuts

Brooke's arrival in Samoa, his first stop, met, and even exceeded, his primitivistic expectations. 'Great bronze men, with gilded hair, and godlike limbs lay about on the grass.'[11] Watching a Samoan dance, Brooke found it all 'very thrilling and tropical and savage': 'I felt strange ancient raucous jungle cries awaking within me.'[12] But one Samoan image would stick with him through the entire trip:

I went [for] a walk under the coco-nut palms, with a naked baby of five or six holding each hand (one said his name was *Fred*), and several more twining round my ankles. I had a coco-nut – for it was hot – in the house of a white trader who had married a native. Have you ever sent a chocolate-coloured youth up an immense almost perpendicular coco-palm to pick a baby coco-nut, and then drunk the milk? It is the most refreshing thing in the world, on such an occasion.[13]

The image of the tree-climbing native labouring for Brooke's milk-drinking satisfaction stayed with Brooke for the entire trip, turning up repeatedly in his letters. The emotional power of the image seems to draw upon infantile omnipotent fantasy: the satisfaction of the unarticulated demand for milk, the colonial scene in which his demand is satisfied, the atmosphere of babies, the gravity-defying ascent of the phallic tree.

In Hawaii, Brooke stayed at the Moana hotel and found Honolulu 'a dreadfully American place, just like any city in the States or Canada.'[14] In his first important poem of the island trip, 'Waikiki,' the exotic atmosphere becomes a vague correlative of Brooke's troubled erotic feelings:

Warm perfumes like a breath from vine and tree
    Drift down the darkness. Plangent, hidden from eyes
    Somewhere an *eukaleli* thrills and cries
And stabs with pain the night's brown savagery.
And dark scents whisper; and dim waves creep to me
Gleam like a woman's hair, stretch out, and rise;
    And new stars burn into the ancient skies,
Over the murmurous soft Hawaiian sea.

And I recall, lose, grasp, forget again,
    And still remember, a tale I have heard, or known,
An empty tale, of idleness and pain,

> Of two that loved – or did not love – and one
> Whose perplexed heart did evil, foolishly,
> A long while since, and by some other sea.[15]

Here, the extraverted sensation of Brooke's shadow side – the exotic sense-object – merges with the emotions of the primally repressed infantile object relation, and attempts to find expression in language. Melanie Klein's account of the depressive position enables us to sort Brooke's fluid identifications into remnants of the good and bad introjected objects reassembled by the infant to construct the whole object, which has been allowed to disintegrate in the poem. 'Only when the ego has introjected the object as a whole and has established a better relationship to the external world and to real people,' Klein explains, 'is it able fully to realize the disaster created through its sadism and especially through its cannibalism, and to feel distressed about it.' This realization becomes the basis for numerous anxiety situations and feelings of remorse which are 'among the essential and fundamental elements of the feelings we call love.'[16] Anxiety and guilt 'add a powerful impetus towards the beginning of the Oedipus complex,' and thus help to set in motion the process of symbol formation as a means of overcoming the loss of the object.[17] The poem works back toward the emotions of the repressed Thing, heard in the eukaleli that 'thrills and cries / And stabs with pain the night's brown savagery,' and then attempts to make sense of it in the symbolic register as an elusive and empty tale 'Of two that loved – or did not love' – a tale that invites the remorse of 'one / Whose perplexed heart did evil, foolishly' – a tale of remorse over both the phallic aggression of the sexual encounter and the primal aggression against the bad object mother.

From Hawaii, Brooke quickly moved on to Fiji. En route, he wrote to Edward Marsh:

> You think of me in a loin-cloth, brown & wild, in the fair chocolate arms of a Tahitian beauty, reclining beneath a bread-fruit tree, on white sand, with the breakers roaring against the reefs a mile out, & strange brilliant fish darting through the pellucid hyaline of the sun-saturated sea. Oh, Eddie, its all true about the South Seas! I get a little tired of it at moments, because I am just too old for Romance, & my soul is seared. But there it is: there it wonderfully is: heaven on earth, the ideal life, little work, dancing singing & eating, naked people of incredible loveliness, perfect manners, & immense kindliness, a divine tropic climate, & intoxicating beauty of scenery.[18]

Brooke has not even seen Tahiti yet, although he has already completed in his mind the image of himself entwined in 'the fair chocolate arms of a Tahitian beauty.' Brooke's desires are mediated by the images and literary scenes into which he is constantly placing himself. He wants nothing better than to relive a scene from a Gauguin painting or a Kipling story ('It is incredibly like a Kipling story,' he writes, describing his travels, '& all the people are very self-consciously Kiplingesque'),[19] experiencing the appropriate experiences in the appropriate attitudes, while avoiding the unpleasant fates of certain Conrad characters.

Return of the Repressed

In what was to be the most important statement of his primitive ethic, Brooke tried to examine his feelings in a letter from Fiji to Edmund Gosse on 19 November:

> The attraction's queer. It's not really Romance. At least, I associate with Romance, something of veiled ladies, and moonlit serenades, and narrow Venetian or Oriental streets. Something just perceptibly feverish. But this is quite another world. It's getting back to one's childhood, somehow: but not to the real childhood, rather to the childhood that never was, but is portrayed by a kindly sentimental memory; a time of infinite freedom, no responsibility, perpetual play in the open air, unceasing sunshine, never-tiring limbs, and a place where time is not, and supper takes place at breakfast-time and breakfast in the afternoon, & life consists of expeditions by moonlight and diving naked into waterfalls and racing over white sands beneath feathery brooding palm-trees.
>
> Oh, it's horribly true, what you wrote, that one only finds in the South Seas what one brings there.[20]

Brooke's definition of 'Romance,' here, characterized as mysterious, alluring, slightly unhealthy, and associated with the Orient, corresponds roughly to the common characterizations of what I have called 'the exotic.' This is precisely *not* what Brooke finds in the islands; here, he finds, rather, the primitive: 'the childhood that never was,' a world of preadolescent sensuality, the world of *Peter Pan*, which was, as Laskowski points out, Brooke's 'favorite celebration of eternal youth.'[21] The features of Brooke's primitive utopia, infinite freedom, irresponsibility, play, sunshine, nudity, have easily recognizable opposites in modern British urban life: obligations, responsibilities, work, bad weather, lack of play, devotion to time and efficiency, prescribed hours for meals. If Gosse is right that 'one only finds in the South Seas what one brings there,' it may be added that what one brings is the expectation of the opposite of what one has at home: the idyllic primitive is the inverse of the oppressive modern.

Nevertheless, Brooke cannot completely fit in. 'One feels that one's a White Man – ludicrously.'

These dear good people, with their laughter and friendliness and crowns of flowers –

one feels that one *must* protect them. If one was having an evening out with Falstaff and Bardolf themselves, and a small delightful child came up with 'Please I'm lost and want to get home,' wouldn't one have to leave good fellowship and spend the evening in mean streets tracking its abode? That's I fancy, how the white man feels in these forgotten – and dissolving – pieces of heaven, the South Seas. And that perhaps is what Stevenson felt. I don't know enough about him. His memory is sweet there, in Samoa; especially among the natives.[22]

Brooke cannot simply fall into his childhood that never was; rather, he can only approach it here as a colonial father tracking the home of a lost child.

The natives do not figure only as childlike innocents, particularly in Fiji, the legendary Cannibal Islands: 'not so attractive a place as Samoa, but more macabre ... just what I've always imagined Avernus to be like.'[23] Fiji was, he thought, 'heavy with the White Man's Burden,' and he was struck by the 'jolly grinning fuzzy-haired Fijians, who care nothing, and know nothing, of burdens, Empire, or responsibility, nor that they are a dying and defeated race. They merely like sunshine, and people, and fishing, and food and especially swimming in the sea.'[24] To Jacques Raverat he could take a more lurid tone, tantalizing him with descriptions of 'the women with a gait like – oh, like no one you've ever seen in your misty tight-laced feminist lands.'[25] And of course, being in Fiji, there was need for the obligatory cannibal reference, a duty which he discharged in a letter to Violet Asquith, presenting himself in mock danger: 'It's twenty years since they've eaten anybody, in this part of Fiji, and far more since they've done what I particularly and unreasonably detest – fastened the victim down, cut pieces off him one by one, and cooked and eaten them before his eyes. To witness one's own transubstantiation into a naked black man, that seems the last indignity.'[26] And he provocatively asked Cathleen Nesbitt, 'Would you marry me if I turned up with two vast cannibal servants, black-skinned and perpetually laughing – all of us attired only in loincloths and red flowers in our hair? I think I should be irresistible.'[27]

What are we to make about Brooke's jokes to Nesbitt about the primitive life in general and about nakedness in particular? 'I had a great time in Samoa, sharing the sports and festivities of the naked brown savage,' he had written her. 'That's the life for a lad like me.'[28] Nudity has a complex range of meanings for Brooke and his British circle, for whom it served as a marker of difference. For Brooke it appears to generate a certain unease as well as a sense of non-conformist pride, especially in his letters to Nesbitt. The naked brown savage and the naked Black cannibal serve as props for Brooke's fantastic and intentionally provocative scenes, which play on the shock of the primitive as well as the comic-grotesque possibilities of cannibalism. One may also note the ideological functioning of the cannibal joke: though Brooke presents himself as a liberal cultural relativist, vigilantly blaming himself for 'unreasonably' detesting a particularly gruesome form of cannibalism, it is not the act of cannibalism itself around which the joke turns but rather the image of 'one's own transubstantiation into a *naked black man*' (my italics) which is expected to evoke horror in the listener. The understatement of 'the last indignity' merely underscores that what is at stake here is the anxiety related to a collapsing of the distinction between the well-dressed White men and the naked Black men. The acts of vivisection and cannibalism, here merely the relatively insignificant vehicles for his transformation, become themselves the subject for a humorous sonnet, which Brooke thinks would 'do well for No. 101 and last, in a modern sonnet sequence':

> The limbs that erstwhile charmed your sight,
> Are now a savage's delight;
> The ear that heard your whispered vow
> Is one of many *entrées* now;
> Broiled are the arms in which you clung
> And devilled is the angelic tongue; ...
> And oh! my anguish as I see
> A Black Man gnaw your favourite knee!
> Of the two eyes that were your ruin,
> One now observes the other stewing.
> My lips (the inconstancy of man!)
> Are yours no more. The legs that ran
> Each dewy morn their love to wake,
> Are now a steak, are now a steak! ...[29]

Yet the same letter also expresses Brooke's love for the islands. 'Fiji in moonlight is like nothing else in this life or the next,' he remarks. 'I love England; and all the people in it; but oh, how can one know of heaven on earth and not come back to it?'

Although he had injured his foot on a coral reef, he was ready, by late December, to continue to Tahiti. 'I go down to the coast to catch a boat to New Zealand, where I shall post this,' he wrote his mother. 'Thence to Tahiti, to hunt for lost Gauguins. Then back to barbarism in America.'[30] His boat is delayed, however, and he is disappointed to learn, he writes Nesbitt, 'that a man got to Tahiti two months ahead of me, and found – and carried off – some Gauguin paintings on glass.'[31]

There were no undiscovered Gauguins awaiting Brooke in Tahiti, but there was something, from Brooke's point of view, even better, a young Tahitian woman named Taatamata.[32] Brooke could now live out the Gauguin myth himself. He was fully prepared for it. The previous November, while in Samoa, Brooke had observed that

> The Samoan girls have extraordinarily beautiful bodies, & walk like goddesses. They're a lovely brown colour, without any black, Polynesian admixture: their necks & shoulders would be the wild envy of any European beauty: & in carriage & face they remind me continually & vividly of my incomparable heartless & ever-loved Clotilde.[33] Fancy moving amongst a tribe of Clotildes. Can't you imagine how shattered & fragmentary a heart I'm bearing away to Fiji & Tahiti. And, oh dear, I'm afraid they'll be just as bad.[34]

In Tahiti, despite the pretence of resistance, Brooke undoubtedly expected to succumb to temptation. On 7 February, he wrote again to Cathleen Nesbitt. (He had apparently already mentioned the affair in a previous letter, for he tells Nesbitt that he is wearing a flower in his hair from Tuatamata, who is not otherwise identified.) His Britishness seems to be receding and he seems in danger of 'going native': 'Tonight we will put scarlet flowers in our hair and sing strange slumberous South Sea songs to the concertina and drink red French wine and dance obscure native dances and bathe in a soft lagoon by moonlight and eat great squelchy tropical fruits.'[35] He has also, he mentions, decided to stay for another month.

Brooke's most important island poem was also written that month. 'Tiare Tahiti' narrates an amusing attempt to explain the Christian heaven to his island love:

> Mamua, there waits a land
> Hard for us to understand.
> Out of time, beyond the sun,
> All are one in Paradise,
> You and Pupure are one,
> And Taü, and the ungainly wise.
> There the Eternals are, and there
> The Good, the Lovely, and the True,
> And Types, whose earthly copies were
> The foolish broken things we knew ...[36]

The lesson becomes increasingly absurd as the poet describes these Platonic forms:

Never a tear, but only Grief;
Dance, but not the limbs that move;
Songs in Song shall disappear;
Instead of lovers, Love shall be;

and finally reverts to a celebration of life over heaven, the actual over the ideal, concluding that 'There's little comfort in the wise.'[37] In contrast to the number of Brooke's poems in which the poet broods over thoughts of death and the question of the afterlife, the tone of 'Tiare Tahiti' seems especially lighthearted.

On 7 March he wrote to Edward Marsh, 'I have been nursed & waited on by a girl with wonderful eyes, the walk of a goddess, & the heart of an angel, who is, luckily, devoted to me. She gives her time to ministering to me, I mine to probing her queer mind. I think I shall write a book about her – Only I fear I'm too fond of her.'[38] The scene is reminiscent of the conclusion of Gauguin's *Noa Noa* in which the artist devotes himself to probing the 'primitive recesses' of the mind of his native wife. Brooke's ambivalent attraction and distancing from his primitive other suggests the failure of his search for a pre-patriarchal sexuality. The desire to textualize the 'queer mind' of the other expresses the desire to bring the primitive other under the law of patriarchal discourse. It was now important to convey the sense that he was maintaining his distance, to deny that he was going native. His fear of the other and desire to be re-constrained by patriarchal law and (heterosexual) domesticity is expressed in a letter to Marsh: 'O my dear, I really do feel a little anchorless. I shall be glad to be back among you all, & tied to somewhere in England. I'll never never never go to sea again. All I want in life is a cottage & the leisure to write supreme poems & plays.'[39] The feeling of anchorlessness is the inverse of the feeling of enclosure from which the primitive quest begins. The 'successful completion' of the primitive quest is the desire to be re-constrained in familiar boundaries. It is above all this trajectory of the primitive quest that lends it to commodification as a form of twentieth-century tourism.

One observer who was rather doubtful of Brooke's strategy, however, was Ezra Pound, who satirized Brooke's adventures in a poem, 'Our Contemporaries':

When the Taihaitian princess
Heard that he had decided,
She rushed out into the sunlight and swarmed up a cocoanut palm tree,

But he returned to this island
And wrote ninety Petrarchan sonnets.[40]

Pound comically combines Brooke's two objects of fascination – the coconut-gathering boy and the Tahitian love interest. Pound elevates Taatamata's status to 'princess,' but simultaneously dehumanizes her by having her *swarm* up a coconut tree. 'If he went to Tahiti for his emotional excitements instead of contracting diseases in Soho, for God's sake let him have the credit of it,' Pound commented in a letter to Harriet Monroe.[41] The resolution of the poem, with the poet returning to write multitudes of Petrarchan sonnets (the most conventional of erotic forms), emphasizes the bathetic quality of Brooke's dramatic resolution of his sexual problem (his 'decision') and the princess's enthusiastic response. When it appeared, at the height of Brooke's wartime fame, the poem earned Pound severe reprimands from his own contemporaries.

Brooke did admit to some difficulty in his return to civilization. 'I've got out of Tahiti – not without tears' he wrote to Nesbitt in April.[42] San Francisco was an almost unbearable shock. In a state of near-crisis he wrote to Marsh:

> Oh, God! oh, God!
>
> How I hate civilization & houses & trams & collars. If I got on the *Tahiti* & went back again, shouldn't I find a quay covered with moving lights & lovely forms in white & pink & scarlet & green? And wouldn't Taate Mata be waiting there to welcome me with wide arms?[43]

But Brooke quickly adjusted. His 'successful' recuperation of patriarchal and civilized values through the (failed) quest for the primitive is nicely summed up in the role he came to play as spokesman for the ideal of the British nation-state. When the war broke out, shortly after his return, he quickly enlisted, and in October, after brief training, he was off to Antwerp. After his death in the spring of 1915 from an infected mosquito bite his poem 'The Soldier' was to make him the most famous poet of the war. Henceforth he was to be associated not with a tropical paradise but with 'some corner of a foreign field / That is forever England.'[44] His legacy, appropriately enough, centres on the image of the burial of the body. Brooke's embrace of the primitive body, with its laughter at the discourse of immortality, is represented in the Brooke myth as effectively buried, covered over by his final alignment with the myth of the patriarchal nation-state, which guarantees immortality to its members through the spiritualized identification with the eternal name of the father.

In recent studies of Brooke, the poet's complicated sexuality has refused to remain buried, emerging as a primary focus of interest in an alternative approach to the iconic war poet. This resexualized Brooke emerged into prominence in Paul Delany's 1987 biography, *The Neo-Pagans: Friendship and Love in the Rupert Brooke Circle*, but it was only in 1997 that rumours that Taatamata had given birth to Brooke's child, investigated as early as 1930 by Brooke's friend Dudley Ward, were revealed in a sensationalized biography by radio personality Mike Read.[45] Though still a sketchy figure, the Tahitian daughter of Rupert Brooke has been incorporated, along with a letter from Taatamata and additional material concerning Brooke's homosexual affairs, in Nigel Jones's *Rupert Brooke: Life, Death and Myth*.[46] New material continues to emerge, however: a few months after the publication of Jones's biography, a packet of fifty new letters chronicling the poet's somewhat abusive relationship with an art student, Phyllis Gardner, came to light in the British Library. With sexual scandal now an accepted part of contemporary English life, Brooke remains 'forever England' in unexpected ways.

Chapter Seven

The Infant Gargantua on the Wet, Black Bough: Pound's Chinese Object Relations

When Ezra Pound first met Rabindranath Tagore in October 1912, he told his fiancée, Dorothy Shakespear, that the Bengali poet made him feel 'like a painted pict with a stone war club.' It was a felicitous comparison: Pound, the aggressive, flamboyant, barbarian poet from America, had much in common with the war-like, pre-Anglo-Saxon inhabitants of the British Isles, whose name, given by the Romans, denoted their habit of body-decoration. The spiritual, pacifistic Tagore, simple and dignified in manner and dress, was just the person to make Pound self-conscious about his aggressive, dandified persona.

The Seeing Eye

The opposition between Pound and Tagore offers an excellent illustration of two opposing personality types: the extraverted intuitive and the introverted intuitive. The introverted intuition of Tagore, absorbed in contemplation of a stream of images, metaphors, allegories, and parables exploring the nature and problems of consciousness and self, contrasts starkly with the extraverted intuition of Pound, always focused on the external object and in perpetual flight from the self. That flight provided the driving force of Pound's irresistible drive to 'make it new': the extraverted intuitive, Jung writes, 'is never to be found in the world of accepted reality-values, but he has a keen nose for anything new and in the making. Because he is always seeking out new possibilities, stable conditions suffocate him. He seizes on new objects or situations with great intensity, sometimes with extraordinary enthusiasm, only to abandon them cold-bloodedly ... as soon as their range is known and no further developments can be divined.' The extraverted intuitive 'is uncommonly important both economically and culturally,' as he is 'the initiator and promoter of new enterprises' and 'the natural champion of all minorities with a future,' and 'his capacity to inspire courage or to kindle enthusiasm for anything new is unrivalled.'[1]

Since perception is by nature irrational, the personality of extraverted intuitives, orientated toward perception rather than judgment, is essentially irrational, a point that goes a long way toward explaining Pound's idiosyncratic character. Jung cautions that 'it would be quite wrong to regard [extraverted intuitives] as "unreasonable." It would be truer to say that they are in the highest degree *empirical*.' The irrational and unconscious orientation of the type is more pronounced as a result of the repression of the judging functions (thinking and feeling) which 'are none the less present, although they eke out a largely unconscious existence,' the result being that they tend to be expressed in 'apparent sophistries, cold-hearted criticisms, and a seemingly calculating choice of persons and situations.'[2] The repressed judging functions 'come up with infantile, archaic thoughts and feelings' which, in combination with repressed introverted sensation, 'take the form of intense projections ... chiefly concerned with quasi-realities such as sexual suspicions, financial hazards, forebodings of illness, etc.'[3]

Repressed introverted sensation is likely to play a dominant role in the shadow of the extraverted intuitive personality. Yet, like Tagore, who persistently sought out his repressed extraverted sensation, Pound was aware of the repressed quality of his introverted sensation and made the pursuit of it a focus of his work. Pound also attributed repressed sensation to his parents: 'they hadn't the seein' eye,' a failing which resulted in the 'almost complete lack of detail' of their stories, and the fact that they 'never succeeded in conveying the visual appearance of any one of their characters as distinct from any other.'[4] Pound's attempt to confront this failing is apparent in his poem 'The Seeing Eye' (published in *Poetry* in August 1914):

The small dogs look at the big dogs;
They observe unwieldy dimensions
And curious imperfections of odor.
Here is the formal male group:
The young men look upon their seniors,
They consider the elderly mind
And observe its inexplicable correlations.

Said Tsin-Tsu:
It is only in small dogs and the young
That we find minute observation.[5]

Just as the small dogs gather information about potentially important or dangerous big dogs using the seeing eye (and smelling nose), the young men observe the 'inexplicable correlations' of the elderly mind, no doubt for similar reasons. It is noteworthy here that Pound gives credit for the recognition of this repression to an apparently factitious 'Chinese sage,' Tsin-Tsu.[6]

What the small dogs and young men perceive is, in effect, an image. 'An "Image,"' Pound had written in his March 1913 exposition of the concept, 'is that which presents an intellectual and emotional complex in an instant of time.' He added: 'I use the term "complex" in the rather technical sense employed by the newer psychologists, such as Hart, though we may not agree absolutely in our application.'[7] Bernard Hart was a British psychologist who popularized a watered-down version of Freud; his *Psychology of Insanity* (1912) introduced complexes, repression, projection, and other Freudian mechanisms while tactfully avoiding discussion of the sexual basis of Freud's theory. He presented the complex as a 'system of emotionally toned ideas' through the examples of a hobby and the thoughts of a young man in love (Oedipus is nowhere to be seen), and offered an account of some of the mechanisms through which a repressed complex 'obtains an indirect expression' through mechanisms like displacement and projection.[8]

Chinese Secrets

Before we begin probing Pound's complexes, let us first approach his exoticism from another direction by looking at the development of his Far Eastern interests. Pound was introduced to Far Eastern art through Laurence Binyon's lectures on the topic in London in 1909,[9] and was introduced to Japanese haiku around the same time by F.S. Flint, who had taken an interest in the form after reading articles on the subject by a French writer, Paul Louis Couchoud. The Imagist version of haiku, Helen Carr has shown, was already explicit in Couchoud's conception of haiku as 'an image which captures an instantaneous response before its freshness is destroyed by ratiocination.'[10] Flint later recalled how the proto-Imagist group that met at the Tour Eiffel rebelled against the poetry of the day; they 'proposed at various times to replace it by pure *vers libre*; by the Japanese *tanka* and *haikai*; we all wrote dozens of the latter as an amusement.'[11] By 1911, Pound had written his famous haiku-like poem, 'In a Station of the Metro':

> The apparition of these faces in the crowd;
> Petals on a wet, black bough.[12]

The poem was celebrated as exemplary enactment of Pound's Imagist technique, and its relation to the idea of the 'intellectual and emotional complex' is made clear in Pound's explanation of its circumstances of composition:

Three years ago in Paris I got out of a 'metro' train at La Concorde, and saw suddenly a beautiful face, and then another and another, and then a beautiful child's face, and then another beautiful woman, and I tried all that day to find words for what this had meant to me, and I could not find any words that seemed to me worthy, or as lovely as that sudden emotion. And that evening, as I went home along the Rue Raynouard, I was still trying and I found, suddenly, the expression. I do not mean that I found words, but there came an equation ... not in speech, but in little splotches of colour. It was just that – a 'pattern,' or hardly a pattern, if by 'pattern' you mean something with a 'repeat' in it. But it was a word, the beginning, for me, of a language in colour. I do not mean that I was unfamiliar with the kindergarten stories about colours being like tones in music. I think that sort of thing is nonsense. If you try to make notes permanently correspond with particular colours, it is like tying narrow meanings to symbols.[13]

Pound does not attempt to analyse the 'sudden emotion' evoked by the beautiful women's and children's faces; rather, he aestheticizes it, developing a 'language in colour' in which petals on a wet, black bough substitute for faces in the crowd.

'It is usually on the occasion of the aesthetic moment,' writes psychoanalyst Christopher Bollas, 'that an individual feels a deep subjective rapport with an object (a painting, a poem, an aria or symphony, or a natural landscape) and experiences an uncanny fusion with the object, an event that re-evokes an ego state that prevailed during early psychic life.' Bollas argues that such objects evoke the child's primary object-relation to the mother, and calls them 'transformational objects,' a terminology that borrows from D.W. Winnicott's notion of the transitional objects that the infant uses to mediate the loss of its primal relationship with the mother. 'To seek the transformational object is to recollect an early object experience, to remember not cognitively but existentially – through intense affective experience – a relationship which was identified with cumulative transformational experiences of the self.'[14]

For Pound the aesthetic moment of the 'Metro' poem is firmly connected to the strategy of substitution, a strategy that becomes the basis for his new approach to the poetic image through what he called 'super-position': 'The "one image poem" is a form of super-position, that is to say, it is one idea set on top of another. I found it useful in getting out of the impasse in which I had been left by my metro emotion.' That this strategy is, at bottom, irrational may be discerned from the fact that Pound calls this a 'one image poem,' though it would seem to make more rational sense to call it a two image poem. But Pound's explanation here is exclusively interested in the mechanism by which the repressed complex (to use Hart's terminology) finds expression; he is not concerned with its underlying structure. His interest is, in other words, aesthetic rather than psychoanalytic.

Pound's Far Eastern connection showed signs of improving in July of 1911, when he unexpectedly received two books of poems from Yone Noguchi in Kamakura, Japan. Pound did not quite know what to think about them, he told Dorothy Shakespear; they were 'rather beautiful' but somewhat ungrammatical and rather poorly proofread; 'his matter is poetic & his stuff not like everything else, he is doubtless sent to save my artistic future.'[15] But Pound's *Exultations* and *Canzoni*, which he sent Noguchi with his reply, did not engage Noguchi's interest. 'What a difference of your work from mine!' Noguchi wrote back in the polite but curt note that seems to have ended their correspondence.[16]

Japan was then much in the news in England as a result of the Japan British Exhibition in London's Shepherd's Bush and the renewal of the Anglo-Japanese Alliance. Noguchi himself had begun writing regular articles on Japanese topics for such periodicals as the *Graphic*, the *Nation*, and the *Academy*. But in the fall of 1911, attention turned to the revolution in China. In December, Sun Yat-Sen was declared president of the new Chinese Republic, and in February of 1912, the Manchu (Qing) dynasty ended with the abdication of the last Emperor Puyi.

Pound's main personal connection to Chinese and Japanese aesthetics continued to be Laurence Binyon. Pound had attended Binyon's lectures on 'Art and Thought in East and West' in 1909 and became a frequent visitor to the British Museum's Department of Prints and Drawings, where Binyon served as Assistant Keeper. Pound no doubt read *The Flight of the Dragon*, Binyon's small collection of essays on East Asian aesthetics, soon after its publication in August of 1911. There, Binyon wrote evocatively of 'the Taoist genius' that 'embodied its ideal in the wild Rishi, the mountain dwellers.'[17] When Pound, 'fed up with Tagore' in May 1913, declared that 'as a religious teacher he is superfluous. We've got Lao Tse,' he was probably thinking of Binyon's idyllic vision of Taoism. But Binyon was one of a series of more or less knowledgeable Western intermediaries between Pound and the exotic. Pound's tendency to glorify these intermediaries – the Arabists Wilfred S. Blunt and Charles M. Doughty, the Africanist Leo Frobenius, and the Asianists Binyon and Fenollosa – should perhaps be set alongside his tendency to fail in his direct relationships with non-Western poets like Naidu, Tagore, and Noguchi.[18]

Dorothy Shakespear, Pound's main romantic interest at this time, also became deeply involved in Pound's exotic interests. She is presumed to be the 'Love' of 'Plunge,' an important early exotic poem which first appeared in *Ripostes* (1912). The poem expresses Pound's emerging modernist aesthetic in terms of an overpowering desire for the exotic:

I would bathe myself in strangeness:
These comforts heaped upon me, smother me!

I burn, I scald so for the new,
New friends, new faces,
Places!
Oh to be out of this,
This that is all I wanted
  – save the new.
And you,
Love, you the much, the more desired!
Do I not loathe all walls, streets, stones,
All mire, mist, all fog,
All ways of traffic?
You, I would have flow over me like water,
Oh, but far out of this!
Grass, and low fields, and hills,
And sun,
Oh, sun enough!
Out and alone, among some
Alien people![19]

Here, Dorothy Shakespear is associated with 'the new,' the strangeness in which the poet wishes to be bathed as a cure for the smothering comforts perceived as sensations of burning and scalding. As in the 'Metro' poem we find the pleasurable appearance of faces, in the 'New friends, new faces, / Places!' that the poet associates with the circumstances of release.

Ezra and Dorothy's exotic preoccupations developed during her parents' prohibition of their relationship. In December 1912, Dorothy entrusted Ezra with the task of buying her a jade 'gew-gaw,' one that he took up with some earnestness. On 16 December, he reported visiting two shops, finding 'nothing that I should care much for' (a third shop was closed).[20] On 2 January he saw 'a decent jade pendant' but the price was too high; he wondered 'what colour goes with a Chinese skirt.'[21] Two days later he reported having 'spent the day in searches – fruitless & otherwise': the fruitless search was at Liberty's department store, while the 'otherwise' was at the British Museum where, he reported, 'I contemplated mediaeval japanese prints ... & feel ages older & wiser.' He had been with Binyon, who complained that England would never have a[n Oriental art] collection 'comparable to the "Fuller" lot in the U.S.'[22] In February, Dorothy managed to gain entrance into the print room herself, and was able to view a portfolio of Utamaro prints. 'I wonder which you liked so much?' she wrote.[23] She saw more Japanese prints at the home of the artist Charles Ricketts in March.[24] Tales of musical Orientalism in France were brought back by their mutual friend Walter

Rummel in April: 'Debussy & his Chinese things must be charming,' Dorothy mused.[25]

Dorothy's interest in the Far East was sufficiently strong by April that it required an act of will to put it aside while travelling in Italy: with the Vatican statuary and Egyptian collections 'one has to forget Chinese ideas entirely.'[26] But it was again on her mind as she prepared for her return on 13 May: 'we go home tomorrow ... My newly papered room will need some Jap prints perhaps. Or you might like one?'[27] Back in Kensington, however, Dorothy was occupied with other things, including her formal rejection of Ezra's marriage proposal in July. These were also the final months of Tagore's English visit. By the time she revived her interest in the print room in September, it had closed. 'That print-room is closed INDEFINITELY – while they move into the new wing of the museo – which means, I should think, six months,' Pound informed her on 23 September. 'There's small use of your imagining you'll be let into *that* plaisance, and unless there are prints at the S. Kens[ington museum] I don't know what will become of you. You'll have to read the Mahabarata or something else extensive.'[28] Pound understood Dorothy's interest in the print room as a need for exotic stimulation that, if unavailable, would have to be satisfied by alternative means. The difficulty of access also served as a symbolic equivalent of the difficulties of their relationship at this juncture. Dorothy also, independently, attempted to explore alternative exoticisms: she had tried reading a translation of the Koran a few weeks earlier, but found it 'mighty dull,'[29] an assessment with which Pound fully concurred.[30] She was threatening to take up embroidery, but Pound thought it 'not much better than smoking'; and while he would not *forbid* her 'embroidery, or hashish,' he counselled her on the benefits of activities that 'demand complete attention.' 'Anything that demands only partial attention is useless, for developing a vortex,' he explained; 'it would incapacitate one for serious creation of any sort.'[31] Dorothy's Far Eastern interests, on the other hand, were the sort he supported.

In the weeks before the Fenollosa meeting, a final contribution to Pound's Chinese interests came through Allen Upward, who had contributed a series of pseudo-Chinese poems entitled 'Scented Leaves – From a Chinese Jar' to *Poetry* magazine via Pound. Upward was a speculative comparativist of the Frazerian type whose experience as a colonial administrator in Nigeria lent his reductive cultural theories an impressive air of authority. His Chinese poems in *Poetry* were 'worth the price of admission,' Pound informed Shakespear, and Upward himself was 'quite an addition.'[32] In the days before the Fenollosa meeting he travelled to Ryde to visit Upward.

Pound's first meeting with Mary Fenollosa took place on 29 September 1913. 'I seem to be getting Orient from all quarters,' he wrote Dorothy Shakespear on 2 October. 'Have done shows chinesesques, borrowed the Mahabarata, been taken to a new curious & excellent restaurant chinois ... Dined on monday with Sarojini Niadu [*sic*] and Mrs Fenolosa [*sic*], relict of the writer on chinese art, selector of a lot of Freer's stuff [the Freer Collection of Oriental art now at the Smithsonian], etc.' Pound had also been to visit Harriet Shaw Weaver (supporter of the *New Freewoman* and future editor of the *Egoist*) at her home, Cedar Lawn in Hampstead: 'I got real japanese prints – I don't mean on paper – at Cedar Lawn ('Ampstead of all places),' he wrote, 'but I believe the Weavers are leaving it and as I've just met 'em I dont see how you can be set there to paint it.' Dorothy must have been jealous. And finally, he had got hold of some translations of Confucius and Mencius: 'I'm stocked up with K'ung fu Tsze, and Men Tsze, etc. I suppose they'll keep me calm for a week or so.'[33]

On 6 October, he dined with Mary Fenollosa and Sarojini Naidu at the Cafe Royal, this time in the company of William Heinemann, publisher of both Naidu and Ernest Fenollosa.[34] Madame Fenollosa, he noted, 'seems determined that he shall support me.'[35] Pound conveyed some of his thoughts – clearly wavering between India and China – to Dorothy the following day: 'I have a huge hunk of the Mahabarata on the "secretoire." I wonder if I'll ever read it.' Pound's interest in India was waning, particularly since Tagore's departure on 4 September; China was clearly on his horizon. 'I find the chinese stuff far more consoling.'

Pound had already begun reading Herbert Giles's *History of Chinese Literature*. The first chapter on poetry began with Giles's assertion that 'in the fourth century B.C., Ch'ü Yüan and his school indulged in wild irregular metres which consorted well with their wild irregular thoughts. Their poetry was prose run mad.'[36] Giles offered some translations in prose: it seemed to be exactly what Pound was looking for. 'There is *no* long poem in chinese,' he explained to Dorothy. 'They hold if a man can't say what he wants to in 12 lines, he'd better leave it unsaid. THE period was 4th cent. B.C. – Chu Yüan, Imagiste – did I tell you all that before???'[37] Dorothy, happy as ever to receive Pound's spurious Oriental wisdom, wrote back: 'Please tell me about the 4th Cent B.C. Chinese. I expect they're right about having no long poem.' She was, as predicted, deprived of Oriental stimulation: 'that beastly Print Room is shut, with a vengeance. What will yr. poor coz do?'[38] Pound was sympathetic: 'In lieu of the print-room you can have Giles' "Hist. of Chinese Lit," & a book of Japanese ditto [this would have been W.G. Aston's *History of Japanese Literature*], & the new Tagore, & Upward's "Divine Mystery."'[39]

Infant Gargantua

Pound's remarkable receptiveness and sensitivity toward China might be linked to his stated desire in 'Plunge' to be among 'alien people,' but this brings us to the enormously complicated question of his attitudes toward cultural otherness, one of the central problems of his work. On the one hand, we find abundant evidence of his appreciation and intuitive understanding of other cultures in his role as a translator of Latin, medieval European, and East Asian poetry; on the other hand, we can only be amazed at the hatred and paranoia of his anti-Semitic theories, and his condescending and denigrating comments about African Americans. This double affect of attraction and repulsion is characteristic of the exotic as projection, but in Pound's case, the positive and negative poles of the exotic seem to be split between different sets of cultural referents.

Pound's descriptions of his early childhood, though cursory, furnish some interesting clues about the infantile origins of his later exotic preoccupations. Here, we must part company with Jung and take up with the infantile post-Freudians. But before delving into theory, let us consider the biographical material.

It is not usually noticed that the story of Pound's encounter with China actually begins only a few months after his birth. Pound tells the story in 'Indiscretions,' the semi-comical account of his progeniture. The newly married Homer and Isabel Pound had relocated to Bailey, Idaho. They had brought along a servant, 'Mary Beaton, the deep bosomed and affable, the "stylish" New York (City) negress' who had been with the family 'since the Flood,' but Mary Beaton had found Idaho uncongenial and soon 'left at midnight, without her variegated assortment of clothing.'[40] When Mary Beaton's successor quit to get married, Pound's mother went to live at the local hotel, where she was apparently still residing at the time of the birth of 'the infant Gargantua,' as Pound calls himself in this memoir. (The name is well chosen, of course, suggesting the childhood origins of Pound's later, famous egotism, as well as a concern with bodily fluids and excesses which all infants share with Rabelais's famous character.)

Isabel Pound's sister arrived and was appalled at the situation, and it was then, in a second attempt at domesticity, that 'they had a Chinaman to do the cooking,' as Pound explains, 'and he was a model of virtue. Anything he was shown how to do, that did he exactly in replica,' until on one occasion he used a hearth-brush to remove crumbs from the table. 'The company maintained its decorum until he had retired. But from the kitchen he heard their hysteria, and there was a great noise in the kitchen "and you would have thought he was breaking all the dishes" altogether; and after a long and anxious interval the dessert "finally came in."' The event evidently brought the employment of the Chinaman to an untimely end, and Pound's mother and the infant Gargantua returned to the hotel.

Pound devotes considerable space in this memoir to the servant problem, evidently a major factor in the family's subsequent decision to quit Idaho and return to the New York boarding house of Isabel Pound's parents, where Mary Beaton had been reemployed. But one also glimpses through the humorous servant stories another implication: that 'the infant Gargantua' may have been closer to the servants than to his mother, described as 'slightly aloof, socially conscious, restrained, not given to demonstrations of feeling' by Pound's biographer Humphrey Carpenter. Pound himself said in later years: 'I was my father's son in opposition to my mother,' and 'my own case is the farthest removed from the Oedipus complex.'[41] The servants, the primary food-providers of the family, were no doubt entrusted with child-care duties as well. The combination is suggested by one of Pound's earliest remembered utterances: 'at the age of two years and four months he denounced Mary Beaton (in error) for wasting his talcum, when she spilt the baking-powder for the biscuits.'[42] The Black or Chinese servant, in short, was entrusted with providing food and tending to Ezra's physical needs, a situation which would certainly have resulted in an affective attachment; but since a positive attachment would have threatened the position of the mother, the affective tie was turned in a negative direction by dwelling on the failure or absence of the servant, and the associated feeling-sensing values were repressed. Pound tended to describe the supposed feeling-sensing orientation of Black people in a highly derogatory manner: in his discussion of 'the race problem' leading up to his introduction of Mary Beaton, he explains, 'the nigger, like any other fine animal, is very quick to perceive certain tones of personality, of voice, modes of moving, not by cerebral analysis but by "feel."' The race problem was a problem of animal management. 'There are ninety different ways of saying "Damn nigger"; it requires knowledge to use the right ones.'[43]

Although the portrait of Pound's infantile development that emerges in the foregoing anecdotes is hardly a complete one, it does offer a number of suggestive clues concerning the infantile origins of his later psychological orientation. The psychoanalytic object relations approach, developed by Melanie Klein, W.R.D. Fairbairn, and D.W. Winnicott, among others, offers the most useful perspective on the processes through which the infant's subjectivity becomes oriented through interaction with the mother as primary object. Although formulations among the various object relations theorists vary considerably, it is usually agreed that the differentiation of subject and object is the central psychological challenge faced by the infantile consciousness and that this challenge is faced and worked through interactively in the infant's relationship to the mother as primary object. In the Kleinian version of the theory, the infant's split experience of libidinal desire and aggressive hatred for a mother seen as the provider and denier of satisfaction results in split internal representations of good and bad mother-objects. In Winnicott's theory, the infant comes to accept separation from the mother through the discovery of the symbol (in the form of early transitional objects) through which it learns to control the presence and absence of the mother-object. This transitional stage, which plays a major role in the individual's later psychological orientation, is facilitated by the mother, who must first fulfil the infant's omnipotent fantasy and continue to provide an environment in which the infant can gradually discover the limits of its power and the separate existence of objects. In Winnicott's terminology, this is a 'holding environment' provided by a 'good-enough mother' who responds adequately to the infant's needs for the necessary period. Pound's description of his own infantile development, understood in conjunction with his later orientation, suggests that Isabel Pound had difficulty providing an optimal or perhaps even minimally adequate holding environment for the infant Pound, and that the servants were entrusted with the provision of care and food, and therefore came to occupy the position psychologists refer to as the early primary surrogate mother.[44]

Hardin and Hardin's work on early primary surrogate mothering points to serious developmental consequences that may result from 'the trauma experienced by the child when the [early primate surrogate mother] leaves.' Since 'parents are often unable to validate the true nature of their child's relationship with the EPSM,' the mourning process associated with the loss of a loved object is often inhibited or disrupted.[45] A more detailed analysis of Pound's case might be developed out of the mechanisms described by Klein and Winnicott, such as Winnicott's 'benign circle,' in which the infant in the depressive position, having devoured the mother in feeding, begins to experience guilt, experiences the sorting out of good and bad objects, and attempts to make reparation and restitution through processes associated with digestion and elimination. Whether or not the mother plays her part in receiving the gift gesture, Winnicott suggests, can determine the development of feelings of anxiety and guilt.[46] In Pound's infantile situation, one surmises, mastery of the gift gesture would have involved substitutions and reroutings the nature of which would have been very difficult to comprehend. I suggest that this infantile problem largely determined the major features of Pound's psychological and poetic orientation – his compulsive relationship to the symbol, his strategies of substitution, and his sorting of loved and hated racial others. In short, I believe that Pound's search for a lost Chinese object was an attempt to repay the prohibited and repressed emotional debt he owed his Black mother, Mary Beaton.

Attachment and Loss

I have already suggested that Pound's powerful but unanalysed emotion associated with the 'Metro' poem derived from his problematic object orientation. I am now in a position to take this identification a step further and link the emotion specifically to the figure of the Black mother, Mary Beaton, through the image of the black bough. This linkage is reinforced by Pound's extended comments on 'a language of colour,' when, in fact, the only colour mentioned in the poem is black, which is, properly speaking, only a 'colour' when used in a racial context. The association of the Black and Chinese surrogate mothers becomes more significant as we look at the development of Pound's early Chinese poetics, picking up our story from where we left Ezra and Dorothy in early October of 1913, after the initial meetings with Mary Fenollosa.

Although Pound would not get the Fenollosa notebooks for some months, he began testing out the possibilities of Chinese poetry using Giles's *History of Chinese Literature*. Giles was in fact mistaken about the early Chinese poems resembling 'prose run mad,' as Ming Xie has pointed out; it was simply that the metre and rhyme schemes had become obscured over time.[47] But the mistake was useful for Pound. He reworked one of the poems as 'After Ch'u Yuan' and later wrote in an essay for *Poetry* magazine about 'the great *vers libre* writers before the Petrarchan age of Li Po ... a treasury to which the next century may look for as great a stimulus as the renaissance had from the Greeks.'[48] The rest of the poems in Giles were translated into conventional and rather oppressive Victorian forms, but Pound attempted to liberate three of these into free verse as well.

Pound's exotic strategies emerge through these reworkings in the thematic concerns of the selections and in his specific alterations. Robert Kern points out that two of the poems share with the 'Metro' poem a 'common image of a personified "clinging" which suggests an experience of loss and a reluctance to let go of what is lost and thus available only as an "apparition."'[49] It is a simple enough matter to link these images of clinging and loss to separation from the mother-object, especially when we recall the specific woman-child imagery associated with the 'Metro' poem and observe the repeated concern with wetness, sensation, and, one may say, the sensation of wetness. I would suggest that these images hark back to Pound's tactile and emotional connection to the lost talcum-wielding Black surrogate mother. The change Pound made to the ending of the poem he entitled 'Liu Ch'e' pushes it in a remarkably similar direction: from Giles's version, 'For she, my pride, my lovely one, is lost, / And I am left, in hopeless anguish tossed,'[50] Pound inexplicably arrives at the mere phrase: 'A wet leaf that clings to the threshold.' The 'depersonalization of the poem,' to use Kern's phrase, has often been praised as an example of imagist strategy; Kern suggests it is an orientalizing strategy as well, on the grounds that the absence of the 'subjective "I"' is 'an absence also common in Chinese poetry.' But one might rather say that the leaf is personalized: it is made to carry the emotional weight of an image of the infant separated from the mother. 'Anxiety in these early stages of the parent-infant relationship relates to the threat of annihilation,' Winnicott writes. 'The alternative to being is reacting, and reacting interrupts being and annihilates. Being and annihilation are the two alternatives.'[51] One may also view it in the context of the reparation and the gift, noting their association with excrement. In any case, Pound's substitution is certainly curious. The tactile theme appears again in the poem entitled 'Ts'ai Chi'h':

> The petals fall in the fountain,
>   The orange-coloured rose-leaves,
> Their ochre clings to the stone.[52]

All of these scenes attach a strong emotion to a crushed flower or leaf clinging to a hard object – black bough, threshold, or stone – and all involve wetness. All involve identification with a rejecting or rejected object, as does another re-worked Giles poem, 'Fan-Piece, For Her Imperial Lord':

> O fan of white silk,
>   Clear as frost on the grass-blade,
> You also are laid aside.[53]

To call these poems depersonalized is to miss the point that 'from the standpoint of the extravert,' as Jung writes, 'we would have to say that the person reveals itself simply and solely in its relatedness, in the function of relationship to the object. For only with the introvert is the "person" exclusively the ego; with the extravert it lies in his affectivity and not in the affected ego.'[54] For the extraverted Pound, the image of the crushed flower or dying leaf clinging to the hard object functions as a core image of personality, organized around object-attachment and object-loss.

The object would always elude Pound's valiant efforts to attach subject to object via the symbol. In a late Canto he seems to have come to some understanding of his symbolic compulsion and its causes:

> Tho' my errors and wrecks lie about me.
> And I am not a demigod,
> I cannot make it cohere.
> If love be not in the house there is nothing.
> The voice of famine unheard.
> How came beauty against this blackness,
> Twice beauty under the elms –
>   To be saved by squirrels and bluejays?
>   'plus j'aime le chien'
> Ariadne.[55]

As if following Ariadne's thread out of the labyrinth, the symbolic compulsion is still able to trace its origins back to the loveless house of childhood, and to child's 'voice of famine unheard.'

Pining for Hieroglyphs

Mary Fenollosa wrote Pound from Alabama on the 24th of November, 'I know you are pining for hieroglyphs and ideographs: but I must keep to our plan and send the No stuff first. That is a complete book in itself.'[56] The first package was shipped, as promised, on the 25th, and Pound's craving for 'hieroglyphs and ideographs' – significant, as it illustrates that Pound was already contemplating uses for ideograms before reading Fenollosa's 'Chinese Character' essay – was apparently not long kept unfulfilled, for Pound reported to William Carlos Williams on 19 December, 'I am very placid and happy and busy. Dorothy is learning Chinese. I've all old Fenollosa's treasures in mss.'[57]

Dorothy, already busy trying to teach herself Chinese, was anxious to see the new poems. On 20 November she began her letter to Pound with the Chinese ideogram for hair and the salutation, 'Beloved "Mao"' – having evidently noticed the fortuitous resemblance between the character and Pound's 'uncombed hair where pigeons might like to be nesting,' as Yone Noguchi memorably described it – and demanded, 'can *I* have any of the Chinese poems to read – some time?' Pound wrote back, 'I will copy those – no I won't I'll bring 'em on Wednesday,' explaining in in mock Chinese-pidgin: 'Them Chineze (Chinese poems). They are only very small 3 1/2 poems.' Pound was by this time secluded with Yeats at Stone Cottage in Sussex for the first of three winters he spent there as Yeats's secretary. He wrote Dorothy shortly after arriving, 'I read Kung-fu-tse, & a barbarous Indian thing and I read ghosts to the eagle [Yeats].'[58]

The Fenollosa translations, when they arrived, all proved to be of the later 'Petrarchan age of Li Po,' and here, Giles was quite clear about the rigid schemes whereby 'the poet is hampered not only by rhyme but also by tone'; and 'as a consequence, the natural order of words is often entirely sacrificed to the exigencies of tone, thus making it more difficult than ever for the reader to grasp the sense.'[59] But Pound simply ignored this obvious fact and continued to identify Chinese poetry with free verse.

Dorothy, meanwhile, was continuing her efforts to immerse herself in Orientalia. 'I have found a nice portrait of you in one of my Japanese picture books!' she jokingly reported on 22 November. In early December, she was anxiously awaiting the reopening of the print room: 'Are there any old Chinese M.S.S. at that blooming museum that you will want copied?' she wrote to him, wanting to be helpful, though the silliness of the idea immediately occurred to her: '(Brilliant idea! how can he want them copied until he knows what they're about?)' In the meantime, 'there is said to be a marvellous collection of Jap. prints at S. Kensington Museum now – a Loan Exh: & worth seeing.'[60] By January 1914 she had set her sights on the main reading room instead: 'I am in communication about an entrance ticket for British M[useum] reading room – where I *say* I am studying Symbolisme – but where I mean *privately*, to study Ching Chang Chinese!'[61] Pound replied that it was not necessary to bother with the *Symbolisme* pretext, since no one at the museum cared, but suggested that 'the oriental room is a much pleasanter place to work in than the "reading-room,"' and she would be able to pursue her study of Chinese there, since he had written to Mary Fenollosa again for 'that simple introduction to Chang.'[62] Dorothy's response is a revealing one: 'My only reason for wishing to pursue Symbolisme is that I shall have to tell my parents what I am doing – at first anyway – and I would much rather keep the Chinese secret – as it amuses me much more, & I am likely to go on longer if amused! Comprends-tu?'[63] The forbidden pleasures of the Orient had to retain an aura of secrecy, even if it was not necessary.

Fortunately, the Noh plays were very secret, according to Ernest Fenollosa. Fenollosa was intrigued by elements of secrecy surrounding the Noh, and his writings conveyed an aura of penetration into forbidden spaces undoubtedly relished by Pound and Dorothy Shakespear. 'Morse and I are the only foreigners who have ever been taught Noh,' Fenollosa claimed, 'and I am the only foreigner now practicing it.'[64] Fenollosa depicts the Noh as secret not only to foreigners but to most Japanese as well: 'When a Noh actor was engaged by the Shogun he had to sign long articles to the effect that he would never divulge even to his wife or his relatives any of the doings or descriptions of things in the palace, also that he would not visit houses of pleasure or go to the theatre.' Several plays were 'so secret that they were told and taught only by father to eldest son.'[65]

But Pound was careful not to play up Fenollosa as an obsessive exoticist. Fenollosa 'cannot be looked upon as a mere searcher after exotics,' wrote Pound in his introduction to 'The Chinese Written Character as a Medium for Poetry' (1919). Pound meant that Fenollosa did not simply wish to immerse himself in the exotic for its own sake: 'his mind,' he wrote, 'was constantly filled with parallels and comparisons between eastern and western art. To him the exotic was always a means of fructification. He looked to an American renaissance.'[66] For Pound, exoticism 'as a means of fructification' – like sex for the sake of reproduction – is healthy (one notes also the association with food); whereas 'mere' exoticism for its own sake is not. The significant word is 'mere,' for elsewhere, Pound goes all out presenting Fenollosa as a romantic hero of the scholarly exotic quest:

The life of Ernest Fenollosa was the romance par excellence of modern scholarship. He went to Japan as a professor of economics. He ended as Imperial Commissioner of Arts. He had unearthed treasure that no Japanese had heard of. It may be an exaggeration to say that he had saved Japanese art for Japan, but it is certain that he had done as much as any one man could have to set the native art in its rightful pre-eminence and to stop the apeing of Europe. He had endeared himself to the government and laid the basis for a personal tradition. When he died suddenly in England the Japanese government sent a warship for his body, and the priests buried him within the sacred enclosure at Miidera. These facts speak for themselves.[67]

Not all the facts did speak for themselves: Fenollosa had in fact had difficulty finding work during his second stay in Japan, the warship story was simply untrue, and Fenollosa's actual burial site is in a small sub-temple a good twenty minutes' walk from the main temple of Miidera. Pound was not really exaggerating Fenollosa's accomplishment, which was extraordinary, but his way of viewing it is marked by exoticist strategies: romance, discovering secrets, unearthing treasure, attaining a high position in a strange land, being worshipped as a divine figure – all of which are typical components of exoticist narrative. Pound views Fenollosa as a sort of American hero who saves Japan from the evils of Western cultural imperialism by setting 'the native art in its rightful pre-eminence' and stopping 'the apeing of Europe.' In fact, Fenollosa's contribution to Japanese cultural nationalism also helped Japan ape Europe in a much more troubling way, by enabling it to use its cultural traditions as a support for its own imperialistic expansion. Moreover, Fenollosa was quite clear about what he saw as the West's need to culturally colonize the East. True, this was part of his visionary outlook toward the future, in which 'vistas of strange futures unfold for man, of world-embracing cultures half weaned from Europe, of hitherto undreamed responsibilities for nations and races.' But Fenollosa framed his project unambiguously in the service of American power over China: 'The Chinese problem alone is so vast that no nation can afford to ignore it. We in America, especially, must face it across the Pacific, and master it or it will master us. And the only way to master it is to strive with patient sympathy to understand the best, the most hopeful and the most human elements in it.'[68] The phrase 'the Chinese problem' reminds us that this is an essay written in the years of Western and Japanese imperial squabbling over Chinese possessions, a period in which Chinese sentiments wavered dramatically between anti-Westernism and Western-influenced political radicalism, in which the political future of the vast country was up for grabs. Fenollosa appears nevertheless overtly opposed to imperialism and current strategies of trade-by-force: 'The duty that faces us is not to batter down their forts or to exploit their markets, but to study and to come to sympathize with their humanity and their generous aspirations. ... We need their best ideals to supplement our own – ideals enshrined in their art, in their literature, and in their lives.'[69]

Meeting in Cho-fu-Sa

English poetry offered a very limited field for the application of the ideogrammic method, as Pound called it. The appeal of *Cathay* no doubt owed more to other factors. One was simply the excellence of the Chinese originals, nearly unknown to British and American readers at this stage. Another, as Hugh Kenner has suggested, was the timeliness of the volume's poems that 'paraphrase an elegiac war poetry nobody wrote.'[70] But the most impressive poems in *Cathay* – 'The River-Merchant's Wife: A Letter' and 'Exile's Letter' – are powerful, I would suggest, because they provided Pound an opportunity to continue and expand the 'Chinese' exotic strategy I have described as a projection of emotional complexes associated with object relations anxieties of attachment and loss. Ronald Bush finds Pound 'obviously moved' by the section in 'Exile's Letter' where the poet recalls the sensations associated with a past reunion with a separated friend, and suggests that he 'gave to it some of his finest inventions.'[71] Bush suggests that because the personality of the Li Po encountered by Pound was 'dim and fluid,' as was his language and culture, the encounter 'recalls what happens in a psychiatrist's office when a patient invests a companionable stranger's voice with part of his own identity.'[72] This takes us closer to an understanding of the psychological basis of Pound's creativity. But we also need a psychological account of the popularity of the poem, which is widely considered to be Pound's greatest success in the exotic mode, what Robert Kern calls 'the quintessential Chinese poem in English, the single poem that comes closest to evoking and confirming the Western sense of China.'[73] Although it has been called 'the most celebrated piece in *Cathay* – indeed, the most appealing poem of Ezra's whole career,' the 'Changkan Song,' on which it is based, 'is not commonly considered as one of Li Po's great poems.'[74] Its success, I will argue, derives not only from Pound's evocation of repressed emotions associated with attachment, loss, and cathexis, but also from the way the poem fortuitously organizes these emotions into a narrative of erotic attachment that is simultaneously an allegory of attachment to the exotic.

'The River-Merchant's Wife' begins by evoking a repressed childhood world of sensation, play, and aggression:

> While my hair was still cut straight across my forehead
> I played about the front gate, pulling flowers.
> You came by on bamboo stilts, playing horse,

You walked about my seat, playing with blue plums.
And we went on living in the village of Chokan:
Two small people, without dislike or suspicion.[75]

Aside from Pound's substitution of 'bamboo stilts' (a fortuitous mistake that heightens the sense of precarious strangeness), the translation follows Fenollosa's notes fairly closely.[76] The brilliance of Pound's contribution inheres mainly in the poem's rhythmical features, which provide a sort of musical gloss that follows the sense of the lines. The sharpness of the girl's haircut is suggested by the missing expected end stress that would have provided a smooth closure to the iambic rhythm of the first line, while the reversal from iambic to trochaic rhythm in the second line suggests the oppositional aggressiveness of 'pulling flowers.' The straightforward iambic progress of 'You walked about my seat' leads into the curious, attention-fixing adonic (dactyl + spondee [$'\smile\smile''$]) rhythm of 'playing with blue plums.' The rhythm is allowed to become ambiguous in the next two lines, appropriate to the sense of doubt experienced by 'two small people' drawn into the unstructured largeness of worldly space and time.

There is a sense in which this approach to free verse may be considered maternal or pre-Oedipal – rhythm provides a kind of holding environment for the meaning of the poem; the meaning is not asked to conform to a rhythmical law as in traditional verse forms; rather, the impression is that sound and meaning accompany each other as a mother's behaviour accompanies an infant's desire. All poetry, perhaps, by pulling the sign back to its acoustical materiality through the emphasis on sound and rhythm, exerts a regressive pull toward the maternal substrate of language. As I have argued that 'The River-Merchant's Wife' and Pound's other early Oriental poems draw their emotional power from his object attachment problems, I would here suggest that the rhythmical evocation of the mothering relation can be a powerful poetic force, not only as an emotional reservoir for the poet to draw upon, but also as a prelinguistic, orientating language that provides extradiscursive cues guiding the reader's relationship to the object of the poem.

And the reader's relationship to this poem is by no means a simple matter, as we will see shortly. If one begins with the conclusion that the poem succeeds as the quintessential exotic poem, we might describe the reader's relationship to it in terms of desire for the exotic. Such a formulation is very close to Lacan's famous formulation, 'man's desire is the desire of the Other.'

Let us then look at the poem through a Freudian-Lacanian lens, at the way desire develops in the poem. The cut hair of the first line suggests castration and entry into Lacan's symbolic, where the two children play into their gender roles, the girl by pulling the flowers of her penis envy, the boy with his comic effort to overcome castration and master the phallus with his blue plums and bamboo horse. Encountering each other during this period of early symbolic play, the two children regard each other as 'Two small people, without dislike or suspicion.' With their marriage, however, their relations are structured by the symbolic and the law of the father. As they are married without the question of sexual desire intruding, the question remains of where this desire might come from, for it certainly seems absent in the speaker:

> I never laughed, being bashful.
> Lowering my head, I looked at the wall.
> Called to, a thousand times, I never looked back.

The girl's abjection in the face of the wall might be read as her exclusion from the symbolic in the awareness of her lack. Barred from possession of the phallus, she responds by refusing the name. There is nothing in this refusal, but in this nothing she is able to discover her relation to the symbolic as the Other, the One-missing. This position, confirmed by repetition 'a thousand times,' locates her relation to desire: man's desire.

From the husband's perspective, the call evokes the primal symbol substituted for the absent mother. The wife cannot but fail to meet this call, since she cannot be the missing mother-object. But her refusal appears to the husband as proof that she is in fact concealing the object that he lacks, and therefore confirms her position as *object a* of the desiring gaze. At this point we can say a sexual relationship exists, the relationship which Lacan characterizes as impossible. The impossibility appears here in its symptom of exhaustion, the repetition of the forever-ness of the approach of desire to the absent object. It is also staged in the paradoxical question of why she should climb the look-out: the answer being that she must place herself on this substitute phallus in order to demonstrate her situation as object of the gaze; to stop doing so would be to relinquish her status as object of desire, but the repetition merely confirms that she lacks a phallus and that her husband believes her to be in possession of one. It is true that in the reenactment of this scene they can both find the trace of the absent object, and can repeat the discovery 'forever and forever and forever' until their dust is mingled after death, a beautiful thought, if we follow Keats and Stevens in supposing that 'death is the mother of beauty.' Nevertheless, there a sense of futility involved in the repetition, and it is the recognition of this futility, and its implied orientation toward death, that opens up the space for what Lacan calls love's most sublime moment, in which, if I may borrow Slavoj Žižek's formulation, 'the beloved object endeavors to deliver himself from the impasse of his position, from the impossibility of complying with the lover's demand, by assuming himself the position of the lover, by reaching his hand back to the lover and thus answering the lover's lack/desire with his own lack.'[77]

Pound is skilful in evoking the abyss of this space of love which cannot directly enter into the poem but can only hover around the spaces he inserts between lines and in what may be called the failed symbol, the exotic word that threatens to fail to signify, a description that may be applied to the place names in the poem, the first of which is 'far Ku-to-yen,' the place 'by the river of swirling eddies' where the husband has gone. It is up to the reader to hold together this broken signifier, an unexplained Japanese rendering of a Chinese place name. Holding this symbol together imaginatively is easy enough; what counts is rather the reader's willingness to jump in and save the symbol, at exactly the point at which the husband, the love object of the speaker, is in danger of being lost in the abyss of swirling eddies. No doubt this is the same abyss Žižek identifies in his Lacanian reading of Hitchcock's *Vertigo* as 'the hole in the Other (the symbolic order), concealed by the fascinating presence of the fantasy object.'[78] Thus, it provides an imaginary site in which the wife is able to restage her loss of the phallic mother as the death of the husband, thus enabling the husband to emerge as her object of desire. His role as object of her desire is as paradoxical as hers is for him, since he only fully achieves it in absence or under threat of disappearance. The swirling eddies are thus a symbol of the way the wife's jouissance remains bound up with what Lacan calls the cut. If we imagine the husband as the phallus in the swirling eddies, repeatedly entering, potentially lost, found, and departing again, we clearly see the form of the wife's sexual desire.

All, then, would seem to be happy, for the husband and wife are now enabled to enjoy their sexual relation until they are both mingled in dust. But if this were all there were to it, there would be no enjoyment left for the reader. How is it that we come to enjoy the poem? The answer is that we are expected to enjoy it in the place of the husband, the supposed recipient of the letter who is in turn a substitute for the poet, Li Po. The river merchant is missed by his wife, which ought to be pleasurable to him, although it must be a vertiginous pleasure for him, if he realizes how it depends on his absence. It must be even more vertiginous for Li Po, who is actually writing the desire of his Other, for unlike the fictitious husband, he knows it is he and not the other writing the other's desire, and, even if his wife existed, how could he know her desire? And finally, it is vertiginous for the reader, who in reading the poem is required to pose as the double of 'My Lord you,' the missing phallus-husband-author whose absence has structured the wife's phallic fantasy, or would, if she existed, and the poem were true. The reader no doubt began innocently enough but has now become actively involved in holding together the defective signifier of Ku-to-yen, complicit in a perverse sex act that goes beyond voyeurism to the impersonation of a missing husband. Should the wife (who also began innocently) object to this impersonation, of course, it may be pointed out that, having arrived at her desire only through the imagined death of her husband, she is in no position to complain about this substitution, since one absent husband should be as desirable as any Other.

This terrifying vertigo that threatens to engulf the whole set of relations governing the poem is nevertheless evaded: the speaker does not fall into the abyss, nor, presumably, do most readers, or the poem could hardly be as popular as it is. The vertigo is appropriated for its pleasurable *frisson* as the speaker veers around the abyss, which then emerges in the form of a symptom: conveniently enough, the symptom we have been studying all along as characteristic of the exotic, that of projection. Monkeys begin making sorrowful noises overhead, different mosses begin growing over the place where the husband dragged his feet before leaving, leaves fall early, the paired butterflies are already yellow with August. These painfully paired butterflies draw the speaker into the realization of her emotion in the projection and its cause:

> They hurt me. I grow older.

Pound scores the intense emotion brilliantly with the poem's only mid-line full stop, the caesura's silence evoking the emotional weight of loss in the passage of time, and suggesting the (unspeakable) possibility of love.

The clincher, however, is in the wife's offer in the final lines of the poem:

> If you are coming down through the narrows of the river Kiang,
> Please let me know beforehand,
> And I will come out to meet you
>> As far as Cho-fu-Sa.

In this imaginary climax, the lovers will offer to be each other's missing object: the husband will be the phallic substitute and the wife will be the woman who comes when called. This meeting is to be arranged at a place named by another defective signifier, the uninterpretable 'Cho-fu-Sa' that Pound chose, rather defiantly, over two alternatives provided by Fenollosa: the evocative character translation 'long wind sand' and the identification of the place as 'a port on the Yangtse.'

Pound's phrase 'the narrows of the river Kiang' does attempt to take advantage of Fenollosa's note on the place named as 'sam pa' (three whirls) identifying it as the 'name of [a] spot on [the] Yangtse Kiang, where waters whirl.' Dorothy Shakespear seems to have taken an interest in this place, for when she bought an apparently Chinese tortoiseshell snuffbox during the Oriental shopping spree of December 1913, she inquired whether 'tortoises grow in the Yangtse Kiang.'[79]

Pound would not have been much help on this point since he was unaware that 'Kiang' was not the name of a river but actually the word for river.

The conventional wisdom is that the defectiveness of these signifiers is insignificant because they are merely unimportant geographical details. Any exotic-sounding name would be as good as any other. But why, then, did Pound choose not to go with 'Long Wind Sand,' a referentially effective, metrically equivalent phrase, one that most other translators have chosen to use? Why not end the poem in that evocatively named place, instead of nowhere?

Of course, the answer is that we need to end up nowhere, because the meeting cannot take place. As noted above, impersonation of the phallic lord is the structural requirement for the reader's pleasure in this epistolary poem, the practical import of which is to inform the reader that his formerly apathetic sixteen-year-old wife, having become aware of her amorous feelings during his absence, is anxious to arrange a meeting at the place named by the signifier in question. For the recipient, therefore, the referentiality of the name is of considerable importance, and the reader who fails to attend to it is at the very least failing to enter the poem's imaginative space. Although we have little expectation of arriving at the designated spot, something is lost if we cannot believe it to be a real place. The river Kiang loses its sparkle when we know it is the river River, because the signifier no longer flows in our exotic imagination. On the other hand, Ku-to-yen and Cho-fu-Sa are defective in a more successful way; they are, in fact, the best sort of exotic signifiers because, although the reader cannot get to the signified, there is every reason to suppose it might be possible, and, as in a treasure hunt, having to go to Japan en route makes it all the more exotically interesting. We are allowed to believe in a Chinese object that is endlessly deferred along a chain of signifiers possessed by others who are supposed to know: from Pound to Fenollosa to Mori to Li Po to the river merchant's wife.

Why should the question of referentiality make any difference here? As I have suggested, the poem may be read allegorically as a poem about desire for the exotic. In this allegorical reading, the defective symbol is like the absent husband. Thus, as the girl's pleasure is bound up with the possible loss of the husband, through which she rediscovers the emotional trace of the lost object, our pleasure as readers is bound up with the possible loss of the signified, through which we rediscover the importance of the original symbol, the infantile transitional object that allowed us to understand the loss of the mother. This original symbol will always be defective, because it will never adequately substitute for what was lost. In the poem, the place of the symbol is promised as *the place of love*, but that is because the symbol has *replaced love*: wherever the symbol is, love is not. Thus the symbol is by nature defective because it never delivers the absent object, just as all phallic husbands are defective, because they can never restore the castrated phallus. By arranging a meeting at a place named by a signifier which he has made defective, the promise will certainly fail, and we can say that *it is Pound's fault*. In taking ownership of this fault through the offer of the defective symbol, Pound covers over the greater defect that threatens to undermine the symbol as such. The exotic symbol, as constructed in the poem, is that which sets up the promise of the return of the woman who comes when called, then attaches that promise to a defective exotic signifier, so that the meeting does not take place. And it is Pound's fault; it is Pound who, like a petal on a wet black bough or a leaf clinging to a threshold, reaches across the abyss to where the object should be and fails to grasp it, who cannot finally make the *Cantos* cohere. But in placing himself into the fault, in offering himself as the symbol that covers over the abyss of love, Pound, failed master and masterful failure, succeeds in bringing into sight the receding Chinese object.

Chapter Eight

The Red Man in the Drawing Room:
T.S. Eliot and the Nativists

'War-Paint and Feathers,' by T.S. Eliot, appeared in the 17 October 1919 number of the London periodical *The Nation and Athenaeum*. It begins as follows:

> The Ustumsjiji are a vanishing race. The last repositories of the Monophysite heresy, persecuted and massacred for centuries (on religious grounds) by the Armenians, the remnants of a unique civilization have taken refuge in the remote gorges of the Akim-Baba Range. Here the explorer discovered them, and was privileged to hear their Shikkamim, or wandering bards, prophets, and medicine-men, recite or chant, to the music of the pippin or one-stringed gourd, the traditional poetry of love, warfare, and theology.
>
> But suddenly, egged on by New York and Chicago intelligentsia, the romantic Chippaway bursts into the drawing-room, and among murmurs of approval declaims his

> MAPLE SUGAR SONG
> Maple sugar
>   is the only thing
>   that satisfies me.

The approval becomes acclamation. The Chippaway has the last word in subtlety, simplicity, and poeticality. Furthermore, his continent is backing him. For, says the editor,

> it becomes appropriate and important that this collection of American Indian verse should be brought to public notice at a time when the whole instinctive movement of the American people is for a deeper footing in their native soil.

> The Red Man is here: what are we to do with him, except to feed him on maple
> sugar? And it is not only the Red Men, but the aborigines of every complexion and
> climate, who have arrived, each tribe pressing upon us its own claims to distinction
> in art and literature.[1]

The reader eventually comprehends that the Red Man in question is a representative poet whose translated song may be found in *The Path on the Rainbow*, a new
anthology of Native American poetry in translation, and that Eliot, in staging this
little drawing-room extravaganza, is having a bit of fun. The fun comes at the
expense of the reader, failing to recognize that there are no Shikkamim among
the imaginary Ustumsjiji in the non-existant Akim-Baba mountains; it comes at
the expense of the aspiring Chippaway, whose poetic performance seems unim-
pressive, and of his drawing-room audience, who nevertheless revel in it; and it
comes at the expense of the pompous cultural nationalism of the Chippaway's
supporters: *The Path on the Rainbow*'s editor and the 'New York and Chicago
intelligentsia.'

But Eliot's interest in this review is not to denigrate the importance of the 'savage.' 'Just as it is necessary to know something about Freud and something about
Fabre,[2] so it is necessary to know something about the medicine-man and his
works,' Eliot writes. 'The maxim, Return to the sources, is a good one.' More specifically, Eliot is interested in appropriating the primitive poet *as a poet*. 'Primitive
art and poetry,' he writes, 'help our understanding of civilized art and poetry' and
'can even, through the studies and experiments of the artist or poet, revivify the
contemporary activities.' Nor is the poet's interest in the primitive merely incidental; for, as Eliot sees it, 'the poet should know everything that has been accomplished in poetry (accomplished, not merely produced) since its beginnings – in
order to know what he is doing himself.' Although Eliot does not explicitly link
this knowledge to the modernist reconfiguration of poetic practice, the implication is clear: reorienting poetry toward the primitive could provide a crucial
justification for the rejection of what modernists viewed as outworn poetic methods. The poet and artist – like the anthropologist – 'will be the last people to tolerate the whooping brave, with his tale of maple sugar, as a drawing-room
phenomenon.'

Modern Poets and Native Americans

There was already a lengthy prehistory to these debates, and a long tradition of
poetry about Native Americans, reaching back to the Romantics, with their
Rousseau-influenced notions of the Noble Savage, a tradition which culminated
in Longfellow's immensely popular *Hiawatha* (1855). In the early twentieth cen-

tury, the Indian as Noble Savage was being transformed into a figure for all that was perceived to be lost in American urban culture: community, cultural identity, unity with nature, a sense of connection with the land, and a purposeful poetry integrated with the rhythms of life. The Native American came to be seen as an antidote to modern urbanism, industrialism, and the loss of spirituality. The neutralization of the Indian threat by the end of the nineteenth century had foregrounded the sufferings of Native Americans and rendered it acceptable to take up their plight as a moral cause. Thus, when Louis Untermeyer, commenting on the new interest in the Indian as poet, quipped that 'a good Indian, according to his students, is not so much a dead Indian as a singing one,' he was making a genuine observation, since allowing that the Indian had a culture, and moreover, an interesting and even important one, had to involve a radical restructuring of the American colonialist ideology which saw the Indian as an uncultured and dangerous savage.

Of all the uses of the Native American for the modern poet, the most important – that of providing a grounding for a distinctive, indigenous American tradition – was also the most patently unrealistic. As Americans had historically been much more interested in exterminating or at least removing Indians than in learning from them (in 1910, the Indian population was the lowest ever), the idea of deriving an American poetic tradition from the American Indian necessitated a deep denial of history. But, as Walter Benn Michaels points out about American novels of this period, 'killing Indians is no obstacle to being Indians.'[3] In Britain, the acceptance of the (Asian) Indian as a primitive ancestor was a comparatively simple matter, since it was the ancient Aryan Indian rather than the contemporary one who was of interest, and the linguistic commonality of English with ancient Aryan Sanskrit had long offered an accepted link between the British and the imperial subjects on whom they lavished so much scholarly attention. One solution to this difficulty was to establish linkages through the land and the names attached to places. Whitman, in 'Starting from Paumanok,' described

> The red aborigines,
> Leaving natural breaths, sounds of rain and winds, calls as of birds and animals in the
>   woods, syllabled to us for names,
> Okonee, Koosa, Ottawa, Monongahela, Sauk, Natchez, Chattahoochee, Kaqueta,
>   Oronoco, Wabash, Miami, Saginaw, Chippewa, Oshkosh, Walla-Walla,
> Leaving such to the States they melt, they depart, charging the water and the land
>   with names.[4]

Whitman's sentiments are with the pioneer, not the Indian; the Indian simply melts away, 'A new race dominating previous ones and grander far,' leaving 'A world primal again.' Another solution was to adopt Native American figures such as Hiawatha or Pocahontas as part of the new American mythology. 'We here renounce our Saxon blood,' Vachel Lindsay declared in 'Our Mother Pocahontas,' announcing a new race 'born of her resilient grace.'[5]

The Discovery of Native American Poetry

The first important book to introduce the Native American as poet to the American public was Natalie Curtis's *The Indians' Book* (1907), actually a collection of songs, complete with translations, transliterations, and musical transcriptions. Despite the resistance of the Bureau of Indian Affairs to her efforts to collect materials on government reservations (she went over their heads, enlisting the help of President Roosevelt), Curtis succeeded, with the help of Charlotte Osgood Mason, later 'Godmother' of the Harlem Renaissance, and others, in producing a volume which she hoped 'might help to revive for the younger generation that sense of the dignity and worth of their race which is the Indians' birthright, and without which, no people can progress.'[6] There was some contradiction, as Helen Carr points out, in the fact that the introduction was 'clearly directed to Anglo-Saxon Americans.'[7] The success of the collection, which Carr calls 'the beginning of a Western aesthetic reading of Native American poetry,' hinged rather on the fact that Curtis made the translations 'recognisably poetic to her readers, even if in a rather faded Victorian way, and argued for their status as art.'[8] It was reviewed widely and favourably by such publications as the *Dial*,[9] which placed it at the head of its list of holiday books. 'To most White readers,' the review suggested, 'this book will be a revelation of the vaguely stirring genius and the art, mystic in its intent, spontaneous in its symbolism, of a child race.' The question of what 'The Indian' may have thought of *The Indians' Book*, with its ostensible function of preserving his birthright, was not a question addressed by reviewers.

In addition to providing the first popular introduction to Native American verse, *The Indians' Book* was also significant, Michael Castro suggests, as 'the first major statement of the theme that has characterized twentieth-century writers' interest in the Indian: that the red man represented in some way the missing aspects of the American self.'[10] As Curtis wrote elsewhere, 'The undeveloped talents native to the aboriginal American are precisely those in which the Anglo-Saxon is deficient.'[11] Such views were controversial. When a similar note was sounded in Frederick R. Burton's *American Primitive Music* (1909), the response in the *Dial* was critical: 'Mr. Burton suggests the use of the Indian melodies as thematic material for American composers. He deplores the dearth of folk-music among us, and thinks that our poverty in this respect may change into something approaching the European opulence by turning to the unexpected sources of wealth furnished by our mountains and prairies. He also alludes to the abundance of tunes, mostly religious, thrust into our lap by the negro. It must, however, occur to everyone that this is after all alien material.'[12] These two reviews in the *Dial* illustrate divergent racialist characterizations of the American Indian: in the Curtis review the Indian is characterized as a member of 'a child race,' while in the Burton review he is thought of as 'alien.' Over the course of the next decade, the 'child race' view would gain ascendancy, as American poets wondered whether and how to find their own absent poetic childhoods in the primitive song of the Native American.

Poetry Goes Native: Henderson, Monroe, and Pound

Harriet Monroe's interest in the primitive was evident as early as 1914, when, introducing Vachel Lindsay's *The Congo* to the literary public as an example of 'primitive' poetry, she wrote of the healthier conditions for poetry of 'the primitive nations [which] may still be found, if the world only knew it, in the wonderful song-dances of the Hopis and others of our aboriginal tribes.'[13] But *Poetry*'s advocacy of Native American poetry later in the decade owed substantially less to Monroe than to her former assistant editor, Alice Corbin Henderson. Henderson became a Native Americanist almost accidentally, when, having contracted tuberculosis, she moved to Taos, New Mexico, for the sake of her health. 'Great God,' wrote Pound, in June of 1916, on hearing of the unexpected retirement of his preferred correspondent at *Poetry*, 'what classics are you to read, without greek or latin?'[14] Fortunately, the Pueblo Indians of Taos were available to provide Henderson with intellectual stimulation. Six months later, she wrote enthusiastically to Pound,

> I am *much* interested in the Indian dances – have seen two. Not at all what one might expect – The Eagle dance as fine as Pavlova – Their sense of costume – Works, etc. in manner of these Pueblo Indians [in Paris, Chicago or New York][15] – They would not lack interpretation. A *theatric* interpretation, I mean. There has never been a shred of it that I can find! – I hope to see the *Buffalo Dance* on the 23rd. – (My remissions are rare, however.) When you get through with China, come out here and do the Indian. Not the 'big injun' of commerce but the ones that *you* would find. W.P.H. is making some fine things of the dances.[16]

Henderson's suggestion to Pound to 'come out here and do the Indian' failed to produce any response from Pound, whose apparently complete lack of interest was somewhat ironic, given that he had an unusually close connection to Native

Americans: his father had grown up in Wisconsin's Chippewa country when 'aborigines still strolled through the settlement at Minnehaha' and 'had one for a nurse.'[17] But Henderson was not deterred. The Buffalo Dance became the subject of a poem (entitled 'Buffalo Dance'), which appeared with others in *Poetry*'s 'Aboriginal Poetry' issue of January 1917.

> Strike ye our land
> With curved horns!
> Now with cries
> Bending our bodies,
> Breathe fire upon us;
> Now with feet
> Trampling the earth,
> Let your hoofs
> Thunder over us!
> Strike ye our land
> With curved horns![18]

'By now you've seen the aboriginal number, ye gods!' she wrote Pound in February. 'I had no idea that my things were to be so determined! I'll work on the things before they go into a book.'[19] Again, no response. Native Americans became Henderson's major literary preoccupation in the following decades,[20] as Taos blossomed as a Southwestern nativist-modernist Mecca, attracting writers like D.H. Lawrence, Carl Sandburg, Willa Cather, and Witter Bynner, and a number of influential artists, including Marsden Hartley and Georgia O'Keeffe.

The *Path on the Rainbow*

Henderson's translations were typical of a new approach to Indian poetry: like the translations of Constance Lindsay Skinner, Mary Austin, Pauline Johnson, and Frank Gordon, they were usually presented as 'interpretations' rather than as literal translations. As Skinner put it, 'authors of these Interpretations who have been inspired by the Native poems – have yielded to Indian beauty, willingly sought to enter into the Indian consciousness and to sing of it from within, interpretatively.'[21] Though most of the interpreters drew on first-hand experience of Native cultures – one, Pauline Johnson, was even part Mohawk – they permitted themselves substantial freedom of translation, and rarely offered contextual explanations or footnotes. This made their work more palatable to the general public than that of the ethnographers, but also more subject to criticism regarding their claims of authenticity.

By 1918, a substantial body of Native American poetry in translation and 'Native-inspired' poetry existed, covering the full range from the painstakingly documented translations intended, at least, to be literal to the most whimsical Indian-inspired primitivist flights of fancy. Moreover, a wide range of tribes had been subjected to the efforts of ethnographers, translators, and interpreters. There was enough material, in short, for a new anthology, which George Cronyn (author of an undistinguished 1914 collection of poems, entitled *Poems*) undertook to edit, delegating the introduction and afterword to the better-known Mary Austin and Constance Lindsay Skinner.

The commanding tone of Austin's introduction must certainly have made an impression on 'those unaware until now of the very existence of such a body of aboriginal verse.' No mere collection of literary curiosities, this 'first authoritative volume of aboriginal American verse,' she argued, was of interest because of 'the relationship which seems about to develop between Indian verse and the ultimate literary destiny of America.'[22]

> That there is such a relationship any one at all familiar with current verse of the past three or four years must immediately conclude on turning over a few pages. He will be struck at once with the extraordinary likeness between much of this native product and the recent work of the Imagists, *vers librists*, and other literary fashionables. He may, indeed, congratulate himself on the confirmation of his secret suspicion that Imagism is a very primitive form; he may, if he happens to be of the Imagist's party, suffer a check in the discovery that the first free movement of poetic originality in America finds us just about where the last Medicine Man left off. But what else could he have expected?[23]

Such claims could hardly have been made while Imagism remained under Pound's stewardship, but Pound had by then moved on to Vorticism, surrendering 'Amygism' to the forceful Amy Lowell, who was herself interested in Indians, and on good terms with Austin. But Austin's arguments are not entirely convincing, and her phrase 'this native product' seems to intentionally obscure the question of whether the alleged Imagist elements were present in the original or, as seems more likely, were artifacts of the translation process. That the difficulties of translation made free verse a more convenient form seems hardly an adequate basis upon which to equate the two forms, and Austin further undermines the force of the comparison by lumping together Imagists and *vers librists* with 'other literary fashionables,' as well as by her slightly malicious confirmation of the reader's 'secret suspicion that Imagism is a very primitive form.' This comment is reminiscent of Victor Plarr's 1914 'Note on a Savage Poet,' which humorously compared the products of an imagined 'savage poet' (an Australian aborigine) with 'the verse of the moment,' at the expense of the latter.[24] There was, indeed, a long association between American free verse and 'savagery,' extending back to Whitman, whose poems, an early reviewer wrote, 'resemble nothing so much as the war-cry of the Red Indians.'[25] The debate over whether the translations were *Imagist* poems may, however, have helped obscure the deeper question of whether many of them were 'poems' in the Western sense at all.

But the comparison to contemporary American verse is only part of Austin's argument for the importance of Native verse. There was also the direct appeal to nationalist sentiments. The poetic faculty was not only 'of all man's modes, the most responsive to natural environment,' but also 'the first to register the rise of his spirits to the stimulus of new nationalist ideals.' 'If this were not so there would be no such thing as nationality in art, and it is only by establishing some continuity with the earliest instances of such reaction that we can be at all sure that American poetic genius has struck its native note. Therefore it becomes appropriate and important that this collection of American Indian verse should be brought to public notice at a time when the whole instinctive movement of the American people is for a deeper footing in their native soil.'[26] Austin's point that poetry is the first to register nationalist ideals is debatable, but she was certainly right about the presence of a 'movement ... for a deeper footing in their native soil,' as wartime books like Van Wyck Brooks's *America's Coming of Age* (1915) and Waldo Frank's *Our America* (1916), as well as postwar works like William Carlos Williams's *In the American Grain* (1925), attest. That the Native American was the perfect vehicle for this nativist movement was demonstrated, as Austin saw it, by (Euro-)American poets' and artists' 'instinctive' and 'unconscious' attraction to the Native American: 'It is the certificate of our adoption, that the young genius of our time should strike all unconsciously on this ancient track to the High Places.'[27] But Austin, in her zeal to promote the Native arts, seems too willing to sell readers on this spurious 'certificate of our adoption' – hardly, in the end, less exploitative than the misunderstood treaties by which the land itself had been appropriated by Euro-Americans – and too accepting of the Euro-American poets' and artists' 'unconscious,' 'instinctive' attractions to the Native American. For the Native American poet who emerged in this period was a projection of American poets' desire to be 'native' American poets – to be rooted in traditions linked to place – and a projection of the American public's desire for such a tradition, as an adjunct to the new international stature of the United States. The literally repressed Native American, embodying American difference and antiquity, was the natural figure to embody this Euro-American desire.

The Maple Sugar War of 1919

In spite of Austin's inspired rhetoric, the critics were not entirely pleased with *The Path on the Rainbow*. Surveying the 'fragmentary' offerings of Native American verse to date, Louis Untermeyer found 'singularly little ... that is either thorough or convincing.'[28] Untermeyer, a poet, critic, and editor, may not have known much about Indians, but he claimed to know a poorly edited poetry anthology when he saw one. His complaint about *The Path on the Rainbow*, the same one T.S. Eliot would make seven months later, concerned the problem of translation: 'Translation, at the best, is a difficult and ungrateful performance for both interlocutor and audience. But the translating of folk songs and aboriginal chants is an even more hazardous matter. So much that is idiomatic escapes or is distorted or is, most often, entirely misunderstood.' Overcoming these barriers was, in Untermeyer's view, the task of the editor. 'If Mr. Cronyn is a genuine student of Indian folklore,' Untermeyer wrote, 'he is to be blamed for not having made the volume more communicative and less cryptic; many of these songs cry aloud for nothing so much as footnotes.' There were other problems: 'the arbitrary arrangement of words and a pretentious typography that is foreign to our native – though it may be native to Ezra Pound, "H.D." and Richard Adington [*sic*].' The poem 'Maple Sugar,' though 'redolent of Others and the Kreymborg-Johns' naivete,' was a good example. Though Untermeyer conceded that 'as an ethnic document this anthology is of indubitable value,' it was also, he felt, 'a rather forbidding pile' and 'a crude and top-heavy monument.'[29]

This was criticism Austin and Cronyn were not going to take lying down. Austin responded first, beginning with a general attack on the *Dial*'s decision to give 'a book of such national, one might say international interest to be reviewed by one whose mind has so evidently never visited west of Broadway.' 'It begins to be a question in America,' Austin wrote (anticipating the arguments of latter-day multiculturalists), 'whether a man is entitled to describe himself as a man of letters at all who so complacently confesses his ignorance of and inability to enter into the vast body of aboriginal literature of his country, literature that rises to the saga form easily comparable to the great works on which European literature is built, and to epics that for sonority and richness of figure approach and at times equal the epics of Homer.' Austin defended the charge of mistranslation by observing that 'when one considers how many readings of Sappho and even of Shakespeare are in doubt, it is not surprising that Indian verse should occasionally suffer at the hands of the translator.' But in responding to Untermeyer's charge concerning the poems' occasional banality, Austin unwittingly conceded the weightiest of Untermeyer's charges: the need for footnotes. 'Indian poets are like other poets, occasionally banal and commonplace, but it is again pertinent to suggest that something more than a "mere man of letters" is required for the appreciation of literature which is different from one's own, or the fashion of the hour.'[30]

Austin proceeds to offer a more nuanced interpretation of the 'Maple Sugar' song, illustrating its emotional charge by invoking the recently ended war: 'Ten thousand American boys in a foreign land singing Home Sweet Home is a very moving thing, and twice ten Indians at the ragged end of Winter, when the food goes stale and their very garments smell of wood smoke, singing their maple sugar song might sing a great deal of poetry into it – poetry of rising sap, clean snow water, calling partridge, and the friendly click of brass bowls and birch-bark sap buckets.'[31] The somewhat gratuitous 'Home Sweet Home' comparison was no doubt intended as a reminder that Untermeyer had come under fire for opposing American involvement in the war, an issue that had finally forced his magazine, *The Masses*, to cease publication in 1917. In return, Untermeyer chose to misconstrue her point, reading the rather spurious interpretive note as just the sort of helpful 'documentation' of the sort he found wanting. 'This,' he declared his reply, 'is the sort of interpretive note that would have made valuable much that at present is inconsequential.' But, he adds, 'a whole volume of footnotes would not have explained the inclusion of Carl Sandburg's "translation" of a non-existent Indian croon, the sentimental jingling of Miss Johnson's The Lost Lagoon, and the too frequent attempts to make an obvious primitive emotion look like a piece of preciosity.'[32]

At this point Cronyn felt obligated 'to emerge in self-defense from what the critic evidently considers a purely nebulous state, and take up arms in his own behalf.'[33] He blamed the damaging Sandburg misattribution on a printer's error, and Pauline Johnson's inclusion – which he, too, opposed – on 'deference to wishes of the publishers,' whose arguments hinged on Johnson's Canadian popularity and Indian ancestry. 'There remain,' he continued, 'the questions of footnotes and of the value of some of the songs themselves.' This, of course, could only be resolved by reopening the case of the mysterious Maple Sugar song. 'It is so unintelligible, inconsequential ... dressed in its absurd pretentious vers libre make-up!' writes Cronyn sarcastically, 'but when Mrs. Austin explains the primitive background, the thing at once becomes illuminatingly satisfying.' Untermeyer is taken to task for his desire 'to have all the poems similarly bulwarked by picturesque explanatory matter.' 'You see, the real secret of the poetry of the above song is, that the Indians are hungry, hungry for maple sugar. To critics who have lost their primitive gusto for maple sugar that sensation may well be a riddle.'

Sarcasm aside, at the core of Cronyn's defence was an essentially primitivist argument: there is no real need for footnotes because the Indian is a primitive version of us; we have only to look within ourselves and find our 'primitive gusto for maple sugar' to understand the meaning of the song. Another example, a brief love song, is offered, with comic 'picturesque notes' added. 'All of this may make Mr. Untermeyer happy and contented, but personally I have cherished a passionate distaste for footnotes ever since that wretched academic period when, for every line of poetry or drama read, one had to plough through a jungle of notes at the bottom of the page, or at the back of the book. It seemed to me then that there was only one creature more horrible and contemptible than the teacher who sandbagged poetry, and that was the editor who crucified it with unnecessary notes.'[34]

The battle may at this point have been left as a standoff: no doubt, the reader is as likely as not to side with Cronyn against the 'teacher who sandbagged poetry' and 'the editor who crucified it with unnecessary notes.' But Cronyn's response was not quite the end of the *Dial* debate; Mary Austin had not yet responded to Untermeyer's response to her earlier response to his now five-and-a-half-month-old review. Moreover, she seemed determined not only to have the last word on the Maple Sugar question, but to defend her argument about the Imagism of the poems as well: 'Mr. Untermeyer speaks of the Indian verse as a "crude reduction to Imagist verse form." What I tried to say before and Mr. Untermeyer still misses, is that Indian verse form *is* Imagism. It was not "reduced" to that form, it was made that way originally.'[35] The 'Maple Sugar' song is dragged out one last time to support this claim; but Austin's arguments do more harm than good to her Imagist claim: 'In its original form the Maple Sugar song reads exactly as it was written in the Anthology. It is a three phrase song literally translated by one of the most careful students of Indian poetry, Frances Dinsmore. The Indian words being longer, fill out the measure of the rhythm, and in case the words do not quite fill out the measure, the Indian poet, contrary to our modern use, does not add more words, but fills in the measure with meaningless musical syllables.' The Imagists who claimed to 'use no superfluous word, no adjective, which does not reveal something' would have had difficulty tolerating 'meaningless musical syllables,' even if they were not technically words. Austin damages her case further with a more technical discussion of the translation question:

> Miss Dinsmore's translations are ethnic rather than poetic. I do not happen to know the Chippewa language in which the song was originally written, but I do know the genius of Indian languages in general. They are holophrastic, that is to say, one word is actually made up of the essential syllables of a whole descriptive phrase. For example, there is an Algonquian word which an ethnologist would translate accurately as Dawn. But a poet would translate it no less accurately and more ade-

quately and more Indianly as 'Hither-whiteness-comes-walking.' In the same manner the word which Miss Dinsmore translates as maple sugar, might actually have been something like this 'the sweet-white-downdripping-blood-of-the-maple-tree' or 'the-sweetness-which-I-draw-from-the-maple-with-my-flint-knife.'

The problem of the holophrastic linguistic features calls into question the possibility of a literal translation, which must choose at least between holophrastic adequacy and reduced simplicity. Austin may have been hoping that the argument would have the effect of Fenollosa's essay on 'The Chinese Written Character as a Basis for Poetry,' much cherished by Pound, but since her revelations illustrate Dinsmore's failure to accommodate these interesting linguistic features, they seriously undermine her earlier claim that the translation reads exactly like the original.

Austin does concede some ground in the end, even as she launches a final attack against Untermeyer's authority as reviewer:

> Now my contention has been from the beginning that unless Mr. Untermeyer knew something of the genius of the aboriginal Indian language, unless he knew something of Imagism besides what it looks like on paper, he had no right to review this book. Certainly he had no right to condemn it because it does not come within his notion of what poetry is in New York today. I admit the errors in editing the book, and particularly I admit my own liability to err in a subject so broad and so little studied, but I deny Mr. Untermeyer's right to object to the inclusion of particular poems in the book because they do not please him. Many Indian poems are banal, many are 'jinglingly sentimental' as he describes Miss Johnson's Paddle Song, albeit Miss Johnson is, I understand, the only contributing translator with Indian blood, and probably closer than any of us to the genuine poetic values of what she translates.

Who, then, is authorized to validate the adequacy of the translations? Apparently not the editors themselves, who hardly come off as authorities on Native American languages, and not 'the only contributing translator with Indian blood,' whom Austin – on racial grounds – sees as 'probably closer than any of us to the genuine poetic values of what she translates.' Pauline Johnson, the would-be Red Woman in the drawing-room, seems to be an embarrassment to the serious students of Indian poetry, the scandal of her performance underscoring for both sides the necessity that the Indian must be interpreted and re-presented. Thus the *Dial* debate ended – and it did end here, in the 23 August 1919 issue, the editors firmly regretting 'that pressure of space on this department compels them to announce this discussion of Mr. Untermeyer's review as closed.'

It is at this point that T.S. Eliot enters the picture. Coming to his October *Nation and Athenaeum* review through this history, we can now better understand Eliot's decision to begin 'War-Paint and Feathers' with his romantic Chippaway bursting into the drawing room, egged on by the New York and Chicago intelligentsia, and among murmurs of approval declaiming his 'Maple Sugar Song.' Eliot's review is almost identical in tone to Untermeyer's: both begin with sarcastic references to the faddishness of the primitive, and work their way into a discussion of the need to take the Indian seriously and the need to properly edit his works. What distinguishes Eliot's review is his insistence that poets, rather than editors or translators, ought to be the ultimate authorities on the question of Native American poetry, assisted by anthropologists. The poet, according to Eliot, 'is the first person to see the merits of the savage, the barbarian and the rustic, he is also the last person to see the savage in a romantic light, or to yield to the weak credulity of crediting the savage with any gifts of mystical insight or artistic feeling that he does not possess himself.' These shared gifts of mystical insight and artistic feeling, rather than any nativist agenda, form the basis of Eliot's interest in the 'Red Man.'

Eliot's Primitive Mysticism

As William Harmon has argued, the conception of the primitive in both Eliot's criticism and his creative work owes 'its contours and emphases to Lévy-Bruhl ... more than to any other single source.'[36] Lucien Lévy-Bruhl's *Les fonctions mentales dans les sociétés inférieures* was published in 1910, and Eliot probably came across it in Paris in 1910–11; he had certainly read it by the time of his 1913 Harvard graduate seminar with Josiah Royce when he used it in his seminar paper on the interpretation of primitive ritual.[37] Lévy-Bruhl's book was framed as an attack on what he considered to be a mistaken premise of the rationalistic English comparative ethnography school: the belief in 'the identity of a "human mind" which from the logical point of view, is always exactly the same at all times and in all places.'[38] In place of this assumption, Lévy-Bruhl proposed that there was a clear distinction between 'primitive mentality' and 'our own.' Whereas 'our' mentality is based on laws of logic, primitive mentality, he argued, is indifferent to contradiction and essentially mystical – its operations based on 'the law of participation,' according to which subjects and objects are capable of merging with each other. His favourite example – and a favourite of Eliot as well – was the Bororo tribe of northern Brazil, who 'boast they are red araras (parakeets).' 'It is not a name they give themselves, nor a relationship that they claim,' Lévy-Bruhl argued. 'What they desire to express by it is actual identity ... To the mentality that is governed by the law of participation there is no difficulty in the matter.'[39]

Lévy-Bruhl saw the totemic identification of the Bororo as an example of what he called, borrowing from sociologist Emile Durkheim, 'collective representations.' These collective representations, he argued, are the primary factor in primitive mental life.

Even as a graduate student Eliot could see that Lévy-Bruhl 'appears ... to draw the distinction between primitive and civilized mental process altogether too clearly.'[40] Perhaps the most intriguing aspect of Lévy-Bruhl's book was the way its painstakingly constructed dichotomy between primitive and civilized mentalities collapses in the last chapter. The Western idea of God turns out to be a remnant of primitive mentality, and Lévy-Bruhl argues that 'the need of participation assuredly remains something more imperious and more intense, even among people like ourselves, than the thirst for knowledge and the desire for conformity with the claims of reason.'[41]

Another reader upon whom *Les fonctions mentales* made a powerful impression was Jung, who came across Lévy-Bruhl's book soon after its publication in 1910. As Jung began to differentiate his theory from Freud's, Lévy-Bruhl's account of the transition from primitive to civilized mentality became a key element in Jung's conception of the modern personality. Jung followed Lévy-Bruhl in supposing that the primitive 'is still more or less identical with the collective psyche' and argued that 'repression of the collective psyche was absolutely necessary for the development of the personality.'[42] The collective unconscious, the cornerstone of Jung's theory of the mind, comprises the remnants of this repressed collective psyche, based on Lévy-Bruhl's conclusion that 'the collective representations of the social group, even when clearly prelogical and mystic by nature, tend to subsist indefinitely.'[43] Jung came to believe these remnants were preserved in the form of archetypes.

Eliot was aware of Jung's use of Lévy-Bruhl, for in another one of his discussions of the Bororo, he notes that Lévy-Bruhl's theory 'has much in common with the analysis of mythology recently made by disciples of Freud.'[44] Moreover, Eliot's orientation to primitive mentality bears a striking resemblance to Jung's. Where Jung wrote of archetypes, Eliot wrote of culture, but both believed in the necessity of returning to an unconscious, instinctual core. Eliot explains in 'War Paint and Feathers': 'Primitive art and poetry can even, through the studies and experiments of the artist or poet, revivify the contemporary activities. The maxim, Return to the sources, is a good one. More intelligibly put, it is that the poet should know everything that has been accomplished in poetry (accomplished, not merely produced) since its beginnings – in order to know what he is doing himself. He should be aware of all the metamorphoses of poetry that illustrate the stratifications of history that cover savagery.'[45]

These observations may be read alongside Eliot's more famous, contemporaneous essay, 'Tradition and the Individual Talent': 'The historical sense compels a man to write not merely with his own generation in his bones, but with a feeling that the whole of the literature of Europe from Homer and within it the whole literature of his own country has a simultaneous existence and composes a simultaneous order.'[46] 'War Paint and Feathers' extends this Eurocentric conception of the tradition to include Lévy-Bruhl's mystical primitive mentality, and the result might be described as a poetic version of Jung's collective unconscious. In their theories of personality, Eliot and Jung are also remarkably similar. Eliot's theory of 'dissociation of sensibility' is essentially identical to Jung's theory of differentiation of personality. The Metaphysical Poets, able to integrate thought and feeling, 'possessed a mechanism of sensibility which could devour any kind of experience,' according to Eliot. But 'in the seventeenth century a dissociation of sensibility set in, from which we have never recovered,' and the Metaphysicals, with their integrated sensibility, were displaced by the 'masters of diction,' Milton and Dryden, who 'performed certain poetic functions so magnificently well that the magnitude of the effect concealed the absence of others' – they 'triumph with a dazzling disregard of the soul.'[47]

Eliot believed that 'the prelogical mentality persists in civilized man, but becomes available only to or through the poet,'[48] and he made deliberate efforts to use it in his own poetry. An interesting early example is 'Afternoon,' an unpublished poem (probably written in 1914) which pursues 'The ladies who are interested in Assyrian art' as they 'Gather in the hall of the British Museum' and finally 'fade beyond the Roman statuary ... Towards the unconscious, the ineffable, the absolute.'[49] In another poem of the same period, 'Suppressed Complex,' the poet becomes a woman's projected shadow, 'Dancing joyously in the firelight,' while she sleeps.[50] These early examples of Eliot's 'studies and experiments' in poetic primitive mentality prefigure the more successful opening stanzas of 'The Love Song of J. Alfred Prufrock,' where we find:

> The yellow fog that rubs its back upon the window-panes,
> The yellow smoke that rubs its muzzle on the window-panes,
> Licked its tongue into the corners of the evening,
> Lingered upon the pools that stand in drains,
> Let fall upon its back the soot that falls from chimneys,
> Slipped by the terrace, made a sudden leap,
> And seeing that it was a soft October night,
> Curled once about the house, and fell asleep.[51]

Eliot here has gone beyond the Bororo to an animistic perspective in which inanimate natural phenomena are considered to have animate, subjective qualities.

But what stands out in these efforts to recover a primitive sensibility is their deliberate, studied character; Eliot appears to be testing his powers of projection like a young Harry Potter performing his first magical experiments. And in spite of his knowing references to 'the unconscious,' 'suppressed complexes,' and 'disciples of Freud,' Eliot seems as oblivious to the psychoanalytic significance of Prufrock's phallic yellow smoke and licked maternal house as Pound was unaware of the identity of his wet, black bough.[52] The Red Man in the drawing room also functions as a projection of repressed elements of Eliot's personality, as becomes apparent when we place him beside his drawing-room double, Prufrock, too nervous to 'perform' and intensely aware of his neurotic difficulties with sensory pleasure ('Do I dare to eat a peach?') – a difficulty shared by Eliot, who 'acknowledged that his early training in self-denial left him with an inability to enjoy even harmless pleasures,' as his biographer Lyndall Gordon has observed.[53] The two sides of Eliot's primitive – idealized mysticism and repressed object-sensation – lead to the figure of Eliot's mother, Charlotte Stearns Eliot, who 'felt an assurance of grace her son could not share,' but also enforced the family ethic of 'self-denial and public service' promulgated by her father-in-law, Unitarian minister William Greenleaf Eliot.[54]

The Red Man, as a savage American poet, also serves as an appropriate hook for the projection of Eliot's rejected American identity. 'Every nation, every race, has not only its own creative, but its own critical turn of mind.' Cultural tradition, in Eliot's view, was national, racial and also linear, accumulative, and totalizing. The poet, he argued, 'must be aware that the mind of Europe – the mind of his own country – a mind which he learns in time to be much more important than his own private mind – is a mind which changes, and that this change is a development which abandons nothing en route, which does not superannuate either Shakespeare, or Homer, or the rock drawing of the Magdalenian draughtsmen.'[55] There is no doubt some truth to Delmore Schwartz's comment on Eliot's internationalism, that 'only an American with a mind and sensibility which is cosmopolitan and expatriated could have seen Europe as it is seen in *The Waste Land*.'[56] But insofar as Eliot recognized a distinctive American tradition, he saw it as built on a European tradition, and thus closer to the ancient Indic tradition he studied at Harvard and employed in *The Waste Land* than to the American Red Man, a late arrival to the cultural accumulation comprising modern American culture. Eliot has little interest in the idea that Native American verse might provide 'a certificate of our adoption' for the American poet, since Eliot, in returning to the colonial mother-country of England (where he would acquire British citizenship in 1927 and exchange his Unitarian roots for the Church of England) has already refused this adoption.

In the end, the Maple Sugar wars ended in a compromise. The criticism of

Untermeyer and Eliot provided a corrective for some of the more egregious excesses of the nativists, but milder formulations survived, and even Untermeyer recognized the movement in the 1921 revised edition of his *Modern American Poetry* anthology. In the preface to the original edition, dated August 1919, the very month the *Dial* controversy ended, he had written, 'I will not go into greater detail concerning the growth of an American spirit in our literature nor point out how, in many of the poems in the present collection, the authors have responded to indigenous forces deeper than their backgrounds. I will, however, call attention in passing to the fact that, young as this nation is compared to her transatlantic cousins, she is already being supplied with the stuff of legends, ballads and even epics. The modern singer, discarding imported myths, has turned to celebrate his own folk-tales.'[57] For Untermeyer, in 1919, a series of poems treating 'the figure of Lincoln' provided the sole representation of this folk element. But in the preface to the revised, 1921 edition, Untermeyer recognized 'The New Folk-Poetry,' a category which included not only 'adaptations and localized versions of English ballads and border minstrelsy' and the cowboy songs of John A. Lomax, but also 'those who have attempted to bring the spirit of Indian tunes and chants into our poetry,' of whom 'Mary Austin, Natalie Curtis Burlin and Lew Sarett are chief.'[58] In his 1923 study, *American Poetry since 1900*, Untermeyer devoted three pages to 'The Amerindian' (slightly more than the two pages devoted to 'the Aframerican'), rehashing his earlier critical discussion of the translation problem, but conceding the 'brave attempts ... to re-express the spirit of the original songs and chants' by Burlin, Skinner, Fletcher, and Henderson, and singling out Austin (whose book *The American Rhythm* had appeared earlier in the year) and Sarett as 'the workers in this field who have plowed deepest.'[59] Though continuing to deny Austin's central claim – Native verse did not need to be 'brought into' American poetry, Austin would have insisted, since it was already there – Untemeyer's book clearly represented an effort to bury the hatchet by recognizing the importance of nativist verse.

Chapter Nine

The Last Nostalgia:
Wallace Stevens in the Shadow of the Other

In the previous chapters I have taken the position of the analyst attempting to discover the meanings of the primitive and exotic as symptoms of repressions in modern poets and their readers. But what happens when a poet, armed with some familiarity with psychoanalytic theory, a philosophical inclination, and an accommodating attitude toward the contents of his unconscious, takes up as a conscious poetic project the pursuit of the primitive and exotic into the space of the unconscious? The conjunction of poetry and analysis that we find in the case of Wallace Stevens is one possible result, and one that reveals a great deal about the psychological function of primitivism and exoticism.

Stevens had a deeper affinity with Jung than any other major poet of his age; although he did not refer to Jung specifically in his published work, he did, as Jacqueline Brogan has pointed out, respond very favourably to a 1935 Jungian reading of his work by Howard Baker ('no one,' he wrote, 'has ever come as close to me as Mr. Baker does in that article').[1] Stevens was also evidently interested in the Freudian school, although his comments on Freud tend to be somewhat contradictory: in a response to an October 1934 questionnaire, he disclaimed Freudian influence and said the only Freud he had read was *The Interpretation of Dreams*, yet two years later, in a Harvard lecture on 'The Irrational Element in Poetry,' he acknowledged Freud as 'one of the great figures in the world,' who, though 'responsible for very little in poetry ... has given the irrational a legitimacy that it never had before.'[2] He shared the common objection to the sexual emphasis of Freudian theory: 'If some really acute observer made as much of egotism as Freud has made of sex, people would forget a good deal about sex and find the explanation for everything in egotism.'[3] In the mid-forties there is another burst of Freudian interest. In the poem 'Mountains Covered with Cats' we find Freud's eye, 'the microscope of potency,' an eye that discerns 'The spirits of all the impotent dead' and 'How truly they had not been what they were.'[4] That Stevens's poetics were a means of avoiding this self-alienating fate has been suggested by Joan Richardson, who argues that 'the process of going back over the past, looking at it again and again, finding words to embody buried feelings, was not different from what Sigmund Freud intended as the purpose of his "talking cure."'[5]

The poem in which Stevens most clearly acknowledges an explicit psychoanalytic orientation – one that resembles both Freudian object relations theory and the Jungian theory of the anima – is his 1944 poem 'Esthétique du Mal,' where we find the following extraordinary passage:

> He had studied the nostalgias. In these
> He sought the most grossly maternal, the creature
> Who most fecundly assuaged him, the softest
> Woman with a vague moustache and not the mauve
> *Maman*. His anima liked its animal
> And liked it unsubjugated, so that home
> Was a return to birth, a being born
> Again in the savagest severity,
> Desiring fiercely, the child of a mother fierce
> In his body, fiercer in his mind, merciless
> To accomplish the truth in his intelligence.
> It is true there were other mothers, singular
> In form, lovers of heaven and earth, she-wolves
> And forest tigresses and women mixed
> With the sea. These were fantastic. There were homes
> Like things submerged with their englutted sounds,
> That were never wholly still. The softest woman,
> Because she is as she was, reality,
> The gross, the fecund, proved him against the touch
> Of impersonal pain. Reality explained.
> It was the last nostalgia: that he
> Should understand.[6]

Here Stevens, unsubjugated animal of his anima, shows himself familiar with the implications of the Jungian anima concept. At the same time, however, the emphasis on the maternal as 'the last nostalgia' is not quite Jungian, because for Jung the anima, linking the personal unconscious with the collective unconscious, is really the *first* nostalgia within the pantheon of collective archetypes. Stevens does attempt some accommodation of these 'fantastic' other mothers, but they are distinctly secondary. Stevens's anima is the 'grossly maternal,' the 'fierce mother,' the mother of the primary object relation. And when, a few lines later, the poet comes away from that mother declaring to his fellow 'Natives of poverty, children of malheur' that 'The gaiety of language is our seigneur,' we are in distinctly Lacanian territory. As M. Keith Booker has argued, 'once the connection with Lacan has been made, its relevance resounds throughout Stevens' poetry, demonstrating many obvious parallels.'[7] With his emphasis on the centrality of language in the organization of personality, Lacan proves to be Stevens's most faithful analytic companion, helping us to (not) arrive at an understanding of Stevens's cross-culturalism as the search for the Other.

The Poet as Analyst

As I have suggested, what distinguishes Stevens from most of the poets treated in this book is his development of, and commitment to, a kind of poetic self-analysis. Stevens succeeds in consciously integrating the strategies of projection that remained predominantly unconscious in the cases of most of the other poets treated in this book. Stevens seems to have developed this mode of analysis on a fairly limited acquaintance with psychoanalytic theory. Of the other factors contributing to this development, perhaps the most important point is that poetry can be said to have evolved naturally for Stevens out of the object relation, that is, his earliest poems seem to have been written for his mother, and to a lesser extent his father, as the primary audience. This would be a critical factor in the development of Stevens's analytical poetics because it offered a solution to the central technical problem of psychoanalysis, the establishment of the transference, through which the analysand accepts the analyst as a parental substitute. For Stevens, the transference was already built into the situation of the poem.

There is, of course, more to the development of poetic self-analysis than writing poems to one's mother. Psychoanalysis is always a struggle, and 'The Comedian as the Letter C,' Stevens's first great effort at self-analysis, may be read as a document of that struggle: a fitful narrative appropriate to what Stevens saw as his own fitful poetical development, in which 'all my earlier things seem like horrid cocoons from which later abortive insects have sprung.'[8] Having completed it, he supposed that 'after a while' the poem would 'become rudimentary and abhorrent,' and indeed, in 1938, he wanted to exclude it from a proposed collected edition of his work on the grounds that it 'has gathered a good deal of dust.'[9] Many critics have had similarly doubtful feelings about the poem. 'The narrative progress,' Helen Vendler argues in her discussion of it, 'was deeply uncongenial' to Stevens's mind, 'which moved in eddies, never in dramatic sequence.'[10] But just as the reconstruction of narrative sequence is crucial to psychoanalysis, it is crucial to an understanding of the development of Stevens's analytic poetics.

The objective of analysis, Lacan writes, is that 'the subject must constitute the history of his ego.' 'So that he can recognise all the stages of his desire, all the objects which have given consistency, nourishment and body to [the image of his ego], he has to perceive it in its completeness, to which he has never had access.' 'In the analytic relation,' Lacan says, 'the initial task is to untie the moorings of speech.' This means untying the symbol from its established mediating position between subject and object.[11] 'The analytic experience is founded on Freud's first discoveries, on the tripod dream, slip, joke,'[12] all of which represent features of language or speech that disrupt its normal discursive, referential functions. 'For the subject, the uncoupling of his relation to the other causes the image of his ego to fluctuate, to shimmer, to oscillate, renders it complete and incomplete ... It is the breaking of the moorings of speech which allows the subject to see, at least as a sequence, the diverse parts of his image, and to procure what we can call a maximal narcissistic projection.'[13] The poet, of course, has access to an elaborate arsenal of tools for disrupting the discursive, referential functions of speech: tools to focus attention away from the transparency of signifiers and toward their materiality and non-referential aspects, their ability to function simultaneously within multiple systems: grammatical, rhythmical, alliterative, etymological, visual, temporal, ironic. The poet may attempt to control these multiple dimensions consciously or allow them to operate more or less unconsciously. Stevens's mastery of these linguistic devices is perhaps less important than the way he positions his use of them so that they have freedom to operate both consciously and unconsciously. While his linguistic effects often show conscious control, he gives the highest priority to the imagination and the irrational, thus allowing the unconscious as much freedom as possible in controlling the poetic process. Stevensian poetics is thus conceived as a bridge between unconscious and conscious, parallel to Freud's 'where id was, there ego shall be' and Jung's transcendent function.

Stevens's poetics, unlike Eliot's, is therefore openly anchored in personality. 'There can be no poetry without the personality of the poet,' he argues in one lecture.[14] 'It is often said of a man that his work is autobiographical in spite of every subterfuge.' Personality, in Stevens's view, is something over which one 'has little control and possibly none, except superficially.'[15] It is a kind of 'biological mechanism'[16] which develops in a manner reminiscent of Jung's conception of individuation, though in a rather more deterministic manner. 'A man's sense of the world is born with him and persists, and penetrates the ameliorations of education and experience of life.'[17] Stevens's writing is for the most part an attempt to grasp the mechanisms and sources of personality.

If the household in which Wallace Stevens was raised retained an atmosphere of Puritanism, as Joan Richardson has argued, it was primarily through the efforts of Kate Stevens, Wallace's mother, who read the children Bible chapters nightly and played hymns on the piano on Sundays. But Stevens's parents were, as Richardson observes, 'already somewhat distanced from the primal communion with the soil of their peasant ancestors.'[18] John Zeller, Kate's father, left farming to establish himself as a shoemaker in Reading, Pennsylvania, while Garrett Stevens, Wallace's father, left his family farm at the age of fifteen to educate himself in Reading: first as a teacher, and later, as a lawyer. Though largely self-educated, Garrett Stevens was remarkably cosmopolitan in outlook; it was he who bore the largest share of the transition to modernity, and for the most part he absorbed it with an extraordinary sense of balance and irony. 'A little romance is essential to ecstasy,' he advised Wallace, nearly eighteen and in his first year as a special student at Harvard. 'I do not believe in being so thoroughly practical that what is beautiful, what is artistic – what is delicate or what is grand – must always be deferred to what is useful.'[19] Garrett was sympathetic to poetry and the arts and encouraged Wallace's early literary efforts, and when it seemed necessary he also performed the obligatory castration on Wallace's poetic 'afflatus,' advising him, in his second year at Harvard, that it was 'not serious – and does not interfere with some real hard work,' thus guiding him to a recognition of the economic reality principle of poetry.[20] Garrett Stevens was even something of a Jungian *avant la lettre*. 'One never thinks out a destiny –' he observed in another fatherly letter of the Harvard period. 'If a fellow takes Peach Pie – he often wishes he had chosen the Custard.'[21] Stevens later needed no Jungian analyst to find the shadow of his Custard pie; elaborating his father's wisdom into a poetic philosophy, it became for him a question of the pie of the mind, the man contemplating pie, the Custard of the imagination, the man who identifies with the man who says 'That's what I call red cherry pie.'[22]

Crispin at Sea

'The Comedian' begins with the irreconcilable paradox of identity, framed in the place of the symbolic:

> Nota: man is the intelligence of his soil
> The sovereign ghost.

In a poem that will demand heightened attention to etymology, 'intelligence' brings us back to *logos*, the word, the space of language, the masculine law declaring its governance of the feminine earth, the soil. The symbolic gendering is of particular importance in a psychological poem concerning a character who is apparently without actual parents. The paradox is that of the object relation, namely how the (masculine) spirit inhabits the space of the (feminine) body. Crispin is,

>   As such, the Socrates
> Of snails, musician of pears, principium
> And lex. Sed quaeritur: is this same wig
> Of things, this nincompated pedagogue,
> Preceptor to the sea? Crispin at sea
> Created, in his day, a touch of doubt.[23]

The fluid and responsive sea is an apt symbol for the undifferentiated infantile consciousness responsive to inexplicable maternal forces. This is the state of omnipotent fantasy: Crispin appears to be in control and, in the infant state, it is by no means certain that he is not. That certainty will arrive, but only with recognition, the entry into symbolic: the division of subject and object through the introduction of the mediating symbol.

Like Lacan, Stevens is fond of the use of eye as symbol of the subject. Crispin is at this stage represented by an eye:

> An eye most apt in gelatines and jupes,
> Berries of villages, a barber's eye,
> An eye of land, of simple salad beds,
> Of honest quilts, the eye of Crispin, hung
> On porpoises, instead of apricots,
> And on silentious porpoises, whose snouts
> Dibbled in waves that were mustachios,
> Inscrutable hair in an inscrutable world.[24]

This is still the world of the primary object relation. The etymology of 'apt' gives us 'attachment'; thus, the apt eye aptly describes the attachment stage. Attachment is followed, of course, by loss. In Lacan, the loss stage is mediated not with the aid of the transitional object, as in Winnicott, but rather through visual, or rather specular, identification, in what he defines as the mirror stage, the stage at which the infant recognizes his identity with the image of the other. For Crispin,

> It was not so much the lost terrestrial,
> The snug hibernal from that sea and salt,
> That century of wind in a single puff.
> What counted was mythology of self,
> Blotched out beyond unblotching. Crispin,
> The lutanist of fleas, the knave, the thane,
> The ribboned stick, the bellowing breeches, cloak
> Of China, cap of Spain, imperative haw

> Of hum, inquisitorial botanist,
> And general lexicographer of mute
> And maidenly greenhorns, now beheld himself,
> A skinny sailor peering in the sea-glass.[25]

The mirror stage will enable a mythology of self to emerge in the space of the omnipotent fantasy, now 'blotched out beyond unblotching.' Omnipotence is replaced by impotence, identification with a name, a word among a multitude of words within the overwhelmingly vast system of language:

> What word split up in clickering syllables
> And storming under multitudinous tones
> Was name for this short-shanks in all that brunt?
> Crispin was washed away by magnitude.
> The whole of life that still remained in him
> Dwindled to one sound strumming in his ear,
> Ubiquitous concussion, slap and sigh,
> Polyphony beyond his baton's thrust.[26]

The sea, formerly the space of Crispin's infantile fantasy, is transformed by the symbolic. In this new condition, the symbolic structures relationships between the subject (now identified with the ego) and objects. But there remains something left over from the earlier stage, and this remnant is split in two directions, first suggested here by the sigh and the slap (Stevens always insisted that the 'Letter C' of the title referred to the 'comical' ambivalence of its K/S sound) which point in the directions Lacan names the imaginary and the real.

The imaginary is the function that produces identifications, whose great accomplishment in the normal individual has been in enabling the subject's identification with the mirror-stage imago. Although it responds to the real, accommodation of the real is only one aspect of the function of the imaginary, and in the wake of the psychic reorganization of the mirror stage, the imaginary becomes a repository of identifications rejected by the ego in response to the real, most importantly the subject's rejected identification with the object. Stevens uses the idea of the imagination in much the same way; in 'Imagination as Value' he calls it 'the power of the mind over the possibilities of things.'[27] In the developmental narrative of 'The Comedian' the emergence of Crispin's imaginary takes the form of Triton, a shape-changing Greek sea god, child of Poseidon and the sea nymph Amphitrite, who possessed power to quell sea turbulence with the blowing of his conch. Triton appears as a fatherly figure whose language holds the elusive promise of the imaginary:

Could Crispin stem verboseness in the sea,
The old age of a watery realist,
Triton, dissolved in shifting diaphanes
Of blue and green?[28]

The symbol initially appears as a means to master the sea that both connects and separates subject and object. But this promise is imaginary and thus problematic, hallucinatory, as Crispin recognizes. Triton represents the 'wordy, watery age' of the symbol as transitional object, whose hallucinatory elements must be rejected through play, revealing a 'Triton incomplicate with that / Which made him Triton.' (Lacan's problem with Jung, it is worth noting, is much like Crispin's with Triton: 'For Jung, the two domains of the symbolic and the imaginary are there completely confused.')[29]

Opposite the imaginary, in Lacan's scheme, is the real, that which is beyond language, the other remnant of the pre-symbolic stage. Again, Stevens's conception of the real closely parallels Lacan's, and Crispin, coming away from his encounter with Triton, ventures off toward it:

Bordeaux to Yucatan, Havana next,
And then to Carolina. Simple jaunt.
Crispin, merest minuscule in the gales,
Dejected his manner to the turbulence.
The salt hung on his spirit like a frost,
The dead brine melted in him like a dew
Of winter, until nothing of himself
Remained, except some starker, barer self
In a starker, barer world

...

Here was the veritable ding an sich, at last,
Crispin confronting it, a vocable thing,
But with a speech belched out of hoary darks
Noway resembling his, a visible thing,
And excepting negligible Triton, free
From the unavoidable shadow of himself
That lay elsewhere around him. Severance
Was clear. The last distortion of romance
Forsook the insatiable egotist. The sea
Severs not only lands but also selves.
Here was no help before reality.[30]

Orientation toward the real strips away the imaginary buildup of the omnipotent ego that Stevens identifies with romance, resulting in a 'starker, barer self / In a starker, barer world.' Stevens's conception of the real, like Lacan's, borrows from Kant's notion of the *ding an sich*, or thing-in-itself, the unknowable-through-the-senses (but nevertheless known) transcendent real, the something out there that must exist separately in order to explain the otherness of the phenomenal world. The *ding an sich*, although unknowable, enables the formation of 'real' objects and selves out of the fluid identifications of the fused subject-object world, like lands and selves formed out of the sea. But the real is ultimately, as Stevens recognizes, a kind of fiction, 'something given to make whole among / The ruses that were shattered by the large.'

The Symbol of the Other

With Crispin's arrival in the symbolic, and the imaginary and real in their proper places, part II of the poem begins with Crispin in Yucatan, the first of a series of encounters with exotic others through which he will orient his relation to the symbolic, his poetics:

> In Yucatan, the Maya sonneteers
> Of the Caribbean amphitheatre,
> In spite of hawk and falcon, green toucan
> And jay, still to the night-bird made their plea,
> As if raspberry tanagers in palms,
> High up in orange air, were barbarous.
> But Crispin was too destitute to find
> In any commonplace the sought for aid.
> He was a man made vivid by the sea,
> A man come out of luminous traveling,
> Much trumpeted, made desperately clear,
> Fresh from discoveries of tidal skies,
> To whom oracular rockings gave no rest.
> Into a savage color he went on.[31]

Crispin here has no desire to imitate the Maya sonneteers because their object, the night-bird, is not his object. (This was clearer in an earlier version of the poem, where the object is not a night-bird but rather a bulbul, the Asian nightingale, which Stevens probably eliminated for geographical accuracy.)[32] Nevertheless, it is clear to Crispin that the Maya sonneteers are the others who demonstrate the relation of poetry to object that he must emulate in forming his own poetics.

The other has its origins in Lacan's mirror stage, in the identification with the infant's imago, coalescing in the realization, through repeated specular evidence, that, as Rimbaud once wrote, 'Je est un autre' (I is an other). The mirror stage is 'a sort of structural crossroads,' an 'erotic relation, in which the human individual fixes upon himself an image that alienates him from himself.'[33] This alienating identification will 'crystallize in the subject's internal conflictual tension, which determines the awakening of his desire for the object of the other's desire'; in Lacan's preferred formulation: 'man's desire is desire of the other.' Stevens explored this idea more fully in later poems and offered a very clear formulation of it in a 1943 letter to Hi Simons: 'We live in a place that is not our own and, much more, not ourselves. The first idea, then, was not our own.'[34] Crispin, however, begins by refusing to accept the other's desire as his desire, because his lost object is not the lost object of the Maya sonneteers.

Critics have read a variety of meanings into this refusal, and I would propose several others. Rather than debate which meaning is the correct one, it is more useful to deploy Freud's notion of condensation, introduced in *The Interpretation of Dreams* to refer to the overdetermination of dream contents that enables the formation of symbolic nodal points in which numerous dream thoughts intersect. As Lacan writes, 'Verdichtung, or "condensation," 'is the structure of the superimposition of the signifiers, which metaphor takes as its field, and whose name, condensing in itself the word Dichtung, shows how the mechanism is connatural with poetry to the point that it envelops the traditional functions proper to poetry.'[35]

Thus, Hi Simons, in his 1940 reading of the poem, argues that the Maya sonneteers were 'the minor romantics who were still dealing with sentimental conventions and ignoring the crude splendors of the contemporary when Crispin entered the literary scene.'[36] Harold Bloom contends that '"The Maya Sonneteers" may include such Harvard poets as Trumbull Stickney, George Cabot Lodge, and even Santayana,' while for A. Walton Litz they suggest 'the "local color" work of his American contemporaries' that Stevens found irrelevant.[37]

These readings seem somewhat plausible, but they do seem to miss the point that Stevens was interested in Mayans, and interested in a way that links them to the nationalist concerns that develop later in the poem. Within the discourse of a newly energized US cultural nationalism, Mayan civilization had emerged as a symbol of the achievement of the Amerindian culture that might be taken as a precursor of modern America. Waldo Frank wrote in *Our America* (1919): 'In the central lands of Yucatan and Guatamala, this world perhaps reached its apogee. The Mayas built great cities, and made beauty out of rock and upon walls, for whose like in profundity of form one must go back to India and Egypt. They wrote books that are still undeciphered ... But the ruins of their greatness in the tropic forests are not hard to read. They bespeak a rich and fertile people, accomplished in spiritual and aesthetic works.'[38] Two letters Stevens wrote in the 1940s suggest that this was not the sort of cultural nationalism that interested him. 'One great difficulty about everything Mexican is the appalling interest in the Indians: the Mayas and so on,' he wrote in a 1946 letter to José Rodríguez Feo. 'It is just as if every time one picked up a number of the New Yorker one found a dozen illustrations of life among the early Dutch settlers.' Actually, Stevens regarded himself as descended from the early Dutch settlers, and was at this time involved in researching his ancestry, so it is not quite clear why he should regard the Mexican interest in ancestry as appalling. He continues, 'After all, few writers tell us what we really want to know about the Indians. One sees pictures of the Mayas, and this, that and the other. These things never take one below the surface and I have yet to feel about any Maya that he was made out of clay. Publications like Cuadernos Americanos convince one that he was made of putty.'[39] So the problem seems to be not the interest in the Mayans but rather the adequacy of the information about them. However, a 1948 letter to Leonard van Geyzel in Ceylon (who supplied him with South Asian artifacts) gives a fuller account of Stevens's ambivalent interest in the Mayans:

> I was interested in your remark about the indifference to Hindu art. I don't know whether you know about Maya art. This consists very largely of glyphs and sacrificial and calendar stones, all of them completely hideous. They are found in Mexico and in the jungles of Central America, Yucatan, and so on. Many people believe that these early Indians came from the South Pacific. We feel a special interest in things of this sort because they give us the antiquity which the English like to deny us. The English insist that Americans have no background. But after all, Ceylon belongs as much to us as it does to them so far as such a background belongs to either. Aside from that special interest, I think we feel the same aversion to Maya art that we feel to Hindu art even after we have taken into account the fact that Maya art is almost brute art while Hindu art is just the opposite. Both spring from alien imaginations and while the imaginations are different, the effect of each is pretty much the same. I am generalizing. There are certain Indian schools, particularly of painting, which come through perfectly.[40]

This passage provides a good example of a thought process based on introverted feeling; the goal is not to objectively analyse cultural relationships but rather to find a way of balancing the various feelings – aesthetic, ancestral, nationalistic, competitive, etc. – evoked by Mayan and Hindu cultural artifacts. The ideas clustering in the background, organizing these feelings, that Stevens cannot quite articulate, are the ideas of colonialism and its associated network of ideologies,

ideologies that remain in a flux, subject to the constant interplay of competing interests of colonial agents and subjects. Thus the rejection of the Maya sonneteers can be read as the outcome of Stevens's evaluation of his own position in relation to the competing colonial ideologies of his age, centring on a unifying and empowering cultural nationalism and concomitant exclusion of the 'alien imagination.'

Among the other condensed meanings of this episode, however, a reader sensitive to Freud and the sound of words may find another, psychoanalytic subtext in Crispin's rejection of the Maya sonneteers. In this reading, the Maya sonneteers may be read as another version of the father, the one who *may*, the *you* who *can* (or perhaps *can't*) possess the mother. A potential way around this Oedipal prohibition is suggested in the proposed 'green toucan,' implying that *two can* (possess the mother), but Crispin's destitution, associated with the 'luminous' and 'vivid' otherness-recognition of the mirror stage, rightly calls this solution into doubt. The sought-for aid (in recovering the lost object) cannot be found 'in any commonplace,' i.e., any *common place* – alternatively, not any place that can be found, nor any common (shared-with-the-father) place – thus the object is missing from the common place: the place of language. In light of this multiply inscribed absence, it is not surprising that 'Oracular rockings,' the promise of the big Other, give him no rest.

One more thread of meaning should be tied into the curious knot of condensed significations that may be the 'Maya sonneteers,' for 'Maya' is not only the Sanskrit word for illusion, but also the name of the mother of the Buddha, significations that may well have been known to Stevens, as they were known to Jung, who used them in shaping his conception of the anima.[41]

Combining all of these condensed meanings, we can say that the Maya sonneteers offer a poetry that speaks to the object, but it is an alien and perhaps illusory object. The rejection leaves Crispin 'desperately clear' – desperate because he retains his drive toward the absent object, and clear in his rejection of the other's object. But the rejection of the alien object reaffirms Crispin's poetic commitment in the idea that there *is* a poetic relation to the object, as the example of the Maya sonneteers suggests. The reaffirmation of this idea depends on the alienation of the other, and thus resituates the poetic impulse in a space marked by culture, nation, and race, a space Crispin will attempt to navigate with his feelings as he goes on 'into a savage color.'

A Ring of Savages

To understand what the 'savage color' Crispin goes into might signify, it is helpful to look at the development of primitivism in Stevens's earlier poems, particularly in 'Sunday Morning,' his important early meditation on the primitive sources of religion and poetry. In this poem, Stevens begins from the contemporary Christianity of 'Complacencies of the peignoir,' a kind of dissociated religious sensibility where

> Coffee and oranges in a sunny chair,
> And the green freedom of a cockatoo
> Upon a rug mingle to dissipate
> The holy hush of ancient sacrifice.[42]

The green cockatoo might recall the red parakeets of Lévy-Bruhl's Bororo, but here, the 'mingling' of objects suggests only a faint trace of the *participation mystique* of subject-object fusion. The poem then proceeds to trace this lost mystical sensibility through the sun of Sunday morning, first returning the 'ancient sacrifice' of the Sabbath to its proper place in Palestine, 'Dominion of the blood and sepulchre,' then tracing the unfortunate fate of Christ's precursor, Jove, who 'moved among us, as a muttering king,' and finally projecting a primitive scene where

> Supple and turbulent, a ring of men
> Shall chant in orgy on a summer morn
> Their boisterous devotion to the sun,
> Not as a god, but as a god might be,
> Naked among them, like a savage source.[43]

The poem concludes that 'We live in an old chaos of the sun,' suggesting that an original religious idea of sun worship has become distant but is still discernible in the worship of Sunday morning, and after tracing this chaos to its source, the poem ends with the contented but melancholy observation of casual flocks of pigeons making ambiguous undulations in the isolation of the sky.

Although at Harvard Stevens did not, like Eliot, immerse himself in anthropology, the anthropological ideas in the poem were built into the literary theory of the age that an advanced student of English would have been likely to encounter. These ideas were probably derived from two prominent scholarly authorities: F. Max Müller and Francis B. Gummere. Müller's controversial solar theory seems to be responsible for the 'old chaos of the sun,' a crucial idea for Stevens that later reappears as 'the first idea' in 'Notes toward a Supreme Fiction.' Müller argued that the name Zeus and the word *deus* derived from an original root meaning 'to shine,' associated with the sunny sky. This original metaphorical meaning was replaced by a personified deity, effacing the original metaphor and beginning what Müller considered the 'disease of language' associated with the mythological stage, in which the original idea became fragmented into a pantheon of gods.[44]

The image of a ring of men chanting their boisterous devotion seems to derive from the work of Francis Barton Gummere, a Haverford College English professor and proponent of the communal origins theory of poetry. Stevens could have picked up most of what he needed from Gummere's popular *Handbook of Poetics for Students of English Verse* (1885), in its third edition during Stevens's college days. In this guide to English metrical forms Gummere extended his historical account of English poetics back to the days of primitive man with a combination of philological methods reminiscent of Müller and anthropological theories derived from E.B. Tylor and others. His account of the epic began with the primitive Germanic tribe:

> The tribe boasted its origin from a god, and at stated seasons joined in solemn worship of its divine ruler and progenitor. To this god the assembled multitude sang a hymn, – at first merely chorus, exclamation and incoherent chant, full of repetitions. As they sang, they kept time with the foot in a solemn dance, which was inseparable from the chant itself and governed the words (*c.f.* our metrical term 'foot'). As order and matter penetrated this wild ceremony, there resulted a rude *hymn*, with intelligible words and a connecting idea. Naturally this connecting idea would concern the *deeds* of the god, – his birth and bringing up and his mighty acts. Thus a thread of *legend* would be woven into the hymn.

A third *mythological* element entered in through the attempt to explain natural processes: 'Something dimly personal stood behind the flash of lightning, the roaring of the wind.'[45] Gummere applies this theory to *Beowulf* in a manner reminiscent of Müller's solar theory: thus Beowulf becomes a personification of Beowa, 'the gentle spring-god, the god of warmth and calm,' while 'Grendel and his mother may fairly be taken as types of ... storms.'[46]

Gummere further developed his theory of communal origins in *Germanic Origins: A Study in Primitive Culture* (1892) and *The Beginnings of Poetry* (1901). It is the latter book that provides the most likely source for Stevens's 'ring of men' image. Tracing out the origins of poetry, Gummere wrote, 'we see no dignified old gentleman in flowing robe, with a long white beard, upturned eyes, and a harp clasped to his bosom, but rather a ring of savages dancing uncouthly to the sound of their own voices in a rhythmic but inharmonious chant.' Though the picture may not be an appealing one, he added, it 'is only what one ought to expect from the doctrine of evolution, applicable in this case as in any other case,'[47] and moreover, Gummere argued, this primal poetry possessed a force largely lost in modern poetry: 'The modern reader is passive; even hearing poetry is mainly foreign to him; active poetry, such as abounded in primitive life, is to him the vagary of a football mob, the pleasure of school children; and to such a reader the words of Wallaschek are salutary indeed, insisting that not the sense of hearing alone is to be studied when one takes up the psychology of music, but the muscular sense as well, and that the muscular sense has precedence.'[48] 'This muscular sense was the basis of rhythm, Gummere argued (supported by ethnomusicologist Richard Wallaschek).[49] 'The main external source of rhythm, then, is the habit of accompanying bodily movements with sounds of the voice, and these bodily movements were primarily movements in man's work.'[50] Elsewhere, in a footnote, Gummere concedes that there is something to be said 'for the partial origin of poetry in choral songs of a sexual character sung after the communal feast of the horde or clan' although 'this "sex-freedom,"' might be 'revolting to modern ideas.'[51] Stevens fortuitously manages to capture both of these suggestions in his phrase 'chant in orgy,' since 'orgy' is etymologically related to 'work.'

Stevens did not, however, share Gummere's view that rhythm provided an essential emotional link to the origins of poetry. 'In rhythm, in sounds of the human voice, timed to movements of the human body, mankind first discovered that social consent which brought the great joys and the great pains of life into a common utterance,' Gummere argued. 'This, then, is why rhythm will not be banished from poetry so long as poetry shall remain emotional utterance.'[52] Gummere was not necessarily advocating a return to primitive communal rhythm. Rather, he was interested in the historical development of poetry, and believed that poetry had diverged along an upward and a downward path.

> The story of the poet is simple. Detaching himself from the throng in short improvisations, he comes at last to independence, and turns his active fellows into a mute audience; dignity and mystery hedge him about, his art is touched with the divine, and like his brother, the priest, he mediates between men and an imaginative, spiritual world, living, too, like the priest, at the charges of the community. This was the upward path; another path led the minstrel into ways of disrepute, where dignity and mystery were unknown, where the songsmith was made a sturdy beggar and an outlaw by act of parliament, and where there was little comfort even in being the singing-man at Windsor.[53]

Stevens was inclined toward Gummere's upward path, that of the priest-poet, although in his essays he attempted to distinguish priest from poet and made gestures toward an incorporation of Gummere's downward path. 'The poet cannot profess the irrational as the priest professes the unknown,' he wrote in 'The Irrational Element in Poetry.' 'The poet's role is broader, because he must be possessed, along with everything else, by the earth and by men in their earthy implications.'[54] But Stevens clearly links the poet and the priest in a late lecture elaborating on the ideas of 'Sunday Morning,' proposing that 'the great and true priest of Apollo was he that composed the most moving of Apollo's hymns.'[55] The modern poet, on the other hand, arrives after the disappearance of the gods, 'one of the great human experiences' but one that 'left us feeling dispossessed and alone in a solitude, like children without parents, in a home that seemed deserted.' The poet's role is not to *take* the place formerly occupied by the gods, but it does have some relation to that place, for 'while it can lie in the temperament of very few of us to write poetry in order to find God, it is probably the purpose of each of us to write poetry to find the good which, in the Platonic sense, is synonymous with God.'[56] And as he says in 'The Noble Rider and the Sound of Words,' the poet's function 'is to make his imagination theirs' and his role 'to help people live their lives.'[57] A return to the communal poetic impulse represented by the ring of savages remained beyond Stevens's range of possibility, but he did insist that modern poetry, as he wrote in his famous poem on the subject, 'has to be living, to learn the speech of the place. / It has to face the men of the time and to meet / The women of the time.'

Other poets of the day did succeed in getting much closer to the sort of primitive, communal, rhythmical poetry suggested by Gummere. The primitive bard had already begun to threaten 'Omer with his 'bloomin' lyre' in the satirical poems of Kipling, the leader of the so called 'virile school' of poetry in the 1890s:

In the Neolithic Age savage warfare did I wage
For food and fame and woolly horses' pelt;
I was singer to my clan in that dim, red Dawn of Man,
And I sang of all we fought and feared and felt.[58]

Kipling's was virile, rhythmical poetry to stir the blood in the manner of the communal English music hall sing-along. Among the American modernists, Vachel Lindsay's highly rhythmical experiments became the subject of discussion in 1913. 'What are we going to do to restore the primitive singing of poetry?' W.B. Yeats asked Lindsay in 1914.[59] Lindsay's answer was a table-pounding, chanting poetics he called 'the higher vaudeville.' Harriet Monroe claimed Lindsay as one of *Poetry* magazine's great discoveries, and in her introduction to Lindsay's *The Congo* hoped to harness his approach to the emerging movement of Native American poetics. 'The return to primitive sympathies between artist and audience, which may make possible the assertion once more of primitive creative power, is recognized as the immediate movement in modern art,' she declared.[60]

Stevens, however, was not impressed with Lindsay. Rachel Blau DuPlessis has persuasively argued that Stevens's 'Bantams in Pine Woods,' with its injunction, 'Chieftain Iffucan of Azcan in caftan / Of tan with henna hackles, halt!' was a direct response and challenge to the primitive poetics of Lindsay, who gave a reading in Hartford in early April 1922, a month before Stevens submitted his poem to the *Dial*.[61] In 'Bantams,' Stevens, as 'inchling,' 'fears not portly Azcan nor his hoos' (recalling the 'hoodoo' refrain of 'The Congo'). Lindsay/Azcan, the 'damned universal cock,' is accused of misunderstanding and misusing the primitive, behaving 'as if the sun / Was blackamoor to bear your blazing tail.' The sun, for Stevens, though a primitive source, is no servile 'blackamoor' – and here, Stevens's tendency to portray Blacks as 'niggers,' 'darkies,' and 'coons' is no doubt relevant.[62] What makes the inchling-poet 'bristle' is not merely Lindsay's Africanism, but also his attempt at universalism: 'I am the personal,' Stevens counters. 'Your world is you. I am my world.' There is no universal cock, only local cocks: bantams in pine woods, for instance. Lindsay, in believing that he can incorporate the spirit of Africa into his poem, instead of pursuing the primitive in his own world, violates what Stevens regarded as the boundaries of personal, racial, national, and cultural identity.

Eye to Gaze

The problem of the local cock brings us back to Crispin, last seen leaving the Maya sonneteers and going on into 'a savage color.' We are told Crispin has 'greatly ... grown in his demesne,' becoming 'difficult and strange / In all desires, his destitution's mark,' and that he has a 'violence for aggrandizement / And not for stupor.' Poetry opens up in the space of the destitution left by the irremediable loss of the object. And this poetry is both primitivist and exoticist:

> He perceived
> That coolness for his heat came suddenly,
> And only, in the fables that he scrawled
> With his own quill, in its indigenous dew,
> Of an aesthetic tough, diverse, untamed,
> Incredible to prudes, the mint of dirt,
> Green barbarism turning paradigm.
> Crispin foresaw a curious promenade
> Or, nobler, sensed an elemental fate,
> And elemental potencies and pangs,
> And beautiful barenesses as yet unseen,
> Making the most of savagery of palms,
> Of moonlight on the thick, cadaverous bloom

That yuccas breed, and of the panther's tread.
The fabulous and its intrinsic verse
Came like two spirits parleying, adorned
In radiance from the Atlantic coign,
For Crispin and his quill to catechize.[63]

The substitute gratifications of the symbolic are not exclusively linguistic; they are linked to what Lacan identifies as the various partial drives, particularly the scopic drive which functions within the dialectic of the gaze. The problem of the gaze is the problem of the other in the visual field: the gaze is the gaze of the other. But just as the other opens up the symbolic as the space of language and meaning, the gaze opens up the visual field as a space of desirable objects.

Crispin, once an eye, is now a gaze. In this transformation, otherness has been relocated from the big Other (the Maya sonneteers) to the objects a, primarily the gaze, which, it should be remembered, is both the way of seeing and the object seen. Thus 'the fabulous and its intrinsic verse' – the object and its symbol – 'come entwined' for Crispin to catechize. The otherness that alienated Crispin's desire from the desire of the Maya sonneteers has been transferred to the objects themselves. What makes this possible is that one cannot see the object and the seeing of the object at the same time. 'A picture,' Lacan suggests, 'is a trap for the gaze. In any picture, it is precisely in seeking the gaze in each of its points that you will see it disappear.'[64] Crispin is able to grow large in the gaze because the gaze opens up a space for infinite signification, by virtue of its detachment from the scene of absence. But the scene of absence is still very much a feature of the field of the gaze, though now in traces glimpsed as the signs of the primitive and exotic.

These traces link the object a to the lost object which persists in the imaginary as the Thing, signified by the phallic mother. To pursue the trace, therefore, is to approach this primally repressed sexual mother, and therefore the pursuit of the primitive-exotic becomes an engagement with an earth 'like a jostling festival / Of seeds grown fat, too juicily opulent, / Expanding in the gold's maternal warmth.' That last phrase, which reveals the concealed aim of desire, produces a sudden shift in the direction of Crispin's desire:

So much for that.
The affectionate emigrant found
A new reality in parrot-squawks.
Yet let that trifle pass.[65]

Lacan's distinction between the aim and goal of the drive explains this apparent shift: 'the aim is not what he brings back, but the itinerary he must take.'[66] The storm that subsequently erupts as Crispin, the 'odd / Discoverer,' examines the façade of a cathedral might be taken as a projection of the emotional power controlled by the object a. This is 'the span of force ... that a valet seeks to own,' and the unentered cathedral stands here as a reminder of the claim to this span of force offered by the priest.

Having discovered the power of the drive and its object, Crispin now needs to learn its vicissitudes. In the approach to the Thing, what Crispin is trying to see is the object as absence, a shadow behind the curtain, but 'what one looks at is what cannot be seen.'[67] In the recoiling which is represented in the poem as Crispin's Arctic moonlight phase, the inverse is true: Crispin avoids looking at the place of the absent object, or gazes at the reflected object of the moon. The substitute object is essentially a fetish, and Crispin recognizes that it is 'perverse, / Wrong as a divagation to Peking ... an evasion, or, if not, / A minor meeting.'[68] Crispin is thus caught in 'A fluctuating between sun and moon' which forms the circuit of the scopic drive, a movement outwards around the absent object and back, forming a dialectic whose poles are the poles of seeing and being seen. The movement forms an erogenous zone, highly appropriate to Stevens's observation that these movements 'grind their seductions' on Crispin. 'This subject, which is properly the other, appears in so far as the drive has been able to show its circular course.'[69] As we have seen, it also gives form to objects, so that Crispin and his world effectively emerge out of the grinding relation produced by the circuit. The drive represents, although only partially, the curve of fulfilment of sexuality in the biological sense, and is thus 'bound up with death.'[70] The objects of Crispin's emergent world literally reek of death: they are rancid, decaying, rank, rotten, but nevertheless purifying and savoured, because they represent 'the one integrity' in 'a world so falsified.' The sense of death enables Crispin to 'round his rude aesthetic out,' for as the poet of 'Sunday Morning' puts it,

> Death is the mother of beauty, mystical,
> Within whose burning bosom we devise
> Our earthly mothers waiting, sleeplessly.[71]

The Idea of a Colony

In the fourth part of the poem, 'The Idea of a Colony,' we arrive at a central allegorical crossing, in which poet and poem are equated with colonizer and colony. In fact, the colony is explicitly a poetic colony. That Stevens, like Crispin, equated poetry with colonization is made clear by a comment Stevens made responding to Marianne Moore's request for a review of his friend William Carlos

Williams: 'What Columbus discovered is nothing to what Williams is looking for. However much I might like to try to make that out – evolve a mainland from his leaves, scents and floating bottles and boxes – there is a baby at home. All lights are out at nine. At present there are no poems, no reviews. I am sorry. Perhaps one is better off in bed anyhow on cold nights.'[72] The idea of a colony is an allegory based on the similarity between the development of a poetic world – and therefore of personality – and the process of colonization. This allegory reveals the aggressive, competitive impulse at the heart of Crispin's project:

> What was the purpose of his pilgrimage,
> Whatever shape it took in Crispin's mind,
> If not, when all is said, to drive away
> The shadow of his fellows from the skies,
> And, from their stale intelligence released,
> To make a new intelligence prevail?[73]

As we have seen, this is not an impulse that Stevens disavows – the priestly role of the poet involves just this sort of aggressive intervention.

The poetry-as-colonization allegory is certainly open to criticism, and Stevens himself raises sufficient doubts in the poem to prevent the colonization narrative from reaching a conclusion. The idea of a colony fails in a number of ways. In Lacanian terms, the attempt to dominate and eliminate the other is impossible. In Jungian terms, the tendency of the introverted feeling type to overpower the object comes to grief in the destruction of the object. What Crispin is after here is to develop a form of intersubjectivity, an impossible but nevertheless necessary aim. Intersubjectivity would be preferable to a world of subject and objects, just as cross-culturalism would be preferable to a world of modern civilized people and primitive or exotic others. But intersubjectivity fails for the same reason that the return to the primal object relation fails, and this failure is inscribed in the individual personality in ways that are distinctive but also, to some extent, universal.

Crispin's arrival at the point of colonization is inevitable because colonization is built into language itself. Crispin's purpose, 'to drive away / The shadow of his fellows from the skies,' is actually the purpose of language: to displace the object by serving as its substitute. To speak at all is to engage in a kind of colonial violence, commiting oneself to a hierarchy in which the subject uses the symbol to dominate the object.

What saves Crispin, however, is that, through it all, he has held on to the trace of the primal object. Thus, his rearticulated principle – 'his soil is man's intelligence' – not only reconfirms the central importance of the object relation but withdraws the insistence on the male self as its dominating subject implied by his earlier formulation, 'man is the intelligence of his soil.'

This progress confirms the efficacy of Crispin's ongoing self-analysis. His poem-colony, therefore, initially adopts a therapeutic relation to its inhabitants, for whom he will serve as a sort of poet-analyst-priest-king, producing hymns that celebrate

> The florist asking aid from cabbages,
> The rich man going bare, the paladin
> Afraid, the blind man as astronomer,
> The appointed power unwielded from disdain.[74]

Although apparently irrational, these prescriptions suggest a therapeutic response to personality in which the individual is made to confront his shadow through a particular form of impossibility.

The goal of this process is to bring the colonists into recognition of their relation to their own maternal earth, wherever it might be, a goal expressed more explicitly in the earlier draft of the poem where Crispin delineates his progeny who are to be 'a race of natives in a primitive land ... A race obedient to its origins.' Thus, poetry-as-therapy leads Crispin to an aesthetic of nativism, and his journey joins the movement of American nativist modernism, the 'instinctive movement of the American people ... for a deeper footing in their native soil,' of which Mary Austin wrote in her introduction to *The Path on the Rainbow*.[75] As Waldo Frank argued in *Our America*, the attempt to identify (US) American culture with European culture failed because 'the European cultures, swept to America and there buried, were half-killed by the mere uprooting. They were never American: they could never live *in* America. The principle of death carried them from Europe: gave them the *coup de grâce* when they made their fitful stand for survival in a pioneering world. The Puritan culture also was an impermanent life. It grew to meet a particular condition: a condition at best fleeting and superficial.' (US) Americans therefore needed, Frank argued, to look to the 'great and varied cultural world [that] already lay upon America before the coming of the pioneer.'[76] Latin American cultures offered a model, for in contrast to the US American who 'did not absorb or learn,' 'the true marriage of the Indian and the Spaniard has brought about a native culture.' As a result, 'the lowly Mexican is articulate, the lordly American is not. For the Mexican has really dwelt with his soil, cultivated his spirit in it, not alone his maize.' The US American must also try to 'identify with one's native ground, to try to attune oneself to a place rather than to the expanse of a nation.'[77]

Like Frank, Crispin recognizes that a *native* culture is not a *national* culture, and moreover, that a nativist agenda must respect the geographical and cultural diversity of the continent. Ironically, Crispin himself is more French than American, and must leave to his native progeny the task of 'Evolving the conjectural resonance / Of voice' 'in its land's own wit and mood and mask,' 'a spirit to be singer of the song / That Crispin formulates but cannot sing.'[78] He therefore writes a prolegomenon, inscribed along with 'commingled souvenirs and prophecies,' thus:

> The natives of the rain are rainy men.
> Although they paint effulgent, azure lakes,
> And April hillsides wooded white and pink,
> Their azure has a cloudy edge, their white
> And pink, the water bright that dogwood bears
> And in their music showering sounds intone.[79]

Crispin's unified theory of diversity places him in the role of analyst. Theorizing the diversity of natives, he encounters, as earlier in the case of the Maya sonneteers, the object of the other, but now in the recognition that the other, too, lacks his object. This recognition provides the basis for a theory of intersubjectivity that avoids the invidiousness associated with the big Other's presumed possession of the object in the case of the sonneteers. In the reorganized field of intersubjectivity, the subject relates to the object of the other as another lacking object. The subject can now identify with the subjectivity and objectivity of the exotic other and his exotic object by projecting his own lacking object relation onto them, thus bringing the exoticism of the other into focus in a compelling way:

> On what strange froth does the gross Indian dote,
> What Eden sapling gum, what honeyed gore,
> What pulpy dram distilled of innocence,
> That streaking gold should speak in him
> Or bask within his images and words?[80]

Crispin's poetic colony would attempt to answer such questions. Thus, Crispin arrives at something very similar to the field of late twentieth-century multicultural identity poetry, replete with Georgia pine-spokesman, Floridian banjo player, mescal-bibbling Aztecs, and dark Brazilians 'Musing immaculate, pampean dits.'

Crispin's colony is based on a set of ideas that preoccupied Stevens throughout his life. Another *Harmonium* poem, 'Anecdote of Men by the Thousand,' opens with: 'The soul, he said, is composed / Of the external world.' The examples proposed there are similar to, but broader than, those found in 'The Comedian':

'There are men of the East, he said, / Who are the East.' A much later poem on Africa, 'The Greenest Continent,' has similar concerns. As he explained his intended meaning in a letter to Hi Simons in 1940, 'Consciousness of West (Europe) differs from the consciousness of South (Africa), etc., so the imagination of West differs from that of South, and so the idea of God and the idea of pure poetry, etc. differ.'[81] In his essay on 'Imagination as Value' he offers a hypothetical argument to demonstrate that if a Parisian and a Ugandan could transmit their imaginations to each other, the resulting experience would be incomprehensible.[82]

The idea was clearly capable of a wide variety of forms, from unobjectionable versions positing the formative influence of environment to objectionable forms of racial essentialism. 'The Comedian' has the advantage of delivering the idea in both its most appealing and its most patently dubious forms. In Crispin's colony, it is all about expression and the celebration of diversity. Crispin, in his attention 'to smart detail,' has carried the process all the way down to the level of ordaining complex rituals for melons and peaches, lest any particular fruit should be without its appropriate 'sacrament / And celebration.'[83]

But one of the problems that bothers Crispin is the impossibility of separating the celebration of diversity from the stereotype. To make the man in Georgia pine spokesman is to prescribe his role.

> He could not be content with counterfeit,
> With masquerade of thought, with hapless words
> That must belie the racking masquerade,
> With fictive flourishes that preordained
> His passion's permit, hang of coat, degree
> Of buttons, measure of his salt. Such trash
> Might help the blind, not him, serenely sly.[84]

The recognition entails a warning against prescribing the contents of diversity. Thus,

> His colony may not arrive. The site
> Exists. So much is sure. And what is sure
> In our abundance is his seignory.[85]

In the end, Crispin's idea amounts to a possibility attached to his seignory: his lordship, his signature, the sign of Crispin, his phallus, in an abundance of phalluses, signs, poems. But there is still no sign of the object: the sign, after all, is not the object. Crispin's colony thus comes to a bad end, and it was in this state that he was left at the end of 'From the Journal of Crispin,' the draft sent to Harriet Monroe in late 1921. Crispin acquiesces in his role as 'a clown, perhaps, but an aspiring clown,' serving 'Gross apprenticeship to chance event.'

Shady Home

In the months after Stevens sent off the early version of the poem, 'From the Journal of Crispin,' at the end of 1921, the poem underwent a final metamorphosis in the addition of two more parts, 'A Nice Shady Home,' and 'And Daughters with Curls,' comprising an ending in which Crispin's inconclusive colonial venture segues into marital domesticity.

Marriage in the poem (if it can be called a marriage) is literally an afterthought:

And so it came, his cabin shuffled up,
His trees were planted, his duenna brought
Her prismy blonde and clapped her in his hand.

This casual treatment is even more curious when contrasted to the sense of urgency with which Stevens had once regarded his own marriage quest. 'The proverbial apron-strings have a devil of a firm hold on me & as a result I am unhappy at such a distance from the apron,' he confessed in his journal a few weeks after leaving his Harvard boarding house upon graduation. 'I wish a thousand times a day that I had a wife – which I shall never have... wife's an old word – which does not express what I mean – rather a delightful companion who would make a fuss over me.'[86] It would be another four years before he met Elsie Moll, and it took another five of devoted courtship, and a break with his parents, before he obtained his prismy blonde. During this latter phase Elsie Moll became the primary recipient of Stevens's literary efforts.

There is certainly something anima-like about the elderly Hispanic governess figure of the duenna. As Jung writes, 'In the case of the son, the projection-making factor [of the anima] is identical with the mother-imago, and this is consequently taken to be the real mother. The projection can only be dissolved when the son sees that in the realm of his psyche there is an imago not only of the mother but of the daughter, the sister, the beloved, the heavenly goddess, and the chthonic Baubo. Every mother and every beloved is forced to become the carrier and embodiment of this omnipresent and ageless image, which corresponds to the deepest reality in a man.'[87] If Crispin's duenna represents the fading maternal form of the anima, his prismy blonde seems the place through which the new anima projections will emerge. Jung believed in a strong tendency for men to project the anima onto their wives: 'If the soul-image is projected, the result is an absolute affective tie to the object. If it is not projected, a relatively unadapted state develops, which Freud has described as *narcissism*. The projection of the soul-image offers a release from preoccupation with one's inner processes so long as the behaviour of the object is in harmony with the soul-image. The subject is then in a position to live out his persona and develop it further. The object, however, will scarcely be able to meet the demands of the soul-image indefinitely.'[88] This trajectory seems applicable to Stevens, particularly in a literary sense: Stevens sent his early poetry to his mother; whose place was gradually transferred to his journal; Elsie became the substitute for the journal, but eventually proved an inadequate receptacle for her husband's anima projection, which gradually took on an independent existence in the female spirits of Stevens's later poetry. Elsie's prismy role, then, was to serve as a temporary or partial site for Stevens's anima projections: Stevens ultimately looks through Elsie to something else. Jung might have approved of this development, but it is hardly surprising that Elsie developed feelings of resentment toward her husband's poetry.

Stevens's marital relations have come under a fair amount of critical scrutiny, beginning with their only daughter, Holly. Mark Halliday argues that in Stevens's marriage, the narcissism that generally limited the poet's interpersonal relations was exacerbated by his fear of sexuality. Halliday cites the statement of the family chauffeur that Elsie Stevens 'wouldn't talk on account of he would snap at her quickly. So she got where she just went in a shell, and she wouldn't say anything.' Halliday concludes that Elsie, like Stevens's Susanna, was 'trapped in a poem controlled by Peter Quince.'[89] I would call attention to the correspondence of Stevens's reported behaviour toward his wife with the tendencies of the introverted feeling type: a 'tendency ... to overpower or coerce the object,' a 'powerful feeling submerged beneath a calm demeanor' that is sensed as 'a domineering influence often difficult to define ... a sort of stifling or oppressive feeling which holds everybody around [him] under a spell.'[90] It also needs to be noted that Elsie Stevens was remembered as being even more standoffish than her husband.

Against the view that the Stevenses' marriage was a failure, there is a good deal of evidence of Stevens's powerful and ongoing feelings for his wife. Moreover, Stevens has Lacan to attest that the sexual relation is an impossible one and that Woman, in any case, does not exist. Lacan's view is based on a distinction between love and the sexual relationship. The sexual relationship, Lacan suggests, is 'that which "doesn't stop not being written"' – i.e. that which, approached through the symbolic, can never be attained, as Keats suggested in his 'Ode on a Grecian Urn':

> Bold Lover, never, never canst thou kiss,
> Though winning near the goal yet, do not grieve;
> She cannot fade, though thou hast not thy bliss.

Love, in contrast, is, for Lacan, a recognition associated with the way the impossible sexual relationship stops not being written, 'an illusion ... by which, for a while – a time during which things are suspended – what would constitute the sexual relationship finds its trace and its mirage-like path in the being who speaks.' More simply, love is what 'approaches being as such in the encounter.'[91]

Poetry Terminable and Interminable

In the end, the poem is unable to decide what to make of itself. Is 'The Comedian' Crispin's 'grand pronunciamento and devise' 'muted, mused, and perfectly revolved,' or is Crispin a 'profitless / Philosopher ... distorting, proving what he proves / Is nothing'? Ultimately the poem has to be given to the other for evaluation. To deliver the poem to the other is to accept castration as the requirement of being allowed to speak to the mother, but it also renders the speech empty, since castration means never being able to have the mother: 'what can all this matter since / The relation comes, benignly, to its end?' Still, castration is benign because everyone is castrated; it is the requirement and law of modern civilized adult life: 'So may the relation of each man be clipped.' This clipping has multiple meanings: the relation of the story is clipped by its ending; the child is clipped from the mother at birth; being is clipped at death, and, of course, castration. Although Stevens always insisted that the 'Letter C' of the title referred to the letter's 'comic' ambivalence of sound, it is impossible to ignore a more significant reading in which the C is the clipped circle, the broken whole, the lost womb, the separating sea, the castration. C is the shape of the symbolic that becomes visible only by stepping out of the symbolic. It is also, conveniently enough, the shape of the cross-cultural, which takes us conveniently to our conclusion.

On a psychological level, Stevens's poem is a poem of extraordinary insight. As a cross-cultural poem, it does not arrive at an alternative to colonial ideology. One is reminded of Chinua Achebe's comment on Conrad's *Heart of Darkness* – if 'reducing Africa to the role of props for the breakup of one petty European mind' represents 'a preposterous and perverse kind of arrogance,' as Achebe suggests, there is something equally troubling and exploitative in Stevens's use of the exotic and primitive as signposts to the near-breakup and reconstruction of the mind. The economic aspects of this imaginative relation are drawn out by Fredric Jameson, who reads Stevens's exoticism as reflecting 'a particular moment in the development of modern capitalism,' a moment in which both tourism and Third World objects come to carry special meanings for Americans of a Stevens's social class: 'There is, in other words, a subterranean relationship between the "umbrella in Java" – the fantasy of the exotic holiday – and the "umbrella *from* Java," the luxury item whose own capacity to generate images, daydreams and semic associations lies in its origins in a distant place and culture, and in the momentary function of a Third World handicraft industry to produce just such objects of consumption for the First World.' The exotic, Jameson argues, 'completes' Stevens's poetic world, enabling the production of 'an autonomous or semi-autonomous space ... that can now be felt to "represent" the real world in its fundamental oppositions (nature versus culture, or, in other words, landscape versus luxury consumption objects; and First World versus Third World).'[92]

Stevens cannot finally dissolve the exotic and primitive projections that have become an inseparable part of his psychological economy, signifying objects that continue to reveal the trace of the other remaining in the shadow. As the personal grows under Stevens's 'violence for aggrandizement,' does the absent other in the shadow shrink, or does it also grow? Contemplating the image of the poet reading to 'ghosts that returned to earth to hear his phrases' in 'Large Red Man Reading,'[93] we cannot but be aware that the poet grows large in the face of an enormous emptiness, a gap in the circle of being that cannot finally be closed by the poem, and that while Stevens becomes an increasingly great poet, the other remains at large.

Chapter Ten

Forgotten Jungle Songs: Ambivalent Primitivisms of the Harlem Renaissance

Given the widespread deployment of primitivist strategies in American literary writing in the decades preceding the Harlem Renaissance of the 1920s, it was inevitable that Black writers of the period should come to assess their validity and applicability to questions of Black identities. Virtually all race theories of the day portrayed African cultures (more commonly, African 'culture' or the lack thereof) as primitive; the least objectionable to many Black writers were those that at least attributed a positive value to this primitive state. In the new interest in primitivism, some Black writers recognized the possibility of cultural critique by modifying White conceptions of the primitive or by overturning the hierarchy of modern civilization over primitive savagery; some recognized an opportunity to develop their own versions of the primitive African past that spoke to their own personal concerns. Embracing a primitive identity or history as a means of empowerment and a claim to cultural superiority meant reversing the terms of cultural hierarchy, placing a positive value upon the African's alleged lack of civilization, and a negative value on the Euro-American's repression of primal instincts. Some Black intellectuals, however, strenuously objected to primitivism, pointing to the distance separating the African American from the primitive African, or denying that the African was primitive, and others simply ignored the whole primitivism phenomenon. African American intellectuals, as members of an educated elite, 'the talented tenth,' had substantial investments in the values of civilization. If civilization was repression, most were, no doubt, as repressed as their White counterparts. But the essentialist racial theories of the day stated that Negroes had primitivism in the blood, and Black writers, therefore, had strong encouragement – often, as we shall see, quite direct and explicit – to produce their own versions of the primitive. In doing so, they addressed their own personal psychological concerns and, at the same time, infused cultural energy into a broader process of cultural transformation.

The Poet and the Mask

In analysing primitivist strategies in the work of the writers of the Harlem Renaissance it is important to foreground the question of audience. In 1903 W.E.B. DuBois, in his analysis of the double-consciousness of the American Negro, saw the plight of the Black artist as a split between the competing demands of Black and White audiences: 'The would-be black savant was confronted by the paradox that the knowledge his people needed was a twice-told tale to his white neighbors, while the knowledge which would teach the white world was Greek to his own flesh and blood. The innate love of harmony and beauty that set the ruder souls of his people a-dancing and a-singing raised but confusion and doubt in the soul of the black artist; for the beauty revealed to him was the soul-beauty of a race which his larger audience despised, and he could not articulate the message of another people.'[1]

Until the end of the nineteenth century, Black poetry was also largely viewed as 'a twice-told tale' by the White world. While literary Black poetry was often categorically dismissed as imitative and inferior, there were other possibilities of appealing to the 'larger audience.' Poetry that emphasized the Black poet's racial difference – particularly through the use of stylized 'negro' dialect – could, as Paul Laurence Dunbar discovered, reach a large and enthusiastic audience. But there was a price: 'We wear the mask that grins and lies, / It hides our cheeks and shades our eyes,' he wrote.

> Why should the world be otherwise,
> In counting all our tears and sighs?
> Nay, let them only see us, while
> We wear the mask.[2]

For Dunbar, wearing the mask meant writing the kind of dialect poetry that White audiences had come to understand as an authentic and non-threatening form of Black cultural production. But, as Houston Baker writes, 'it is as though Dunbar's speaker plays the masking game without an awareness of its status as a game. It seems that he does not adopt masking as self-conscious gamesmanship in opposition to the game white America has run on him.'[3]

But the alternatives to 'wearing the mask' tended to lead to an equally problematic racial essentialism. A 1917 review of Fenton Johnson's *Songs of the Soil*, a collection of dialect poems and spirituals, in Harriet Monroe's Chicago-based *Poetry* magazine provides a good illustration of prevailing racialist attitudes. The review, by Alice Corbin Henderson, was essentially favourable, but the strong racialist assumptions offer a glimpse of why the magazine failed to recognize the significance of the Harlem Renaissance over the next decade: 'As soon as the negro is educated he begins to think the white man's thoughts, or to try to think them; it is impossible for him to do otherwise. But his emotional reactions, his religious feeling and his imagination are racially different from those of the white man, and if his art is to amount to anything he will have to seek to give expression to what is essentially his.'[4] 'Usually,' Henderson argues, 'when the negro poet discards dialect for plain English, his language is pale and academic, and his thought, again, is not his own but a weak dilution of some already diluted European model'; she therefore recommends 'that all negro poets make a study of their folk-songs, collecting all they can, for it is through such songs that they will learn to know their own race.'[5]

Pound, Eliot, and Stevens all held strongly racist views about Black people. When Pound learned in 1913 that William Stanley Braithwaite, the poetry editor of the Boston *Evening Transcript* and of the annual *Anthology of Magazine Verse*, was Black, he wrote to Alice Corbin Henderson, 'sorry <to learn that> Braithwaite is a nigger. I have taken the trouble to be more contemptuous to him than I should have ever thought of being to any one but a man of equal race. And now that I know his affliction I shall have to stop saying what I think of him. A Boston coon!! that explains a lot. Still his brand of intelligence is quite indistinguishable from most of his pale-face confreres. Poor devil. Please destroy this <last> sheet.'[6] Afterwards, Pound was even more contemptuous of Braithwaite; when a 1915 Braithwaite article praising Robert Frost irritated him, he wrote to the editor of the *Transcript* chastising 'your (?negro) reviewer' with the observation, 'I think it unwise that you should encourage that type of critic which limits the word "American" to such work as happens to flatter the parochial vanity. It is not even Chauvinism. It is stupid.'[7] Pound knew that 'there are ninety different ways of saying "Damn nigger"' and that 'it requires knowledge to use the right ones.'[8] Stevens also had troublesome views about 'niggers' and 'coons,' as did Eliot. But all three poets enjoyed using Black dialect. All three poets were, in their distinctive ways, primitivists, and Black people figured prominently in their versions of primitivism.

A Zulu from Matabooloo

Pound, Eliot, and Stevens are not our main concern in this chapter, but we are interested in the links and separations between White modernist primitivisms and their Black counterparts.[9] Thus it is useful to begin our study of Black primitivisms with a 'coon song' that was a particular favourite of Eliot's, a song written by James Weldon Johnson, who later became a major Harlem Renaissance figure, and his brother John Rosamond Johnson, with Bob Cole.[10]

'Under the Bamboo Tree' is an example of the infantile primitive, an attempt to reconcile the loss of the mother through the love object. Its narrative is concerned with a romance between 'a maid of royal blood though dusky shade' who lives 'down in the jungles' and 'a Zulu from Matabooloo' who woos her beneath a bamboo tree in an infantile patois reminiscent of the pseudo-Japanese dialect of John Luther Long's *Madame Butterfly*:

> If you lak-a-me, lak I lak-a-you
> And we lak-a-both the same,
> I lak-a say, this very day,
> I lak-a-change your name;
> 'Cause I love-a-you and love-a-you true
> And if you-a love-a-me.
> One live as two, two live as one
> Under the bamboo tree.[11]

Lacan can be of some assistance in sorting out the numerical puzzle of the name that the Zulu wishes to change, which is, of course, the name (and law) of the father. Although ostensibly directed at the love object, the song makes more sense when framed around the problem of the prohibited maternal object, to which it proposes an Oedipal solution: erase the name of the father and marry the mother:

> One day he seized her and gently squeezed her;
> And then beneath the bamboo green,
> He begged her to become his queen

She then 'blush[es] unseen' but expresses her passive agreement by joining him in the chorus. The problem of the subject-object distinction ('one live as two') is apparently resolved and the primal object relation ('two live as one') can continue unhindered. The song then offers a series of rapidly shifting interpretive perspectives on this narrative, first placing it in a mythological space as a 'little story strange but true,' then intimating that it was not, after all, a successful resolution, but, rather, a story about 'how this Zulu *tried* to woo his jungle lady in tropics *shady*' (my emphasis), and then performing a little psychological sleight-of-hand to relocate the story in the space of the imaginary by means of a distancing effect that is immediately rescinded:

> Although the scene was miles away,
> Right here at home I dare to say,

You'll hear some Zulu ev'ry day,
Gush out this soft refrain ... [etc.]

The listener who has followed along has completed a short course of psychoanalysis: having projected his own Oedipal Zulu in the space of the imaginary, and then reclaiming it in the home of the ego, thereby providing temporary relief for the symptoms of primal repression.

'Under the Bamboo Tree' is merely one example of the sort of projective strategy at which Black cultural producers became adept. The Oedipal Zulu was one of the more enduring members of the legions of projected coons, darkies, minstrels, Sambos, Uncle Toms, and so on, that Black performers were obliged to stage for the White gaze, performing resolutions to compulsive White fears of Black power and sexuality. The ambivalence of Black cultural producers regarding these projected figures was quintessentially that of the man in the Woody Allen joke who can't turn in his brother, who thinks he is a chicken, because he needs the eggs. If a Zulu from Matabooloo could pay for James Weldon Johnson's Columbia tuition, why cut down the bamboo tree? Of course, there were good reasons, even with such a relatively innocuous example: the most common being the complaint that such productions contributed to demeaning stereotypes and general misinformation about African peoples. In fact, the casual designation 'Zulu from Matabooloo' is slightly off-kilter, perhaps intentionally, but to explain why requires a short course in South African tribal and colonial history, covering the formation of the Matabele (Ndebele) tribe (by disgruntled generals of Zulu king Shaka in the 1820s), their opposition to the Boers in the late 1830s and subsequent alliance with the British, Matabele king Lobengula's acceptance of a deceptive treaty with Cecil Rhodes and his subsequent, unsuccessful appeal to Queen Victoria in the late 1880s, the two Anglo-Matabele wars, before and after the formation of Rhodesia in the mid-1890s, at which time Matabeleland was officially opened to British settlement, and the Anglo-Boer war, which was further decimating what remained of the displaced Zulu and Matabele populations in 1901 when 'Under the Bamboo Tree' was published. The phrase 'Zulu from Matabooloo' may be seen as a symptom calling attention to the song's blithe repression of these political realities, compared to which its Oedipal repressions seem trivial.

A Negro Stick to Beat the Cunard Mother

Strategies involving primitivism were central to the Black artistic dilemma of audience. For one thing, primitivism was on the mind of many of the White patrons who played major roles in funding artistic and literary projects of the

Harlem Renaissance. Among the most important of these was Charlotte Osgood Mason, who supported a number of writers and artists and funded Zora Neale Hurston's ethnographic expeditions. Mason was the wealthy widow of Rufus Osgood Mason, a prominent New York surgeon and author of books on psychic phenomena. Charlotte Mason had participated in earlier projects involving American Indians, even 'trekking with Natalie Curtis to the Southwest to help gather materials for Curtis's *The Indians' Book*.'[12] She was known as 'Godmother' to writers and artists of the Renaissance. Harvard- and Oxford-educated Alain Locke, whose projects she generously funded, was her 'precious Brown boy,' even if he could not take up her suggestion 'to slough off white culture – using it only to clarify the thoughts that surge in [his] being.'[13] Zora Neale Hurston, another of her 'projects,' recalled her 'curious' relations with Mason, and the way Godmother and her cronies would give her 'a proper straightening' when she had 'broken the law' by 'dissipating [her] powers in things that have no real meaning': 'There she was sitting up there at the head of the table over capon, caviar and gleaming silver, eager to hear every word on every phase of life on a saw-mill "job." I must tell the tales, sing the songs, do the dances, and repeat the raucous sayings and doings of the Negro farthest down. She is altogether in sympathy with them, because she says truthfully they are utterly sincere in living.'[14] As Godmother was providing two hundred dollars a month for Hurston's ethnographic fieldwork, such demands had to be met. 'She possessed the power to control people's lives,' wrote Langston Hughes. Hughes resisted. 'She wanted me to be primitive and know and feel the intuitions of the primitive,' he wrote in *The Big Sea*. 'But unfortunately, I did not feel the rhythms of the primitive surging through me, and so I could not live and write as though I did. I was only an American Negro – who had loved the surface of Africa and the rhythms of Africa – but I was not Africa.'[15]

Claude McKay also 'accepted [Charlotte Mason's] checks gratefully and wrote adoringly, thanking her for news clippings and renewed magazine subscriptions, and in return penned vivid descriptions of "primitive" life in North Africa,' according to David Levering Lewis.[16] But he was outspoken in his autobiography, *A Long Way from Home*, about exploitative primitivists such as Nancy Cunard and Henri Cartier-Bresson. Cartier-Bresson, he wrote, 'had a falsetto voice which was not unpleasant, but it wasn't so pleasant to listen to it reiterating that its possessor could fancy only Negro women because he preferred the primitive. That falsetto voice just did not sound authentic and convincing to me.'[17] Such people, he wrote, reminded him of 'white lice crawling on black bodies.'[18] Cunard, whom he accused of trying to use his work in her *Negro Anthology* without payment, was, according to McKay, similarly exploitative in her negrophilia, which he attributed to unhealthy causes: 'the reader gets the impression,' he wrote, 'that the Cunard daughter enjoys taking a Negro stick to beat the Cunard mother.'[19]

These difficulties contributed to the deep ambivalence many Harlem Renaissance writers felt about the question of audience. Alain Locke argued in his essay on 'The New Negro' that 'the Negro of the Northern centers has reached a stage where tutelage, even of the most interested and well-intentioned sort, must give place to new relationships, where positive self-direction must be reckoned with in ever increasing measure.'[20] On the other hand, he defended a cooperative White interest in the Negro on the grounds that 'carefully maintained contacts of the enlightened minorities of both race groups' would be 'the only safeguard for mass relations in the future,' and suggested that the New Negro 'welcomes the new scientific rather than the old sentimental interest' because science offered a road to self-understanding. 'In the intellectual realm a renewed and keen curiosity is replacing the recent apathy; the Negro is being carefully studied, not just talked about and discussed' and the New Negro was 'keenly responsive' to it; the resulting dialogue, he thought, was 'an augury of a new democracy in American culture.'[21]

But it was not easy to separate the new scientific interest from the old sentimental interest. Indeed, the real problem was the *old scientific* interest, which supported an elaborate system of contradictory racial theories that had developed under the strong impress of European imperialism and American slavery. Anthropology as a discipline emerged in the 1860s as a splinter group of the Ethnological Society, under the leadership of James Hunt, whose first presidential address, entitled 'On the Negro's Place in Nature,' asserted that Negroes were a different species, closer to the ape than to the European, and 'were incapable of civilization, either on their own or through the influence of others; indeed, they were better off as slaves in the Confederate States of America than as Freemen in Sierra Leone.'[22] The polygenist theory of Hunt was somewhat less popular than the monogenist view preferred among members of the Ethnological Society, which emerged out of missionary efforts in the 1830, and tended toward the linear model of cultural development. The linear view became the explicit basis of the comparative ethnography school of Tylor and Frazer, which posited a hypothetical primitive condition that 'corresponds in a considerable degree to that of modern savage tribes, who, in spite of their difference and distance, have in common certain elements of civilization, which seem remains of an early state of the human race at large.'[23] None of these scientific racial theories offered any place for a civilized Negro except, possibly, in an endlessly deferred future. These theories were beginning to give way to the emerging theory of cultural relativism espoused by Columbia anthropologist Franz Boas, teacher of Zora Neale Hurston and Ruth Benedict, among others, but during the Harlem Renaissance, cultural relativism remained on the horizon and had not yet coalesced into the cultural ideology it would become after the Second World War. The scientific arguments and theories of Boas and his followers provided necessary components of this transformation, but they would have been ineffective had they not coincided with a large-scale transformation of the primitive as cultural projection. In this process of transformation, Black primitivism played a key role. In the Harlem Renaissance, Black writers, artists, musicians, and intellectuals owned and dis-owned the Black primitive, refurbished and celebrated it, interrogated and played with it, altered it to suit their own psychological requirements, and repackaged it in various forms, some successful, some merely unsettling.

Vestiges of Pomp

'Race pride' and 'race consciousness,' cornerstones to the New Negro movement, were closely linked to a new understanding of the African heritage of the Black American. By the 1920s the stock images of Africans as cannibals and savages had begun to make room for a new set of images of Africans as proud and exotic, images that contemporary Black Americans could experience as a heritage rather than a curse. The European 'scramble for Africa,' new discoveries in Egyptology, the new interest in African art, the success of Black musical forms and dance – all provided material out of which new images of the African were constructed by the New Negro movement. One strategy was to create an atmosphere of African nobility or royalty within an African American frame. In Helene Johnson's 'Son-net to a Negro in Harlem' (1923), the suggestion of royal African lineage provides a justification for the apparently maladjusted behaviour of the poem's young Black male subject:

> You are disdainful and magnificent –
> Your perfect body and your pompous gait,
> Your dark eyes flashing solemnly with hate;
> Small wonder that you are incompetent
> To imitate those whom you so despise –
> Your shoulders towering high above the throng,
> Your head thrown back in rich, barbaric song,
> Palm trees and mangoes stretched before your eyes.
> Let others toil and sweat for labor's sake
> And wring from grasping hands their meed of gold.
> Why urge ahead your supercilious feet?
> Scorn will efface each footprint that you make.
> I love your laughter, arrogant and bold.
> You are too splendid for this city street![24]

African religion could be refigured from merely 'heathen' to 'mysterious and powerful.' In his 1923 book, *Cane*, Jean Toomer looked at Black men in Georgia and saw

> the men, with vestiges of pomp,
> Race memories of king and caravan,
> High-priests, an ostrich, and a juju-man,
> Go singing through the footpaths of the swamp.[25]

Admittedly, Toomer's publishers, Charles Boni and Horace Liveright, played a backstage role in the staging of Toomer's primitivism: while Toomer wanted to play down his race and did so in later works, Liveright argued that 'right at the very start there should be a definite note struck about your colored blood.' And, as Michael North points out, 'this the ad department of Boni & Liveright did with a vengeance: in ads for *Cane* it offered "negro life whose rhythmic beat, like the primitive tom-tom of the African jungle, you can feel because it is written by a man who has felt it historically, poetically, and with deepest understanding."'[26]

The more successful versions of the Black nobility theme tried to work with, or around, established facts and racial theories of the day. The classic example is Langston Hughes's poem 'The Negro Speaks of Rivers.' Without explicitly endorsing a theory of what constitutes racial identity, Hughes lays claim to a transhistorical racial subjectivity by stating he has 'known rivers ancient as the world and older than the flow of human blood in human veins,' and then, by a merger of subject with river, appropriating experiences in relation to four key rivers associated with Black culture, from the dawn of civilization at the Euphrates and Nile, to the ostensibly less productive experience of sleep near the Congo, to the more recent Black experience of emancipation at the Mississippi. Through these experiences 'My soul,' he concludes, 'has grown deep like the rivers.' Although Hughes avoids espousing a particular race theory, the poem is *about* race and racial experience, and involves a metaphysical component not unlike Jung's theory of the collective unconscious.

Others, like Alain Locke, were more hesitant about these 'race memories.' 'Even with the rude transplanting of slavery, that uprooted the technical elements of his former culture, the American Negro brought over as an emotional inheritance a deep-seated aesthetic endowment,' Locke argued in 'The Legacy of the Ancestral Arts,' an essay printed in *The New Negro*.[27] However, 'this offshoot of the African spirit blended itself in with entirely different culture elements and blossomed in strange new forms.' 'Only by the misinterpretation of the African spirit, can one claim any emotional kinship between them – for the spirit of African expression, by and large, is disciplined, sophisticated, laconic and fatalistic.

The emotional temper of the American Negro is exactly opposite. What we have thought primitive in the American Negro – his naïveté, his sentimentalism, his exuberance and his improvizing spontaneity – are then neither characteristically African nor to be explained as an ancestral heritage. They are the result of his peculiar experience in America.'[28] The influence of African art upon Black American artists was mainly due, he pointed out, to 'a growing influence of African art upon European art in general.' Although 'the American Negro, even when he confronts the various forms of African art expression with a sense of its ethnic claims upon him, meets them in as alienated and misunderstanding an attitude as the average European Westerner,' nevertheless, 'stimulated by a cultural pride and interest,' he 'will receive from African art a profound and galvanizing influence,' an influence not different in kind from that of African art on European modernism but perhaps greater, since Negro artists as blood descendants are 'bound to it by a sense of direct cultural kinship.'[29]

Locke's conclusion that the modern American Negro was as alienated from Africa as any other Westerner did not prevent writers and artists from seeking more than simply 'a galvanizing influence' from Mother Africa and from the 'primitive' folk cultures of the peoples of the African diaspora. Some writers, like Claude McKay, and to a lesser extent Langston Hughes and Zora Neale Hurston, rebelled against Locke's artistic program as promoting middle-class Negro culture at the expense of Negro folk culture. McKay was especially critical: he thought that 'a kink in Dr. Locke's artistic outlook, perhaps due to its effete European academic quality,' made him incapable of leading a Negro renaissance.[30] Michael Stoff has suggested that 'the primitivism in Claude McKay's art manifests itself even in his earliest efforts.'[31] Stoff is thinking of McKay's two volumes of dialect poetry, *Songs of Jamaica* and *Constab Ballads*, both published in 1912, which 'capture the exotic and earthy qualities of the Black peasantry with a lyrical sensitivity reminiscent of Robert Burns.' McKay had previously written poetry in a standard English diction and metre (his preferred form was the sonnet), but he agreed to write the dialect verse under the encouragement of his mentor, Edward Jekyll, an amateur ethnographer with a reasonably good ear for Jamaican English, whose meticulously transcribed and annotated collection *Jamaica Song and Story* indicates a genuine admiration for Jamaican culture. Jekyll was delighted with McKay's dialect poems, and arranged for their publication. McKay clearly appreciated the attention, later offering a kind fictional portrait of Jekyll as Squire Allworthy in his novel *Banana Bottom*.

'Of all the Harlem writers and artists none grasped the lure of Negro Primitivism more eagerly than Claude McKay,' argues Nathan Huggins. 'Again and again, the message: the human and vital black man is alien in the sterile, mechanized European civilization.'[32] This was indeed the message, but McKay's sense of alienation actually ended up much closer to what Locke predicted, as McKay became increasingly troubled by his inability to return to the primitive he idealized. This is the theme of 'Outcast,' a poem from his years on the *Liberator*:

> For the dim regions whence my fathers came
> My spirit, bondaged by the body, longs.
> Words felt, but never heard, my lips would frame;
> My soul would sing forgotten jungle songs.
> I would go back to darkness and to peace,
> But the great western world holds me in fee,
> And I may never hope for full release
> While to its alien gods I bend my knee.
> Something in me is lost, forever lost,
> Some vital thing has gone out of my heart,
> And I must walk the way of life a ghost
> Among the sons of earth, a thing apart.
> For I was born, far from my native clime,
> Under the white man's menace, out of time.[33]

Already, the sense of impossibility permeates the idea of the return to 'the dim regions whence my fathers came.' The poem's emphasis is on the ostensible agent of this impossibility, 'the great western world' and its alien gods, that leave him permanently devitalized and alienated from an idealized but not clearly described primitive state.

In Search of the Father of Enjoyment

Whereas McKay's focus, appropriate to his political interests, remains on the repressive mechanism (identified with White culture), Countee Cullen's 'Heritage' (1927) takes the theme of ambivalent alienation from the primitive into deeper psychological territory. Here, the three elements of McKay's African-American primitive – the alienated 'I,' the externalized (White) repressing force, and the supposedly persisting internal primitive – resolve themselves into the tripartite structure of the Freudian ego, superego, and id. The poem's movement – denial of the primitive alternating with drifting-off into primitive reverie – thus turns out to be the movement between ego and id characteristic of psychoanalysis, a process aided by the poet's use of free association, self-interrogating dialogue, and a kind of play therapy, in which the poet constructs scenes and narratives out of available African symbols and images.

What is Africa to me:
Copper sun or scarlet sea,
Jungle star or jungle track,
Strong bronzed men, or regal black
Women from whose loins I sprang
When the birds of Eden sang?
One three centuries removed
From the scenes his fathers loved,
Spicy grove, cinnamon tree,
What is Africa to me?[34]

The speaker's apparent desire to rediscover a strong, regal, and exotic Africa which is the scene of his birth is countered by the Lockean voice reminding him that he has been literally 'removed' from this paradisal homeland. Thus, the reiterated question 'What is Africa to me?' locates the unconscious projection of Africa in the impossible space between desire and denial. This unconsciously rooted, projected Africa is therefore approached by lying (both in the sense of reclining and of misrepresenting):

So I lie, who all day long
Want no sound except the song
Sung by wild barbaric birds
Goading massive jungle herds,
Juggernauts of flesh that pass
Trampling tall defiant grass
Where young forest lovers lie,
Plighting troth beneath the sky.[35]

The barbaric birdsong offers an alternative speech linking the poet to the animal body, the vehicle that takes him to the scene where 'young forest lovers lie, / Plighting troth.' This marital scene is the representable form of the usual destination of psychoanalysis, namely, the primal scene. The African scene may be identified with the mother's body: the Thing from which the poet is removed, the Thing the father loves. The primal scene's troublesome resonance for the poet is reflected in the fact that, like the poet, the parent-lovers are also doubly lying: indeed, they 'lie, / Plighting troth.'

Cullen's interest in reconstructing this primal scene is shared by his biographers, who have scant knowledge even of the identities of its protagonists. Interpretation of Cullen's poetry remains hampered by the dearth of biographical information about the poet's relationship with his birth parents and other aspects of his upbringing, as well as the crucial question of his later sexual orientation. In the absence of such information, we can identify the content of Cullen's primitive fantasy, but we must leave open the question of its relation to biographical fact. What we can say about this carefully elaborated fantasy is that it offers the form of the poet's alienation, and that this alienation *fuses the parental relationship with the questions of race, ancestry, and religion that are the poem's more overt subjects*: the word 'heritage,' of course, signifying the immediate parental inheritance as well as the more distant ancestral one. If the fantasy of the poem resolves into the neurotic effect of a traumatic parental relationship, it is important to bear in mind the potential for interpretive confusion that results from this fusion of the personal and cultural. Fanon identifies a similar phenomenon in the French colonial context, noting that the psychopathology of the Negro, though often seeming to lead to some repressed, remote experience – like that of the child's father being beaten or lynched by Whites – usually does not point to a real traumatism, but rather to the collective aggression of racist culture.[36] At the same time, we may grant that this cultural violence creates conditions (for example, through the breakup of families that results from economic disenfranchisement) which tend to exacerbate the ordinary traumas that are every child's lot.

If we attempt to disentangle the violent trauma at the centre of the fantasy of 'Heritage,' what we uncover is the other primal scene, hidden by the one where the lovers 'lie / Plighting troth,' namely, the one where the White Christian father rapes the Black pagan African mother. This fantasy seems capable of resolving into a very personal form, in which the Reverend F.A. Cullen, Cullen's adoptive father, is cast as the would-be rapist of his biological mother: a role the father can neither claim nor deny. Alternatively, the confrontation may be viewed in more general terms as that between Christianity and paganism, the West and Africa, the ego and the id, the soul and the body, among other oppositions. Nevertheless it is the Oedipal version that gives the clearest shape to the fantasy. As Fanon observes, 'the Negro is fixated at the genital; or at any rate he has been fixated there.'[37]

A psychoanalytic reading of Cullen's poetry certainly bears out this claim. In 'Heritage,' the repressed primal scene joins up in the unconscious with an Africa abjectly identified in images, gleaned from books, of aggressive (phallic) animals that are 'unremembered' or 'no more'– circling bats and crouching cats 'Stalking gentle flesh' – images that end up in 'bugle-throated roar': the 'Cry that monarch claws have leapt / From the scabbards where they slept,' that may be read as the law-giving, violent voice of an aggressive, phallic father threatening the security of the mother's body. These images are relegated to the *not here*, which is to say, the phallic father has been excluded in a denial of patriarchal law, and thus the *here* of the poem, the space of Cullen's fantasy, remains in a pre-phallic state. Here, desire is attracted to the repressed phallus; the 'silver snakes' that doff the lovely coats they wear, and repelled by the 'leprous flowers' that 'rear / Fierce corollas in the air,' signs of the female genitalia that cannot emerge as objects of desire. Thus, here, 'no bodies sleek and wet ...Tread the savage measures of / Jungle boys and girls in love.'[38]

This suggests, of course, that Cullen is fixated at the genital in a queer way. As we have seen, the poet has suppressed the primal scene, but this means that the excluded Thing has been introjected, resulting in the poet's sense either that he *is* the (mother's) phallus (a writhing 'baited worm' that can 'never quite / Safely sleep from rain at night') or that, alternatively, he must recreate the Black phallus for the mother who has been deprived of it. Thus, the compulsive desire to create a Black Christ that would restore the Black phallus to the mother:

> Lord, I fashion dark gods, too,
> Daring even to give You
> Dark despairing features where,
> Crowned with dark rebellious hair,
> Patience wavers just so much as
> Mortal grief compels, while touches
> Quick and hot, of anger, rise
> To smitten cheek and weary eyes.[39]

The Black Christ is a father-like thing with maternal features that will accept domination and also compel submission. It represents not the excluded *phallic* father, however, but what Žižek calls the 'anal Father' (i.e., the pre-phallic Father) or the Father of Enjoyment: not the dead father of the symbolic, but the reverse of the Name of the Father, 'the part in himself that the subject must murder in order to start to live as a "normal" member of the community.'[40] In Cullen's long poem 'The Black Christ' (1929), we learn much more about this obscene Father of Enjoyment: most importantly, that he is personified by the Black man (the narrator's younger brother) who makes love to a White woman, kills the White Father of the Law, and is resurrected after his own lynching. He is, of course, an entirely sympathetic character.

Žižek argues that the anal Father is key to understanding the psychology of the transition from modernism to postmodernism. 'Modernism endeavors to assert the subversive potential of the margins which undermine the Father's authority, of the enjoyments which elude the Father's grasp, whereas postmodernism *focuses on the father himself and conceives him as "alive," in his obscene dimension.*'[41] Cullen's Black Christ is only obscene to the extent that the reader embodies the perspective of a racist, patriarchal, heterosexual law. The primitive and the exotic,

I have suggested, were the quintessential modernist forms of the enjoyments which elude the Father's grasp; what characterizes their transformation into postmodernism is their relocation from the margins to the centre, the inversion of the hierarchy in which they play second fiddle to civilization, modernity, empire. Žižek's schema enables us to locate the shift between the primitive-exotic cultural formations of modernity and the postcolonial-multicultural formations of post-modernity as part of a broader psychological paradigm shift associated with the failure of colonial/racial law, its subsequent fragmentation and partial collapse. In this movement, the perverse, obscene fetish of the Black Christ is transformed into a natural and sympathetic figure of identification. 'The Black Christ' is 'Hopefully dedicated to White America' in the spirit of this discovery, which may be taken as an invitation to join in the denial of modernity that ends 'Heritage' and marks its transition into the postmodern:

Not yet has my heart or head
In the least way realized
They and I are civilized.

Notes

Abbreviations

CPP   Wallace Stevens, *Collected Poetry and Prose*, ed. Frank Kermode and Joan
       Richardson (New York: Library of America, 1997)
EPDSL *Ezra Pound and Dorothy Shakespear, Their Letters, 1909–1914*, ed. Omar Pound
       and A. Walton Litz (New York: New Directions, 1984)
FFCP   Jacques Lacan, *The Four Fundamental Concepts of Psychoanalysis*, ed. Jacques-
       Alain Miller, tr. Alan Sheridan (New York: W.W. Norton, 1981)
IT   *Imagining Tagore: Rabindranath and the British Press, 1912–1941*, ed. Kalyan
       Kundu, Sakti Bhattacharya, and Kalyan Sircar (Calcutta: Shishu Sahitya
       Samsad, 2000)

Introduction

1 Wallace Stevens, 'The Comedian as the Letter C,' in *Collected Poetry and Prose*, ed.
   Frank Kermode and Joan Richardson (New York: Library of America, 1997), 30, hereafter *CPP.*
2 Yone Noguchi, *The Spirit of Japanese Poetry* (London: John Murray, 1914), 17.
3 Cary Nelson, *Repression and Recovery: Modern American Poetry and the Politics of Cultural Memory, 1910–1945* (Madison: University of Wisconsin Press, 1989), 4.
4 Edward Said, *Orientalism* (New York: Pantheon, 1978), 2–3.
5 An account of scholarly efforts to describe, categorize, and theorize primitivism and
   exoticism might begin with Gilbert Chinard's *L'Amérique et le rêve exotique dans la lit-
   térature française au XVIIe et au XVIIIe siècle* (Paris: Hachette, 1913). Hoxie Fairchild's
   The Noble Savage: A Study in Romantic Naturalism (New York: Columbia University
   Press, 1928) offered a comparative study of primitivist themes in Romantic poetry. In
   the 1930s, A.O. Lovejoy joined forces with George Boas and Lovejoy's student Lois

Whitney, publishing a series of studies attempting to systematically categorize primitivisms in different periods, including Whitney's *Primitivism and the Idea of Progress in English Popular Literature of the Eighteenth Century* (Baltimore: Johns Hopkins Press, 1934), Lovejoy and Boas's *Primitivism and Related Ideas in Antiquity* (Baltimore: Johns Hopkins Press, 1935), and Boas's *Essays on Primitivism and Related Ideas in the Middle Ages* (Baltimore: Johns Hopkins Press, 1948). Thematic studies of primitivism remained the dominant tendency in the resurgence of scholarly interest that accompanied a broader cultural reawakening of interest in the primitive in the 1960s and early 1970s, in works such as Henri Baudet's *Paradise on Earth: Some Thoughts on European Images of Non-European Man* (New Haven: Yale University Press, 1965), Michael Bell, *Primitivism* (London: Methuen, 1972), Edward Dudley and Maximillian E. Novak, eds., *The Wild Man Within: An Image in Western Thought from the Renaissance to Romanticism* (Pittsburgh: University of Pittsburg Press, 1972), and Brian Street, *The Savage in Literature: Representations of 'Primitive' Society in English Fiction, 1858–1920* (London: Routledge, 1975). It was not until the mid-1970s that primitivism in English and American literature began to be reexamined in the light of colonialist cultural historiography, with early efforts like Chinua Achebe's 'An Image of Africa: Racism in Conrad's *Heart of Darkness*,' *Massachusetts Review* 18:4 (Winter 1977): 782–94 provoking considerable controversy. The reinvention of primitivism studies in the 1970s and 1980s owed much to the work of revisionist anthropologists who distanced themselves from the primitivist nostalgia evident in works like Stanley Diamond's *In Search of the Primitive: A Critique of Civilization* (New York: Dutton, 1974) and redefined the primitive as a product of colonialistic and textual practices: Talal Asad, ed., *Anthropology and the Colonial Encounter* (New York: Humanities Press, 1973), Johannes Fabian, *Time and the Other: How Anthropology Makes Its Object* (New York: Columbia University Press, 1983), James Clifford and George E. Marcus, eds. *Writing Culture: The Poetics and Politics of Ethnography* (Berkeley: University of California Press, 1986), James Clifford, *The Predicament of Culture: Twentieth-Century Ethnography, Literature, and Art* (Cambridge, Mass.: Harvard University Press, 1988), Marc Manganaro, *Modernist Anthropology: From Fieldwork to Text* (Princeton: Princeton University Press, 1990), and the anthropological historiography of George Stocking. Examinations of primitivism as a function of colonial discourse became the norm by the late 1980s, in works like Patrick Brantlinger's *Rule of Darkness: British Literature and Imperialism, 1830–1914* (Ithaca: Cornell University Press, 1988). The postcolonial critique of literary primitivism developed further in the 1990s in such works as Marianna Torgovnick's *Gone Primitive: Savage Intellects, Modern Lives* (Chicago: University of Chicago Press, 1990) and *Primitive Passions: Men, Women, and the Quest for Ecstasy* (New York: Knopf, 1997), in Elazar Barkan and Ronald Bush, eds., *Prehistories of the Future: The Primitivist Project and the Culture of Modernism* (Stanford: Stanford University Press, 1995) and Helen Carr, *Inventing the American Primitive: Politics,*

Gender, and the Representation of Native American Literary Traditions, 1789–1936 (Cork, Ireland: Cork University Press, 1996). Parallel tendencies in the field of art history can be traced from Robert Goldwater's *Primitivism in Modern Art* (New York: Harper, 1938); a useful survey may be found in Jack Flam and Miriam Deutch, eds., *Primitivism and Twentieth-Century Art: A Documentary History* (Berkeley: University of California Press, 2003).

There have been far fewer attempts to categorize or theorize exoticisms, most of them, until recently, emerging from the French cultural context. One might begin with Victor Segalen's insightful *Essai sur l'exotisme: une esthetique du divers* (Montpellier: Fata Morgana, 1978), comprising notes written between 1908 and 1918 for a never-completed book project. It was translated by Yaël Rachel Schlick as *Essay on Exoticism: An Aesthetics of Diversity* (Durham: Duke University Press, 2002), and a useful analysis of it may be found in Charles Forsdick, *Victor Segalen and the Aesthetics of Diversity: Journeys between Cultures* (Oxford: Oxford University Press, 2000). Exoticism studies remained predominantly French territory for most of the twentieth century, as Chinard's work was followed by Roger Bezombes's *L'exotisme dans l'art et la pense* (Paris: Elsevier, 1953); Said's *Orientalism* both drew upon and critiqued the French tradition. A rare American contribution is Stephen William Foster's essay, 'The Exotic as a Symbolic System,' *Dialectical Anthropology* 7:1 (1982): 21–30, in which the author notes that 'The subject of the exotic in anthropology has yet to be treated systematically,' a problem that showed little sign of abating despite an onslaught of exoticism studies in the 1990s. Chris Bongie's *Exotic Memories: Literature, Colonialism, and the Fin de Siècle* (Stanford: Stanford University Press, 1991), Tzvetan Todorov's *On Human Diversity: Nationalism, Racism, and Exoticism in French Thought* (Cambridge: Harvard University Press, 1993), and Roger Celestin's *From Cannibals to Radicals: Figures and Limits of Exoticism* (Minneapolis: University of Minnesota Press, 1996) brought French exoticism studies into the postmodern age. Following G.S. Rousseau and Roy Porter, eds., *Exoticism in the Enlightenment* (Manchester: Manchester University Press, 1990), Anglophone exoticism studies took off toward the end of the 1990s, in such works as Peter Mason, *Infelicities: Representations of the Exotic* (Baltimore: Johns Hopkins University Press, 1998), Isabel Santaolalla, ed., *'New' Exoticism: Changing Patterns in the Construction of Otherness* (Amsterdam: Rodopi, 2000), Graham Huggan, *The Postcolonial Exotic: Marketing the Margins* (London: Routledge, 2001), and Justin D. Edwards, *Exotic Journeys: Exploring the Erotics of U.S. Travel Literature, 1840–1930* (Hanover: University Press of New England for New Hampshire, 2001).

6 Wallace Stevens, 'The Irrational Element in Poetry,' in *CPP,* 792.

7 In 'On the Psychology of the Unconscious' (1917), Jung said that 'the personal unconscious ... corresponds to the figure of the shadow so frequently met with in dreams.' See C.G. Jung, *Two Essays on Analytical Psychology,* vol. 7 of *The Collected Works of C.G. Jung,* 2nd ed. (Princeton: Princeton University Press, 1966), 66. A more comprehen-

sive later presentation of the shadow concept may be found in C.G. Jung, *Aion*, vol. 9, part II of *The Collected Works of C.G. Jung*, 2nd ed. (Princeton: Princeton University Press, 1968), 8–10. The shadow concept has recently spawned a whole category of popular 'how-to' psychology books whose range may be surmised from a sampling of titles: John Monbourquette's *How to Befriend Your Shadow: Welcoming Your Unloved Side* (Ottawa: Novalis, 2001), Connie Zweig and Steve Wolf's *Romancing the Shadow: A Guide to Soul Work for a Vital, Authentic Life* (New York: Ballantine, 1999), David Richo's *Shadow Dance: Liberating the Power and Creativity of Your Dark Side* (Boston: Shambhala, 1999), and Robert A. Johnson's *Owning Your Own Shadow: Understanding the Dark Side of the Psyche* (San Francisco: HarperSanFrancisco, 1991).

8 Jung, *Aion*, 9.

9 Naomi L. Quenk, *Beside Ourselves: Our Hidden Personality in Everyday Life* (Palo Alto: CPP Books, 1993), 8.

10 Frantz Fanon, *Black Skin, White Masks*, tr. Charles Markmann (New York: Grove Press, 1967), 165.

11 Chinua Achebe, 'An Image of Africa: Racism in Conrad's Heart of Darkness,' in *Hopes and Impediments: Selected Essays* (New York: Doubleday, 1989), 12.

12 Elazar Barkan and Ronald Bush, 'Introduction,' in Barkan and Bush, eds., *Prehistories of the Future*, 2.

13 Torgovnick, *Gone Primitive*, 21.

14 Jung, *Two Essays on Analytical Psychology*, 157.

15 Ibid., 54.

16 Ibid.

17 On the relationship between the inferior function and the shadow, Naomi Quenk suggests that the shadow represents 'the personal contents that appear when the inferior function is constellated or evoked.' See Quenk, *Beside Ourselves*, 51–2.

18 T.S. Eliot, 'Tradition and the Individual Talent,' in *The Sacred Wood*, 7th ed. (London: Methuen, 1960), 58.

19 Stevens, 'The Figure of the Youth as a Virile Poet,' in *CPP*, 670.

20 For descriptions of the eight personality types, see chapter 10 of C.G. Jung, *Psychological Types*, vol. 6 of *The Collected Works of C.G. Jung*, 2nd ed. (Princeton: Princeton University Press, 1971). Basics of the MBTI extension and systematization of Jung's theory can be discerned in a number of popular texts, including Isabel Briggs Myers, *Gifts Differing: Understanding Personality Type* (Palo Alto: CPP Books, 1993).

21 Jung, 'Psychology and National Problems,' in *The Symbolic Life*, vol. 18 of *The Collected Works of C.G. Jung*, 2nd ed. (Princeton: Princeton University Press, 1976), 577.

22 Fanon, *Black Skin, White Masks*, 188.

23 See Michael Vannoy Adams, *The Multicultural Imagination: 'Race,' Color, and the Unconscious* (London: Routledge, 1996), 37–50.

24 Homi K. Bhabha, *The Location of Culture* (London: Routledge, 1994), 112.

25 Ibid., 113.

26 Ibid., 114.

27 Susan Rowland, *C.G. Jung and Literary Theory: The Challenge from Fiction* (Basingstoke: Macmillan, 1999), 23.

28 William Butler Yeats, 'Ego Dominus Tuus,' in *The Poems*, ed. Richard J. Finneran, 2nd ed. (New York: Scribner, 1997), 162.

1. The Spell of Far Arabia

1 J.C. Squire, 'Introduction,' in James Elroy Flecker, *The Collected Poems of James Elroy Flecker*, ed. J.C. Squire (London: Martin Secker, 1916), xxviii.

2 John Sherwood, *No Golden Journey: A Biography of James Elroy Flecker* (London: Heinemann, 1973), 9.

3 Squire, 'Introduction,' xxviii–xxix.

4 Sherwood, *No Golden Journey*, 66.

5 James Elroy Flecker, 'Laurence Hope,' *Monthly Review* 81 (June 1907): 164–8.

6 Ibid., 164, 167.

7 Ibid., 166.

8 Sherwood, *No Golden Journey*, 151.

9 Said, *Orientalism*, 74.

10 Frances Mannsaker, 'Elegancy and Wildness: Reflections of the East in the Eighteenth-Century Imagination,' in Rousseau and Porter, eds., *Exoticism in the Enlightenment*, 187.

11 Mohammed Sharafuddin, *Islam and Romantic Orientalism: Literary Encounters with the Orient* (London: I.B. Tauris, 1994), 1–3.

12 Ibid., 50.

·13 Marilyn Butler, 'The Orientalism of Byron's Giaour,' in *Byron and the Limits of Fiction*, ed. Bernard Beatty and Vincent Newey (Liverpool: Liverpool University Press, 1988), 78–96.

14 Alfred, Lord Tennyson, 'Recollections of the Arabian Nights,' in *Works*, ed. Hallam Tennyson (London: Macmillan, 1907–8), 41.

15 The poem, 'Looking Eastwards,' *Nation* 6 (29 Feb. 1908), rpt. Sherwood, *No Golden Journey*, 74, was, according to Sherwood, written in Italy the previous September. Flecker never reprinted this poem, Sherwood notes, 'perhaps finding its sentiment embarrassing in the light of the Levant Consular Service.'

16 Sherwood, *No Golden Journey*, 99, 150, 157.

17 Ibid., 164.

18 Ibid., 155.

19 Ibid.

20 Squire, 'Introduction,' xiv.

21 Flecker, *Collected Poems*, 179–81.
22 Ali Behdad, *Belated Travelers: Orientalism in the Age of Colonial Dissolution* (Durham: Duke University Press, 1994), 13.
23 Robert Bly, *A Little Book on the Human Shadow*, ed. William Booth (San Francisco: Harper and Row, 1988), 34.
24 Ibid., 36.
25 Behdad, *Belated Travelers*, 15.
26 C. G. Jung, *On the Nature of the Psyche*, tr. R.F.C. Hull (Princeton: Princeton University Press, 1969), 118.
27 Flecker, *Collected Poems*, 163.
28 Ronald A. Gillanders, *James Elroy Flecker* (Salzburg: Institut für Anglistik und Amerikanistik, Universität Salzburg, 1983), 233.
29 Flecker, *Collected Poems*, 161.
30 Ibid., 151–7.
31 Sherwood, *No Golden Journey*, 148.
32 J.S. Bratton, 'Introduction,' in *Acts of Supremacy: The British Empire and the Stage, 1790–1930* ed. J.S. Bratton (Manchester: Manchester University Press, 1991), 5.
33 Flecker, *Collected Poems*, 149.
34 James Elroy Flecker, *Hassan*, intro. J.C. Squire (London: William Heinemann, 1922), 15.
35 On the history of the English ghazal, see Agha Shahid Ali, ed., *Ravishing Disunities: Real Ghazals in English* (Middleton: Wesleyan University Press, 2000).
36 Gillanders, *James Elroy Flecker*, 332.
37 Sherwood, *No Golden Journey*, xvii.
38 Gillanders, *James Elroy Flecker*, 107.
39 Ibid.
40 Flecker, *The King of Alsander* (London: Max Goschen, 1914), 130.

2. The Ends of the Earth

1 Kipling, *Something of Myself and Other Autobiographical Writings*, ed. Thomas Pinney (Cambridge: Cambridge University Press, 1990), 19.
2 'The Children's Song,' in Rudyard Kipling, *Rudyard Kipling's Verse: Definitive Edition* (London: Hodder and Stoughton, 1940), 574.
3 Rudyard Kipling, *Kipling's India: Uncollected Sketches, 1884–8*, ed. Thomas Pinney (London: Macmillan, 1986), 78.
4 Ibid., 79.
5 Ibid., 83–5.
6 Kipling, *Something of Myself*, 44.
7 Kipling, *Kipling's India*, 89.

8 Ann Parry, *The Poetry of Rudyard Kipling: Rousing the Nation* (Buckingham: Open University Press, 1992), 5.

9 Peter Keating, *Kipling the Poet* (London: Secker and Warburg, 1994), 80.

10 Kipling, *Rudyard Kipling's Verse*, 234.

11 Ibid., 236–7.

12 Ibid., 234, 238.

13 Ralph Durand, *A Handbook to the Poetry of Rudyard Kipling* (London: Hodder and Stoughton, 1914), 47. Godolphus Mitford [Mirza Moorad Alee Beg, pseud.], *Lalun the Beragun: A Legend of Hindoostan* (Bombay: Ránina's Union Press, 1884).

14 Kipling, *Rudyard Kipling's Verse*, 253.

15 Mitford, *Lalun the Beragun*, 196.

16 Ibid., 247.

17 Ibid., 248.

18 Kipling, *Rudyard Kipling's Verse*, 269.

19 Andrew Lycett, *Rudyard Kipling* (London: Weidenfeld and Nicolson, 1999), 62.

3. The Exotic Transgressions of 'Laurence Hope'

1 'Verses,' in Laurence Hope [Adela Nicolson, pseud.], *Complete Love Lyrics* (New York: Dodd, Mead, 1929), 12.

2 'Reverie of Mahomed Akram at the Tamarind Tank,' ibid., 7–8.

3 'Kashmiri Song,' ibid., 99.

4 'Afridi Love,' ibid., 51.

5 [Jeannette Gilder], 'The Lounger,' *Critic* 44 (June 1904): 493.

6 'Recent Verse,' *Athenaeum*, 15 March 1902, 331.

7 [Francis Thompson], 'Hindoo Love-Poems,' *Academy*, 15 March 1902, 263–4. Thompson's authorship of this article, which alluded to the 'open secret that "Laurence Hope" is the pen-name of Mrs. Malcolm Nicolson,' is identified in Terence L. Connolly, ed., *Literary Criticisms by Francis Thompson* (London: E.P. Dutton, 1948).

8 Edith M. Thomas, 'India's Love Lyrics,' *Critic* 40 (1902): 549.

9 William Morton Payne, *Dial* 34 (1 Jan. 1903): 24.

10 'Western Interpreters of Eastern Verse,' *Calcutta Review* 236 (April 1904): 478.

11 Ibid., 480.

12 Ibid., 487, 489.

13 'Songs from Far Lands,' *Spectator* 95 (1905): 391.

14 Brian Hooker, 'Some Springtime Verse,' *Bookman* (New York) 29 (June 1909): 371.

15 [Arthur Symons] 'The Poetry of Laurence Hope,' *Outlook* 16 (26 Aug. 1905): 261–2. Authorship identified in Karl Beckson, Ian Fletcher, Lawrence W. Markert, and John Stokes, *Arthur Symons: A Bibliography* (Greensboro, NC: ELT Press, 1990), 230.

16 A brief biographical summary and survey of source materials may be found in Edward

Marx, '"Laurence Hope" (Adela Florence Cory Nicolson),' in *Late Nineteenth- and Early Twentieth-Century British Women Poets*, vol. 240 of *Dictionary of Literary Biography*, ed. William Thesing (Detroit: Gale, 2001), 88–93.

17 Violet Jacob, *Diaries and Letters from India 1895–1900*, ed. Carol Anderson (Edinburgh: Canongate, 1990), 73–4.

18 W. Somerset Maugham, 'The Colonel's Lady,' in *Creatures of Circumstance* (London: Heinemann, 1947), 5–25.

19 [Thomas Hardy], 'Laurence Hope,' *Athenaeum*, 29 Oct. 1904, 590–1; 'Preface' [to the posthumous poems of Laurence Hope, written by request], [1905], Dorset County Museum; *The Collected Letters of Thomas Hardy*, ed. Richard Little Purdy and Michael Millgate, vol. 3 (Oxford: Clarendon Press, 1982): 142–3.

20 Laurence Hope, *Indian Love* (London: Heinemann, 1905), iii.

21 H[enry] Bruce, 'A True Indian Poet,' *East and West* 52–3 (Bombay, Feb.–March 1906): 160; H. Pearl Humphry, 'The Work of Laurence Hope,' *Acorn* (1905): 144–5.

22 'Requiescat,' *Academy* 69 (5 Aug. 1905): 802; Flecker, 'Laurence Hope,' 164; Harold Herbert Williams, *Modern English Writers* (London: Sidgwick and Jackson, 1918), 142; 'Recent Verse,' 331.

23 [Francis Thompson], 'Poetry of Passion,' *Daily Chronicle*, 12 Nov. 1903, 3.

24 'Verse, Old and New,' *Athenaeum*, 2 Sept. 1905, 299–300.

25 'Some Recent Verse,' *TLS*, 25 Aug. 1905, 267; [Symons], 'Poetry of Laurence Hope,' 262.

26 Jung, *Psychological Types*, 434.

27 Ibid., 355.

28 Hope, 'Song of the Parao,' in *Complete Love Lyrics*, 397.

29 [Symons], 'Poetry of Laurence Hope,' 262.

4. Everybody's Anima

1 Daniel J. Cahill, 'Eunice Tietjens,' in *American Poets 1880–1945, Third Series*, vol. 54:2 of *Dictionary of Literary Biography*, ed. Peter Quartermain (Detroit: Gale, 1987), 516; Eunice Tietjens, *The World at My Shoulder* (New York: Macmillan, 1938), 96.

2 E[unice] T[ietjens], 'From India,' *Poetry* 10 (April 1917): 47–8.

3 'Another Hindoo Poet,' *New Republic* 9 (30 Dec. 1916): 247–8.

4 George Sampson, ed., *Concise Cambridge History of English Literature* (Cambridge: Cambridge University Press, 1941), 914.

5 Nissim Ezekiel, 'On Sarojini Naidu,' *Sunday Standard*, 11 Feb. 1962, 12, quoted in Parama Roy, *Indian Traffic: Identities in Question in Colonial and Postcolonial India* (Berkeley: University of California Press, 1998), 134.

6 M.K. Naik, 'The Achievement of Indian English Poetry,' in *Perspectives on Indian Poetry in English*, ed. M.K. Naik (New Delhi: Abhinav Publications, 1984), 215.

7 Ibid.
8 Sarojini Chattopâdhyây, 'Sunalini: A Passage from Her Life,' unpublished ms., India Office Library, pp. 3–4. I have followed the custom of referring to the poet, as in the case of many other Indian poets, by either first or last name.
9 Arthur Symons, 'Introduction,' in Sarojini Naidu, *The Golden Threshold* (London: Heinemann, 1905), 11.
10 Ibid., 12.
11 Ibid.
12 Jung, *Aion*, 10.
13 Jung, *Two Essays*, 189.
14 Ibid., 207.
15 Izzat Yar Khan, *Sarojini Naidu, the Poet* (New Delhi: S. Chand, 1983), 7.
16 In a letter to Edmund Gosse, 10 Nov. 1896, Sarojini explains that Girton was 'a place for people who are gifted with strong and distinct brain and muscular power ... but there are some temperaments that care passionately for the vivid and vital things of life; for dear-bought experiences and deep thought and keen emotions; and for them, Girton is certainly not an ideal place of education, unless of course, education means one great convention by which all natures are to be reduced to one soulless and uninteresting pattern!' See Sarojini Naidu, *Selected Letters 1890s to 1940s*, ed. Makarand Paranjape (New Delhi: Kali for Women, 1996), 32.
17 A.N. Dwivedi, *Sarojini Naidu and Her Poetry* (Allahabad: Kitab Mahal, 1981), 54.
18 Edmund Gosse, 'Introduction,' in Sarojini Naidu, *The Bird of Time: Songs of Life, Death and the Spring* (London: Heinemann, 1912), 4.
19 Bhabha, *The Location of Culture*, 86.
20 Ibid., 88.
21 Gosse, 'Introduction,' 4.
22 Ibid., 4–5.
23 Ibid.
24 Sarojini Chattopâdhyây to Edmund Gosse, 6 Oct. 1896, *Selected Letters*, 27.
25 Bill Ashcroft, Gareth Griffiths, and Helen Tiffin, *The Empire Writes Back: Theory and Practice in Post-Colonial Literatures* (London: Routledge, 1989), 6.
26 Gosse, 'Introduction,' 6.
27 The first issue of the *Savoy* – marketed, with the help of art director Aubrey Beardsley, as the successor to the notorious *Yellow Book* – had appeared in January.
28 Arthur Symons, *Mes souvenirs* (Chapelle-Reanville: Hours Press, 1929), 33; 'Introduction,' in Naidu, *The Golden Threshold*, 16; Naidu, *Selected Letters*, 233.
29 Letter to Govindarajulu Naidu, 17 Jan. 1896, in Naidu, *Selected Letters*, 7.
30 Sarojini Chattopâdhyây, 'Eastern Dancers,' *Savoy* 5 (1896), n.p.
31 Naidu, *The Golden Threshold*, 71.
32 Symons, 'Javanese Dancers,' in *Poems*, vol. 1 (London: Martin Secker, 1924), 125.

33 Naidu to Gosse, Aug. 1899, *Selected Letters*, 39–40.

34 Ibid., 41, 42.

35 Naidu, *The Golden Threshold*, 13.

36 Saint Nihal Singh, 'The Patriotic Songs and National Poems of India,' *Hindustan Review* 26 (Dec. 1912): 580–1.

37 Naidu, *The Golden Threshold*, 93.

38 Naidu to Gosse, 12 Jan. 1905, *Selected Letters*, 45.

39 See Yone Noguchi, *Collected English Letters*, ed. Ikuko Atsumi (Tokyo: Yone Noguchi Society, 1975), 216, and Arthur Symons, *Selected Letters, 1880–1935,* ed. Karl Beckson and John M. Munro (Iowa City: University of Iowa Press, 1989), 284.

40 Kalyan Kundu, Sakti Bhattacharya, and Kalyan Sircar, eds., *Imagining Tagore: Rabindranath and the British Press, 1912–1941* (Calcutta: Shishu Sahitya Samsad, 2000), 46 (hereafter cited as *IT*).

41 Phiroze Edulji Dustoor, *Sarojini Naidu* (Mysore: Rao and Raghavan, 1961), 3–4.

42 Naidu, 'Foreword,' in H.S.L. Polak, H.N. Brailsford, Lord Pethick-Lawrence et al., *Mahatma Gandhi* (London: Odhams Press, 1949), rpt. <http://www.mkgandhi.org/Sarojini/>

43 'Comment on April 11, 1918,' Appendix II, in E.S. Reddy and Mrinalini Sarabhai, eds., *The Mahatma and the Poetess* (Bombay: Bharatiya Vidya Bhavan, 1998), rpt. <http://www.mkgandhi.org/Sarojini/>

44 Naidu, 'Foreword,' in Polak et al., *Mahatma Gandhi*; Gandhi, 'Comment on April 11, 1918,' <http://www.mkgandhi.org/Sarojini/>

45 Sarojini Naidu, *Speeches and Writings of Sarojini Naidu*, 2nd ed. (Madras: G.A. Natesan and Co. 1919), 174.

46 Ibid., 175.

47 Naidu to Syed Mahmud, 6 Jan. 1916, *Selected Letters*, 109.

48 Naidu to Syed Mahmud, 25 Jan. 1916, ibid., 110, 111. For further background on Syed Mahmud, see Syed Mahmud, *A Nationalist Muslim and Indian Politics*, ed. V.N. Datta and B.E. Cleghorn (Delhi: Macmillan, 1974).

49 With the exception of the collected edition of her poems entitled *The Sceptred Flute: Songs of India* (New York: Dodd, Mead, 1928). A group of poems probably written in the 1920s was published posthumously in 1961 as *The Feather of the Dawn* (New York: Asia Publishing House, 1961).

50 Sarojini Naidu, *The Broken Wing*: *Songs of Love, Death and Destiny, 1915–1916.* (London: Heinemann, 1917), 97.

51 Meena Alexander, 'In Search of Sarojini Naidu,' in *The Shock of Arrival: Reflections on Postcolonial Experience* (Boston: South End Press, 1996), 181.

52 Naidu, 'The Broken Wing,' in *The Broken Wing*, 15.

53 Naidu, 'Devotion,' in *The Broken Wing*, 120.

54 Naidu to Mahmud, 25 Jan. 1916, *Selected Letters*, 111.

55 Naidu, *Speeches and Writings*, 203.

56 Partha Chatterjee, 'The Nationalist Resolution to the Women's Question,' in *Recasting Women*, ed. Kumkum Sangari and Sudesh Vaid (New Brunswick, NJ: Rutgers University Press, 1990), 248.

57 Susie Tharu, 'Tracing Savitri's Pedigree: Victorian Racism and the Image of Women in Indo-Anglian Literature,' in Sangari and Vaid, eds., *Recasting Women*, 261.

58 Naidu, *The Bird of Time*, 87–8.

5. The Tagore Era

1 William Rothenstein, *Men and Memories* (New York: Coward-McCann, 1931–40), 262.

2 William Butler Yeats, 'Introduction,' in Rabindranath Tagore, *Gitanjali (Song Offerings)* (London: India Society, 1912), xiii–xiv.

3 F. Max Müller, *India: What Can It Teach Us?* (London: Longmans, Green, 1883), 46.

4 Ibid.

5 Ibid., 24.

6 Ibid., 52.

7 Ibid., 24–5.

8 Ibid., 106.

9 Ibid., 117.

10 Ibid., 123.

11 Henry David Thoreau, *Journal* 2:36, in *The Writings of Henry David Thoreau*, ed. Bradford Torrey and Francis H. Allen, 20 vols. (Walden ed., 1906; rpt. ed., New York: AMS Press, 1968).

12 http://www.vivekananda.net/commentsparliament9_93.html

13 Jung, *Psychological Types*, 401–2.

14 On Vaishnava poetry see Edward C. Dimock, *In Praise of Krishna: Songs from the Bengali*, tr. Edward C. Dimock, Jr., and Denise Levertov (Garden City, NY: Doubleday, 1967).

15 Jung, *Psychological Types*, 401.

16 Rabindranath Tagore, *Personality: Lectures Delivered in America* (London: Macmillan, 1917), 69.

17 'Dinner to Mr. Rabindranath Tagore,' London *Times*, 13 July 1912, 5; 'The Triumph of Art over Circumstances,' London *Times*, 16 July 1912, 7. Both articles are reprinted in *IT*, 5–7.

18 Rothenstein to Yeats, 24 Aug. 1912, in *Letters to W.B. Yeats*, ed. Richard J. Finneran, George Mills Harper, and William M. Murphy, vol. 1 (New York: Columbia University Press, 1977), 249, 251.

19 Naidu to Tagore, 16 Nov. 1912, *Selected Letters*, 82.

20 Yeats, 'Introduction,' in Tagore, *Gitanjali*, vii.

21 Ibid., xi.

22 Ibid., 11–12.

23 Ibid., 12–13.

24 Rothenstein to Yeats, 24 Aug. 1912, *Letters to Yeats*, 251.

25 'Mr. Tagore's Poems,' *TLS*, 7 Nov. 1912, 492, rpt. *IT*, 8; 'An Indian Mystic,' *Nation* (London), 16 Nov. 1912, p. 320–2, rpt. *IT*, 11; Lascelles Abercrombie, 'The Indian Poet,' *Manchester Guardian*, 14 Jan. 1913, p. 6, rpt. *IT*, 16.

26 Yeats to Edmund Gosse, 25 Nov. 1912, in W.B. Yeats, *Letters*, ed. Allan Wade (New York: Macmillan, 1955), 572–3.

27 Rabindranath Tagore, 'Modern Poetry' (1932), in *Selected Writings on Literature and Language*, ed. Sukanta Chaudhuri (New Delhi: Oxford University Press, 2001), 288. Another translation of the essay appears in *A Tagore Reader*, ed. Amiya Chakravarti (Boston: Beacon, 1961), 241–53.

28 William Butler Yeats, *The Poems*, ed. Richard J. Finneran, 2nd ed. (New York: Scribner, 1997), 127.

29 Tagore to Pound, Feb. 1913, in *Selected Letters of Rabindranath Tagore*, ed. Krishna Dutta and Andrew Robinson (Cambridge: Cambridge University Press, 1997), 106.

30 Ezra Pound to Dorothy Shakespear, 8 May 1913, in *Ezra Pound and Dorothy Shakespear, Their Letters, 1909–1914*, ed. Omar Pound and A. Walton Litz (New York: New Directions, 1984), 224 (hereafter cited as *EPDSL*).

31 'Poems,' a section in *Poetry: A Magazine of Verse* 3:2 (Nov. 1913): 53. The poem also appears in *Lustra* (London: Elkin Mathews, 1916), 25.

32 See Olivia Shakespear to Ezra Pound, 13 Sept. 1912, *EPDSL*, 153–4.

33 Pound to Dorothy Shakespear, 3 Oct. 1912, *EPDSL*, 162–3.

34 Pound to Harriet Monroe, [24] Sept. 1912, in Ezra Pound, *The Selected Letters of Ezra Pound, 1907–1941*, ed. D.D. Paige (New York: New Directions, 1971), 10.

35 See Harold M. Hurwitz, 'Tagore in Urbana, Illinois,' *Indian Literature* 4 (1961): 27–36; Krishna Dutta and Andrew Robinson, *Rabindranath Tagore: The Myriad-Minded Man* (New York: St Martin's Press, 1996), 172–3.

36 Pound to Homer Pound, 12 Dec. 1912, quoted in *EPDSL*, 178; Pound to Dorothy Shakespear, 8 Jan. 1913, *EPDSL*, 179; Pound to Dorothy Shakespear, 21 Jan. 1913, *EPDSL*, 183; Kali Mohan Ghose and Ezra Pound, tr., 'Certain Poems of Kabir,' *Modern Review* 13 (June 1913): 611–13.

37 Pound to Monroe, March 1913, *Selected Letters*, 16.

38 Pound to Monroe, 22 April 1913, ibid., 19.

39 Pound to Henderson, 9 Feb. 1917, in *The Letters of Ezra Pound to Alice Corbin Henderson*, ed. Ira B. Nadel (Austin: University of Texas Press, 1993), 187–8.

40 'An Indian Drama,' *Westminster Gazette*, 10 May 1913, 7, rpt. *IT*, 23–4.

41 *Manchester Guardian*, 15 Nov. 1913, p. 8, rpt. *IT*, 93.

42 'Honour to Indian Poet,' *Daily Telegraph*, 14 Nov. 1913, 15, rpt. *IT*, 81.

43 Dutta and Robinson, *Tagore*, 186.

44 Horst Frenz, ed., *Literature, 1901–1967* (Amsterdam: Elsevier, 1969), 127–8.

45 'Nobel Prize for Indian Poet,' *Daily News and Leader*, 14 Nov. 1913, 1, rpt. *IT*, 79–80.

46 Frenz, *Literature*, 130, 131.

47 My translation of Jean-Jacques Rousseau, *Discours sur l'origine de l'inégalité*, ed. Jacques Roger (Paris: Garnier-Flammarion, 1971), 233.

48 Jung, *On the Nature of the Psyche*, 32–3.

49 Ibid., 34–5.

50 Tagore, *Gitanjali*, 34–5.

51 D.W. Winnicott, 'The Location of Cultural Experience,' in *Transitional Objects and Potential Spaces: Literary Uses of D.W. Winnicott*, ed. Peter L. Rudnytsky (New York: Columbia University Press, 1993), 3–4.

52 This schema is derived from Jung, *Two Essays*, 163–71.

53 'An Attack on the Tagore "Craze,"' *Literary Digest*, 21 Aug. 1915, 352.

54 Joyce Kilmer, *Trees and Other Poems* (Garden City, NY: Doubleday, 1914).

55 'An Attack on the Tagore "Craze,"' 352.

56 Lawrence to Morrell, 24 May 1916, quoted in Alex Aronson, *Rabindranath Through Western Eyes* (Calcutta: Rddhi-India, 1978), 37. On Lawrence and primitivism, see Torgovnick, *Primitive Passions*, 43–57.

57 Harold Monro, 'New Books: English Poetry,' *Poetry and Drama* 5 (March 1914): 58.

58 'Rabindranath Tagore in America,' *Modern Review* 19 (March 1917): 372.

59 Ibid. (April 1917): 422.

60 Rothenstein, *Men and Memories*, 265–6, 283.

61 'Mr. Punch's Own Indian Poet, *Punch*, 10 Dec. 1913, 494, rpt. *IT*, 111; 'Today's Table Talk,' *Evening Standard and St James's Gazette*, 5 Jan. 1914, 10, rpt. *IT*, 136.

62 'Jodindranath Mawhwor's Occupation,' *Little Review* 4 (May 1917): 12–18, rpt. *Pavannes and Divisions* (New York: Knopf, 1918); rpt. *Pavannes and Divagations* (New York: New Directions, 1958), 79–85. This was presumably the 'story with a nice thick nauseous indian atmosphere ... mostly cribbed from the Kamasutra' that Pound mentioned to Alice Corbin Henderson, 26 Aug. 1916, *Letters to Henderson*, 163.

63 Max Beerbohm, *Max in Verse: Rhymes and Parodies by Max Beerbohm*, ed. J.G. Riewald (Brattleboro, VT: Stephen Greene Press, 1963): 63.

64 'Do Prizes and Petting Spoil Poets?,' *Daily Citizen*, 3 Jan. 1914, 4, rpt. *IT*, 134.

65 Dutta and Robinson, *Tagore*, 214.

66 Pound, *Letters to Henderson*, 108.

67 '"League of Vagabonds": Sir R. Tagore's Vision of a Fellowship of Man,' London *Times*, 6 Jan. 1921, 9, rpt. *IT*, 328; 'The West in the East: Sir Rabindranath Tagore on a Great Failure,' *Morning Post*, 9 April 1921, 3, rpt. *IT*, 328.

68 Aronson, *Rabindranath through Western Eyes*, 23–4.

69 Ibid., 14; *Manchester Guardian*, 15 Nov. 1921, 5, rpt. *IT*, 344.

6. The Childhood That Never Was

1 William E. Laskowski, *Rupert Brooke* (New York: Twayne, 1994), 6; Adrian Caesar, *Taking It Like a Man: Suffering, Sexuality and the War Poets* (Manchester: Manchester · University Press, 1993), 34.

2 Nigel H. Jones, *Rupert Brooke: Life, Death and Myth* (London: Richard Cohen Books, 1999), 7.

3 Paul Delany, *The Neo-Pagans: Friendship and Love in the Rupert Brooke Circle* (New York: Free Press, 1987), 204.

4 Laskowski, *Rupert Brooke*, 21.

5 Brooke to Cathleen Nesbitt, 12 Oct. [1913], in *The Letters of Rupert Brooke*, ed. Geoffrey Keynes (New York: Harcourt, Brace and World, 1968), 515.

6 Brooke to Marsh, 1 Oct. [1913], *Letters*, 513.

7 John Dryden, *The Works of John Dryden*, vol. 11 (Berkeley: University of California Press, 1978), 30.

8 Christopher Herbert, *Culture and Anomie: Ethnographic Imagination in the Nineteenth Century* (Chicago: University of Chicago Press, 1991), 158.

9 Herman Melville, *Typee: A Peep at Polynesian Life* (New York: Penguin, 1986), 179–80.

10 Ibid., 225.

11 Brooke to Nesbitt, 28 Oct. [1913], *Letters*, 521.

12 Ibid., 522.

13 Ibid., 521.

14 Brooke to Isabel Brooke, 28 Oct. 1913, ibid., 523.

15 Rupert Brooke, *The Complete Poems*, 2nd ed. (London: Sidgwick and Jackson, 1942), 126.

16 Melanie Klein, *The Selected Melanie Klein*, ed. Juliet Mitchell (New York: Free Press, 1987), 124, 125.

17 Ibid., 204.

18 Brooke to Marsh, 15? Nov. 1913, *Letters*, 525.

19 Ibid., 526.

20 Brooke to Gosse, 19 Nov. 1913, ibid., 530–1.

21 Laskowski, *Rupert Brooke*, 23.

22 Brooke to Gosse, 19 Nov. 1913, *Letters*, 531.

23 Brooke to Edward Marsh, 22 Nov. 1913, ibid., 535.

24 Brooke to Nesbitt, 24? Nov 1913, ibid., 536.

25 Brooke to Raverat, 1 Dec. 1913, ibid., 540.

26 Ibid., 541.

27 Brooke to Nesbitt, 17 Dec. 1913, ibid., 552.
28 Brooke to Nesbitt, 24? Nov. 1913, ibid., 537.
29 Brooke to Violet Asquith, Dec. 1913, ibid., 540.
30 Brooke to Mrs Brooke, Dec. 1913, ibid., 544.
31 Brooke to Nesbitt, 17 Dec. 1913, ibid., 550.
32 Taatamata is also referred to variously in Brooke's writings as 'Tuate Mata' and 'Mamua.' In her surviving letter, she signs herself as 'Tatamata.' See Brooke to Dudley Ward, ibid., 654n1.
33 Clotilde (474–545), the Frankish queen and Catholic saint Brooke apparently refers to here, was often depicted as a savage beauty.
34 Brooke to Marsh, 15? Nov. 1913, *Letters*, 525–6.
35 Brooke to Nesbitt, 7 Feb. [1914], ibid., 563.
36 Brooke, *Complete Poems*, 139.
37 Ibid., 140, 144.
38 Brooke to Marsh, 7 March 1914, *Letters*, 565.
39 Ibid.
40 Pound, *Blast* 2 (July 1915), rpt. in Ezra Pound, *Personae: The Shorter Poems of Ezra Pound*, ed. Lea Baechler and A. Walton Litz (New York: New Directions, 1990), 122.
41 Pound, *Selected Letters*, 64–5.
42 Brooke to Nesbitt, April 1914, *Letters*, 570.
43 Brooke to Marsh, April 1914, ibid., 577.
44 'The Soldier,' in Brooke, *Complete Poems*, 150.
45 Mike Read, *Forever England: The Life of Rupert Brooke* (Edinburgh: Mainstream Publishing, 1997).
46 Nigel H. Jones, *Rupert Brooke: Life, Death and Myth* (London: Richard Cohen Books, 1999).

7. The Infant Gargantua on the Wet, Black Bough

1 Jung, *Psychological Types*, 368, 369.
2 Ibid., 371.
3 Ibid., 370.
4 Ezra Pound, 'Indiscretions, or *Une Review des Deux Mondes*,' *Pavannes and Divagations* (New York: New Directions, 1958), 35.
5 Pound, *Personae*, 106.
6 K.K. Ruthven, *A Guide to Ezra Pound's Personae, 1926* (Berkeley: University of California Press, 1969), 217.
7 Ezra Pound, 'A Few Don'ts by an Imagiste,' *Poetry* 1:6 (March 1913): 200.
8 Bernard Hart, *The Psychology of Insanity*, 3rd ed. (Cambridge University Press, 1916), 61–2, 116.

9 Zhaoming Qian, *Orientalism and Modernism: The Legacy of China in Pound and Williams* (Durham: Duke University Press, 1995), 9.

10 Helen Carr, 'Imagism and Empire,' in *Modernism and Empire*, ed. Howard J. Booth and Nigel Rigby (Manchester: Manchester University Press, 2000), 71.

11 F.S. Flint, 'A History of Imagism,' *Egoist* 2:5 (1 May 1915): 70–1.

12 Pound, *Personae*, 111.

13 Ruthven, *Guide*, 152–3.

14 Christopher Bollas, *The Shadow of the Object: Psychoanalysis of the Unthought Known* (New York: Columbia University Press, 1987), 16–17

15 Pound to Dorothy Shakespear, Aug. 1911, *EPDSL*, 44.

16 Kodama Sanehide, ed., *Ezra Pound and Japan: Letters and Essays* (Redding Ridge, CT: Black Swan Books, 1987), 5.

17 Laurence Binyon, *The Flight of the Dragon* (London: J. Murray, 1911), 108.

18 Pound did apparently get along with Japanese dancer Michio Itow, and had some successful relationships with Asian writers, notably Kitasono Katsue, in later years.

19 Pound, *Personae*, 66–7.

20 Pound to Dorothy Shakespear, 16 Dec. 1912, in *EPDSL*, 165.

21 Pound to Dorothy Shakespear, 2 Jan. 1913, ibid., 175.

22 Pound to Dorothy Shakespear, 4 Jan. 1913, ibid., 177.

23 Dorothy Shakespear to Pound, 22 Feb. 1913, ibid., 190.

24 Dorothy Shakespear to Pound, 14 March 1913, ibid., 191.

25 Dorothy Shakespear to Pound, 8 April 1913, ibid., 198.

26 Dorothy Shakespear to Pound, [18] April 1913, ibid., 204.

27 Dorothy Shakespear to Pound, 13 May 1913, ibid., 175.

28 Pound to Dorothy Shakespear, 25 Sept. 1913, ibid., 259.

29 Dorothy Shakespear to Pound, 9 Sept. 1913, ibid., 254.

30 'The Koran is I suppose a fake and a compromise,' Pound replied on 17 Sept. 1913, ibid., 256.

31 Pound to Dorothy Shakespear, 5 Sept. 1913, ibid., 251.

32 Pound to Dorothy Shakespear, 17 Sept. and 21 Sept. 1913, ibid., 256, 259.

33 Pound to Dorothy Shakespear, 2 Oct. 1913, ibid., 264.

34 Humphrey Carpenter, *A Serious Character: The Life of Ezra Pound* (New York: Dell, 1988), 220.

35 Pound to Dorothy Shakespear, 11 Oct. 1913, *EPDSL*, 270.

36 H.A. Giles, *A History of Chinese Literature* (London: Heinemann, 1901), 50.

37 Pound to Dorothy Shakespear, 7 Oct. 1913, *EPDSL*, 266.

38 Dorothy Shakespear to Pound, 9 Oct. 1913, ibid., 269.

39 Pound to Dorothy Shakespear, 11 Oct. 1913, ibid., 270.

40 Pound 'Indiscretions,' 31, 37. 'Mary Beaton' is presumably a fictitious name, as are the other names in the essay.

41 Carpenter, *A Serious Character*, 12, 11.

42 Pound, 'Indiscretions,' 42–3.

43 Ibid., 31.

44 For a general discussion of these psychological issues, see Harry T. Hardin, 'On the Vicissitudes of Early Primary Surrogate Mothering,' *Journal of the American Psychoanalytic Association* 33 (1985): 609–29 and Harry T. Hardin and Daniel H. Hardin, 'On the Vicissitudes of Early Primary Surrogate Mothering II,' *Journal of the American Psychoanalytic Association* 48 (2000), rpt. <http://www.psychoanalysis.net/JAPA_Psa-NETCAST/hardinandhardin.html>.

45 Hardin and Hardin, 'Vicissitudes II,' para. 1.

46 D.W. Winnicott, *Through Paediatrics to Psycho-Analysis* (New York: Basic Books, 1975), 269–70.

47 Ming Xie, 'Pound, Waley, Lowell, and the Chinese "Example" of Vers Libre,' *Paideuma* 22:3 (1993): 39–68.

48 Ezra Pound, *Literary Essays of Ezra Pound*, ed. T.S. Eliot (New York: New Directions, 1968), 218.

49 Robert Kern, *Orientalism, Modernism, and the American Poem* (Cambridge: Cambridge University Press, 1996), 188.

50 Giles, *History of Chinese Literature*, 100.

51 D.W. Winnicott, 'The Theory of the Parent-Infant Relationship,' in *Essential Papers on Object Relations*, ed. Peter Buckley (New York: New York University Press, 1986), 243–4.

52 Pound, *Personae*, 111.

53 Ibid.

54 Jung, *Psychological Types*, 90.

55 Canto CXVI, in Ezra Pound, *The Cantos of Ezra Pound* (New York: New Directions, 1972), 795.

56 Kodama, *Pound and Japan*, 6.

57 Pound to Williams, 19 Dec. 1913, *Selected Letters*, 27.

58 Pound to Dorothy Shakespear, 21 Nov. and 14 Nov. 1913, *EPDSL*, 276, 274; Yone Noguchi, 'A Japanese Poet on W.B. Yeats,' *Bookman* (NY) 43 (June 1916): 432.

59 Giles, *History of Chinese Literature*, 144.

60 Dorothy Shakespear to Pound, 6 Dec. 1913, *EPDSL*, 285–6.

61 Dorothy Shakespear to Pound, 6 Jan. 1914, ibid., 295.

62 Dorothy Shakespear to Pound, 12 Jan. 1914, ibid., 297. Shakespear, for reasons that are not clear to me, uses 'Chang' to refer to the Chinese language. The 'simple introduction,' according to the editors' note, was probably Walter Caine Hillier's *The Chinese Language and How to Learn It: A Manual for Beginners*, 2nd ed. (1910).

63 Dorothy Shakespear to Pound, 13 Jan. 1914, *EPDSL*, 300.

64 Ezra Pound and Ernest Fenollosa, *The Classic Noh Theatre of Japan* (New York: New Directions, 1959), 28.

65 Ibid., 29–31.

66 Ezra Pound, prefatory note to Ernest Fenollosa, *The Chinese Written Character as a Medium for Poetry* (1919; San Francisco: City Lights, 1968), 3.

67 Pound and Fenollosa, *Classic Noh Theatre*, 3.

68 Fenollosa, *The Chinese Written Character*, 3–4.

69 Ibid., 4.

70 Hugh Kenner, *The Pound Era* (Berkeley: University of California Press, 1971), 202.

71 Ronald Bush, 'Pound and Li Po: What Becomes a Man,' in *Ezra Pound among the Poets*, ed. George Bornstein (Chicago: University of Chicago Press, 1985), 44.

72 Ibid., 36.

73 Kern, *Orientalism*, 197.

74 Carpenter, *A Serious Character*, 268; Anna Xiao Dong Sun, 'The Man That Is Waiting: Remarks on Li Po's "Chokan Shin" and Pound's "The River-Merchant's Wife: A Letter," *Paideuma* 29:3 (2000): 153.

75 Pound, *Personae*, 134.

76 There is an extensive discussion of the Fenollosa notes in Bush, 'Pound and Li Po,' 35–62.

77 Slavoj Žižek, *Enjoy Your Symptom!* rev. ed. (New York: Routledge, 2001), 58.

78 Slavoz Žižek, *Looking Awry: An Introduction to Jacques Lacan through Popular Culture* (Cambridge: MIT Press, 1991), 86.

79 Dorothy Shakespear to Pound, 30 Dec. 1913, *EPDSL*, 289.

8. The Red Man in the Drawing Room

1 T.S. E[liot], 'War-Paint and Feathers,' *Nation and Athenaeum*, 17 Oct. 1919, 1036.

2 Renowned French entomologist Jean Henri Fabre (1823–1915).

3 Walter Benn Michaels, 'Race into Culture: A Critical Genealogy of Cultural Identity,' *Critical Inquiry* 18 (Summer 1992): 665.

4 Walt Whitman, 'Starting from Paumanok,' in *Leaves of Grass* (New York: Kennerley, 1904), 27–8.

5 Vachel Lindsay, *The Chinese Nightingale and Other Poems* (New York: Macmillan, 1917), 42.

6 Natalie Curtis, *The Indians' Book: An Offering by the American Indians of Indian Lore, Musical, and Narrative, to Form a Record of the Songs and Legends of Their Race* (1907; New York: Dover, 1950), xxi.

7 Helen Carr, *Inventing the American Primitive: Politics, Gender and the Representation of Native American Literary Traditions, 1789–1936* (New York: New York University Press, 1996), 218.

8 Ibid., 216.

9 *Dial* 43 (Dec. 1907), cited in Michael Castro, *Interpreting the Indian: Twentieth-Century Poets and the Native American* (Albuquerque: University of New Mexico Press, 1983), 11.

10 Ibid.

11 Curtis, *American Review of Reviews* 36 (Nov. 1907): 63, cited in Castro, *Interpreting the Indian*, 11.

12 Louis James Block, 'The Music of Primitive Man,' *Dial* 48 (Feb. 1910): 84–5.

13 Harriet Monroe, 'Introduction,' in Vachel Lindsay, *The Congo and Other Poems* (New York: Macmillan, 1914), viii.

14 Pound to Henderson, 15 June 1916, *Letters to Henderson*, 150.

15 I am interpolating the apparent sense of the transcription of this phrase. Nadel's transcription of the bracketed passage reads: '... were as even Paris, as they are Chicago or New York ... '

16 Henderson to Pound, 4 Jan. 1917, *Letters to Henderson*, 174. W.P.H., Henderson's husband, the painter William Penhallow Henderson, had begun using Indian motifs in his own work.

17 Pound, 'Indiscretions,' 12–13.

18 Alice Corbin Henderson, 'Buffalo Dance,' *Poetry* 9 (Jan. 1917): 236.

19 Henderson to Pound, 17 Feb. 1917, *Letters to Henderson*, 192.

20 Henderson later published a collection of Native American verse, *Red Earth: Poems of New Mexico* (Chicago: Ralph Fletcher Seymour, 1920), and an edited anthology, *The Turquoise Trail: An Anthology of New Mexico Poetry* (Boston: Houghton Mifflin, 1928).

21 Constance Lindsay Skinner, 'Afterword,' in George W. Cronyn, *The Path on the Rainbow: An Anthology of Songs and Chants from the Indians of North America* (New York: Boni and Liveright, 1918), 347.

22 Mary Austin, 'Introduction,' in Cronyn, *Path on the Rainbow*, xv–xvi.

23 Ibid., xvi.

24 Victor Plarr, 'A Note on a Savage Poet,' *Poetry and Drama* 1 (Sept. 1913): 344–7.

25 Milton Hindus, ed., *Walt Whitman: The Critical Heritage* (New York: Barnes and Noble, 1971), 57.

26 Austin, 'Introduction,' xvii.

27 Ibid.

28 Louis Untermeyer, 'The Indian as Poet,' *Dial* 66 (8 March 1919): 240.

29 Ibid., 241.

30 Mary Austin, 'The Path on the Rainbow,' *Dial* 66 (31 May 1919): 569.

31 Ibid.

32 Louis Untermeyer, 'Footnotes Wanted,' *Dial* 67 (12 July 1919): 30.

33 George Cronyn, 'Indian Melodists and Mr. Untermeyer,' *Dial* 67 (23 Aug. 1919): 162.

34 Ibid., 162–3.

35 Austin, 'Imagism: Original and Aboriginal,' *Dial* 67 (23 Aug. 1919): 163.

36 William Harmon, 'T.S. Eliot, Anthropologist and Primitive,' *American Anthropologist* 78 (1976): 803.

37 See Harry Todd Costello, *Josiah Royce's Seminar 1913–1914*, ed. Grover Smith (New Brunswick, NJ: Rutgers University Press, 1963).

38 Lucien Lévy-Bruhl, *How Natives Think*, tr. Lilian A. Clare (1926, New York: Washington Square Press, 1966), 8.

39 Ibid., 62.

40 Quoted in Robert Crawford, *The Savage and the City in the Work of T.S. Eliot* (New York: Oxford University Press, 1987), 192.

41 Lévy-Bruhl, *How Natives Think*, 345–6.

42 Jung, *Two Essays*, 277.

43 Lévy-Bruhl, *How Natives Think*, 347.

44 T.S. Eliot, review of *Group Theories of Religion and the Religion of the Individual* in *International Journal of Ethics*, Oct. 1916, 116.

45 Eliot, 'War Paint and Feathers,' 1036.

46 'Tradition and the Individual Talent' was first published in the September and December 1919 numbers of the *Egoist*. See Eliot, *The Sacred Wood*, 49.

47 T.S. Eliot, 'The Metaphysical Poets,' in *Selected Essays* (London: Faber and Faber, 1932), 289.

48 T.S. Eliot, *The Use of Poetry and the Use of Criticism* (Cambridge: Harvard University Press, 1933), quoted in David Richards, *Masks of Difference: Cultural Representations in Literature, Anthropology and Art* (Cambridge: Cambridge University Press, 1995), 205.

49 T.S. Eliot, *Inventions of the March Hare: Poems 1909–1917*, ed. Christopher Ricks (New York: Harcourt, Brace and Co., 1996), 53.

50 Ibid., 54.

51 T.S. Eliot, *The Collected Poems and Plays, 1909–1962* (London: Faber and Faber, 1974), 13.

52 In the passage from *The Use of Poetry and the Use of Criticism* cited above, Eliot admits his inability to understand 'why ... certain images recur, charged with emotion,' stating that 'such memories may have symbolic value, but of what we cannot tell, for they come to represent the depths of feeling into which we cannot peer.'

53 Lyndall Gordon, *T.S. Eliot: An Imperfect Life* (New York: Norton, 2000), 14.

54 Ibid., 10, 14.

55 Eliot, *The Sacred Wood*, 51.

56 Delmore Schwartz, 'T.S. Eliot as the International Hero,' *Partisan Review* 12 (Spring 1945): 201.

57 Louis Untermeyer, ed., *Modern American Poetry: An Introduction* (New York: Harcourt, Brace and Howe, 1919), xi.

58 Louis Untermeyer, ed., *Modern American Poetry: An Introduction*, revised and enlarged ed. (New York: Harcourt, Brace and Co., 1921), 19.

59 Louis Untermeyer, *American Poetry since 1900* (New York: Henry Holt, 1923), 375.

9. The Last Nostalgia

1 On Stevens's comments on the Baker essay (to Ronald Lane Latimer, 5 Nov. 1935, *The Letters of Wallace Stevens*, ed. Holly Stevens [New York: Knopf, 1966], 292), see Jacqueline Vaught Brogan, '"Sister of the Minotaur": Sexism and Stevens,' in Melita Schaum, ed., *Wallace Stevens and the Feminine* (Tuscaloosa: University of Alabama Press, 1993), 10. Barbara M. Fisher's essay in the same volume, 'A Woman with the Hair of a Pythoness' (46–57), draws attention to a number of differences between Stevens's 'interior paramour' and the Jungian anima, but does not undermine the basic equivalence of the two figures.

2 Response to inquiry from *New Verse*, Oct. 1934, in *CPP*, 771; 'The Irrational Element in Poetry,' *CPP*, 783.

3 Stevens to Ronald Lane Latimer, 10 Jan. 1936, in *Letters*, 305–6.

4 Stevens, *CPP*, 319.

5 Joan Richardson, *Wallace Stevens*, 2 vols. (New York: Beech Tree Books, 1986–8), 1:111.

6 Stevens, *CPP*, 283.

7 M. Keith Booker, 'Notes toward a Lacanian Reading of Wallace Stevens,' *Journal of Modern Literature* 16:4 (Spring 1990): 493.

8 Stevens to Harriet Monroe, 28 Oct. 1922, *Letters*, 231.

9 Ibid.; Stevens to Ronald Lane Latimer, 29 Jan. 1938, *Letters*, 330.

10 Helen Hennessy Vendler, *On Extended Wings: Wallace Stevens' Longer Poems* (Cambridge: Harvard University Press, 1969), 54.

11 Jacques Lacan, *The Four Fundamental Concepts of Psychoanalysis*, ed. Jacques-Alain Miller, tr. Alan Sheridan (New York: W.W. Norton, 1981), 181, 182 (hereafter cited as *FFCP*).

12 Ibid., 280.

13 Ibid., 181–2.

14 Stevens, 'The Figure of the Youth as a Virile Poet,' *CPP*, 670.

15 Stevens, 'Effects of Analogy,' ibid., 717.

16 Stevens, 'The Irrational Element in Poetry,' ibid., 784.

17 Stevens, 'Effects of Analogy,' ibid., 716.

18 Richardson, *Wallace Stevens*, 40.

19 Garrett Stevens to Wallace Stevens, 27 Sept. 1897, *Letters*, 14.

20 Garrett Stevens to Wallace Stevens, 9 Feb. 1898, ibid., 23.

21 Garrett Stevens to Wallace Stevens, 13 Nov. 1898, ibid., 20.

22 'What They Call Red Cherry Pie,' *CPP,* 561–2.

23 Stevens, *CPP,* 22.

24 Ibid.

25 Ibid.

26 Ibid., 22–3.

27 Ibid., 726.

28 Ibid., 23.

29 Jacques Lacan, *The Seminar of Jacques Lacan,,* vol. 1, ed. Jacques-Alain Miller, tr. John Forrester (New York: Norton, 1988), 117.

30 Ibid., 23–4.

31 Ibid., 24.

32 Stevens, *CPP,* 987.

33 Jacques Lacan, *Ecrits: A Selection* (New York: Norton, 1977), 19.

34 Stevens to Hi Simons, 29 March 1943, *Letters,* 444.

35 Lacan, *Ecrits,* 160.

36 Simons, 'The Comedian,' 456.

37 Bloom, *Wallace Stevens,* 75; Litz, *Introspective Voyager,* 130.

38 Waldo Frank, *Our America* (New York: Boni and Liveright, 1919), 107–8.

39 Stevens to José Rodríguez Feo, 19 Dec. 1946, *Letters,* 543.

40 Stevens to Leonard van Geyzel, 14 Sept. 1948, *Letters,* 614.

41 For Jung's identification of the Indic Maya with the anima, see *Aion,* 11, 13.

42 Stevens, *CPP,* 53.

43 Ibid., 55–6.

44 Lourens P. Van Den Bosch, *Friedrich Max Müller: A Life Devoted to the Humanities* (Leiden: Brill, 2002), 262–3.

45 Francis Barton Gummere, *A Handbook of Poetics for Students of English Verse* (Boston: Ginn and Company, 1885).

46 Ibid., 13.

47 Francis B. Gummere, *The Beginnings of Poetry* (New York: Macmillan, 1901), 347.

48 Ibid., 101.

49 Richard Wallaschek (1860–1917) was the author of *Primitive Music: An Inquiry into the Origin and Development of Music, Songs, Instruments, Dances, and Pantomimes of Savage Races* (London: Longmans, Green, and Co., 1893).

50 Gummere, *Beginnings of Poetry,* 109.

51 Ibid., 8.

52 Ibid., 114–15.

53 Ibid., 454.

54 Stevens, *CPP,* 792.

55 Stevens, 'Two or Three Ideas,' *CPP,* 842, 843.

56 Stevens, *CPP,* 786.

57 Stevens, *CPP,* 660–1.
58 Kipling, 'In the Neolithic Age' (1895), in *Rudyard Kipling's Verse,* 342.
59 Ellen Williams, *Harriet Monroe and the Poetry Renaissance: The First Ten Years of Poetry, 1912–22* (Urbana: University of Illinois Press 1977), 102–3.
60 Harriet Monroe, 'Introduction,' in Vachel Lindsay, *The Congo and Other Poems* (New York: Macmillan, 1914), viii–ix.
61 Rachel Blau DuPlessis, '"HOO, HOO, HOO": Some Episodes in the Construction of Modern Whiteness,' *American Literature* 67:4 (1995), 679.
62 Nielsen, *Reading Race: White American Poets and the Racial Discourse in the Early Twentieth Century* (Athens: University of Georgia Press), 60–5.
63 Stevens, *CPP,* 25.
64 Lacan, *FFCP,* 89.
65 Stevens, *CPP,* 26.
66 Lacan, *FFCP,* 179.
67 Ibid., 182.
68 Stevens, *CPP,* 28.
69 Lacan, *FFCP,* 178.
70 Ibid., 177.
71 Stevens, *CPP,* 55.
72 Stevens to Monroe, 19 Nov. 1925, *Letters,* 246. As noted in *Letters,* 248, Moore later included the comment in the *Dial's* announcement of an award to Williams.
73 Stevens, *CPP,* 29–30.
74 Ibid., 30.
75 Austin, 'Introduction,' in Cronyn, *Path on the Rainbow,* xvii.
76 Frank, *Our America,* 106.
77 Ibid., 96.
78 Stevens, *CPP,* 993.
79 Ibid., 30.
80 Ibid.
81 Stevens to Simons, 28 Aug. 1940, *Letters,* 369.
82 Stevens, *CPP,* 729.
83 Ibid., 31.
84 Ibid.
85 Ibid., 995.
86 Stevens, journal entry for 26 July 1900, *Letters,* 43.
87 Jung, *Aion,* 12–13.
88 Jung, *Psychological Types,* 472.
89 Mark Halliday, *Stevens and the Interpersonal* (Princeton: Princeton University Press, 1991), 47.
90 Jung, *Psychological Types,* 390.

91 Lacan, *On Feminine Sexuality: The Limits of Love and Knowledge*, tr. Bruce Fink (New York: W.W. Norton, 1998), 144–5.
92 Fredric Jameson, 'Wallace Stevens,' in *Critical Essays on Wallace Stevens*, ed. Steven Gould Axelrod and Helen Deese (Boston: G.K. Hall, 1988), 186.
93 Stevens, *CPP*, 365.

10. Forgotten Jungle Songs

1 W.E.B. DuBois, 'The Souls of Black Folk,' *Three Negro Classics* (New York: Avon, 1965), 216.
2 Paul Laurence Dunbar, 'We Wear the Mask,' in *The Collected Poetry of Paul Laurence Dunbar*, ed. Joanne M. Braxton (Charlottesville: University Press of Virginia, 1993), 71.
3 Houston A. Baker, Jr, *Modernism and the Harlem Renaissance* (Chicago: University of Chicago Press, 1987), 39.
4 A[lice] C[orbin] H[enderson], 'Poetry of the American Negro,' *Poetry* 10:3 (June 1917): 158.
5 Ibid., 159.
6 Pound to Henderson, 16 Jan. 1913, *Letters to Henderson*, 15.
7 Pound, *Selected Letters*, 62.
8 Pound, 'Indiscretions,' 31.
9 For more on modernist poets' uses of the African American, see Rachel Blau Duplessis, '"Darken your speech": Racialized Cultural Work of Modern Poets,' in *Reading Race in American Poetry: An Area of Act*, ed. Aldon Lynn Nielsen (Urbana: University of Illinois Press, 2000), 43–83, and Michael North, *The Dialect of Modernism: Race, Language, and Twentieth-Century Literature* (New York: Oxford University Press, 1994).
10 See Eliot, 'Fragment of an Agon,' in *Collected Poems*, 131–2.
11 Cole and Johnson Bros., *Under the Bamboo Tree* (New York: Stern, 1901).
12 Lewis, *When Harlem Was in Vogue*, 152.
13 Ibid., 152, 154.
14 Ibid., 128–9.
15 Langston Hughes, *The Big Sea* (New York: Knopf, 1940), 325.
16 Lewis, *When Harlem was in Vogue*, 154.
17 Claude McKay, *A Long Way from Home* (1937; San Diego: Harcourt, Brace, 1970), 335.
18 Ibid., 337.
19 Ibid., 344.
20 Alain Locke, ed., *The New Negro: An Interpretation* (1925; New York: Arno Press, 1968), 8.
21 Ibid., 9.

22 George W. Stocking, *Victorian Anthropology* (New York: Free Press, 1987), 251.

23 E.B. Tylor, *Primitive Culture*, vol. 1 (London: John Murray, 1871), 21.

24 Maureen Honey, ed., *Shadowed Dreams: Women's Poetry of the Harlem Renaissance* (New Brunswick, NJ: Rutgers University Press, 1989), 99.

25 Jean Toomer, *Cane* (New York: Boni and Liveright, 1923), 15.

26 North, *The Dialect of Modernism*, 164. For more on Boni and Liveright, see George Hutchinson, *Harlem Renaissance in Black and White* (Cambridge: Harvard University Press, 1995), 368–72.

27 Locke, ed., *The New Negro*, 254.

28 Ibid.

29 Ibid.

30 McKay, *A Long Way from Home*, 313.

31 Michael B. Stoff, 'Claude McKay and the Cult of Primitivism,' in *The Harlem Renaissance Remembered*, ed. Arna Bontemps (New York: Dodd, Mead, 1972), 127.

32 Nathan Huggins, *Harlem Renaissance* (New York: Oxford University Press, 1971), 172, 173.

33 Claude McKay, *Selected Poems* (New York: Dover, 1996), 40.

34 Countee Cullen, *My Soul's High Song: The Collected Writings of Countee Cullen, Voice of the Harlem Renaissance*, ed. Gerald Early (New York: Doubleday, 1991), 104.

35 Ibid.

36 Fanon, *Black Skin, White Masks*, 145.

37 Ibid.

38 Cullen, *My Soul's High Song*, 165.

39 Ibid., 107.

40 Žižek, *Enjoy Your Symptom!*, 125.

41 Ibid., 124.

Index